A SENSE OF PLACE AND BELONGING

A volume in the
NIU Series in Southeast Asian Studies
Edited by Kenton Clymer

For a list of books in the series, visit our website at cornellpress.cornell.edu.

A SENSE OF PLACE AND BELONGING

The Chiang Tung Borderland of Northern Southeast Asia

Klemens Karlsson

NORTHERN ILLINOIS UNIVERSITY PRESS
An imprint of
CORNELL UNIVERSITY PRESS
Ithaca and London

Copyright © 2025 by Cornell University

All rights reserved. Except for brief quotations in a review, this book, or parts thereof, must not be reproduced in any form without permission in writing from the publisher. For information, address Cornell University Press, Sage House, 512 East State Street, Ithaca, New York 14850. Visit our website at cornellpress.cornell.edu.

First published 2025 by Cornell University Press

Library of Congress Cataloging-in-Publication Data
Names: Karlsson, Klemens, author.
Title: A sense of place and belonging : the Chiang Tung borderland of northern Southeast Asia / Klemens Karlsson.
Description: Ithaca : Northern Illinois University Press, an imprint of Cornell University Press, 2025. | Series: NIU series in Southeast Asian studies | Includes bibliographical references and index.
Identifiers: LCCN 2024042596 (print) | LCCN 2024042597 (ebook) | ISBN 9781501779756 (hardcover) | ISBN 9781501779763 (paperback) | ISBN 9781501779770 (epub) | ISBN 9781501779787 (pdf)
Subjects: LCSH: Group identity—Burma—Kēng Tung—History. | Shan (Asian people)—Ethnic identity. | Transborder ethnic groups—Burma. | Transborder ethnic groups—Southeast Asia. | Borderlands—Burma. | Borderlands—Southeast Asia. | Kēng Tung (Burma)—History. | Kēng Tung (Burma)—Ethnic relations—History. | Kēng Tung (Burma)—Social conditions.
Classification: LCC DS530.9.K46 K35 2005 (print) | LCC DS530.9.K46 (ebook) | DDC 305.8959/19—dc23/eng/20241203
LC record available at https://lccn.loc.gov/2024042596
LC ebook record available at https://lccn.loc.gov/2024042597

To the people of Chiang Tung, and to the spirit of the place, seen and unseen, which inspired me to write this book

Contents

Acknowledgments	ix
Abbreviations	xiii
A Note on Names, Places, and Ethnonyms	xv
Introduction: The Place, the People, and the Borderland	1
1. Local Belonging	16
2. Myths and Memories	31
3. Precolonial Times	44
4. Foreign Rulers	66
5. Sacred Space	98
6. Religious Culture	123
7. Songkran Festival	164
Conclusion: A Sense of Place and Belonging	190
Notes	199
References	205
Index	217

Acknowledgments

This volume is based on research made during a period of more than ten years, during which time I relied on friends and informants in Chiang Tung, to whom I owe my deepest gratitude. Special appreciation goes to the late Long Haung Kham and members of the committee organizing the Songkran festival and associated cultural activities.

In Chiang Tung I have always been very warmly received by people I have met around town, in discussions, and at dinners with friends and their families. Many thanks go to the Buddhist monks in Chiang Tung and also monks from Chiang Tung studying or living in Chiang Mai. Because of current political circumstances, I chose not to mention by name any of my friends and informants in Myanmar to whom I also owe thanks, but you know who you are. Without your help this book wouldn't be what it is.

My time at the Regional Center for Social Science and Sustainable Development (RCSD), Faculty of Social Science, at Chiang Mai University made it possible for me to carry out my research. Many thanks to the director there, Chayan Vaddhanaphuti, and colleagues and staff at the university. Special thanks to Amporn Jirattikorn, Renoo Wicha, Rawiwan Oranratmanee, Aranya Siriphon, Phailin Tongtammacatt, and Chanida Puranapun for their help. I also thank anonymous peer reviewers who read an early draft of the manuscript and suggested important improvements.

Thanks to Bertil Lintner, who taught me about the various ethnic and political resistance movements in Myanmar. Thanks also to Kazuo Fukuura for introducing me to the Lan Na twelve-month tradition, to Cholthira Satyawadhana for constructive discussions about the culture of Lua/Lawa, to Peter Schalk, my supervisor many years ago at Uppsala University, for introducing me to the writings of Paul Mus, which have been invaluable to this study, and to Aroon and her family for introducing me to the spirits of her home. A special thought to the late Anatole-Roger Peltier, with whom I had interesting talks about Chiang Tung at the beginning of my research. Thanks also to Roger Casas, who kindly guided me around Sipsong Panna and introduced me to the Buddhist culture of Tai Lue in the beginning of my research.

I have spent many valuable days at the library at École française d'Extrême-Orient in Chiang Mai. Thanks to the staff there and to Rebecca Weldon and

Louis Gabaude for organizing the Informal Northern Thai Group and its many interesting lectures. I would also like to thank Rebecca Ahlfeldt for correcting my language mistakes and Daniel Huffman for drawing the map of the Chiang Tung borderland. Thanks also to friends in Chiang Mai and elsewhere in Thailand for making my long evenings not so lonely.

I am grateful to everyone at the NIU Press and Cornell University Press who shepherded this book on the ground: my acquiring editor, Amy Farranto; Kristen Gregg in marketing; the production editor, Susan Specter; and the copy editor, Glenn Novak.

I would like to give special thanks to the organizers and people I met at various conferences: Thanks to Holly High for organizing the conference panel Stone Masters, held in Sydney in 2018 at the 22nd Biennial ASAA Conference. Thanks also to Perry Schmidt-Leukel, Hans-Peter Grosshans, and Madlen Krueger for organizing the conference Ethnic and Religious Diversity in Myanmar, sponsored by the Myanmar Institute of Theology and the Protestant Faculty of Theology / University of Münster in Yangon in February 2019. Thanks also to Erik de Maaker and Monica Janowski for organizing the panel Stories across Borders: Narratives of Origin and Their Contestation in the Borderlands of Asia II, at the Fifth Conference of the Asian Borderlands Research Network, at Kathmandu, Nepal, in 2016. Thanks also to Julius Bautista for organizing the conference New Directions in the Study of Material Religion, in Singapore in 2008. I also am grateful to the organizers and people I met at the conference on Shan Buddhism and Culture at SOAS London, at the International Conference on Shan Studies, Institute of Asian Studies, Culalongkorn University, Bangkok, in 2009, and the 13th international conference on Thai Studies at Chiang Mai, in 2017.

This volume is the result of several research projects carried out during a period of more than ten years, all focused on different aspects of Chiang Tung and the borderland of northern Southeast Asia. These research projects were made possible by generous funding by the following foundations: Lars Hiertas minne, Helge Ax:son Johnsons stiftelse, Stiftelsen Längmanska kulturfonden, and Margot och Rune Johanssons stiftelse. The present volume is completely revised, but the research results have also been reported and published in my following journal articles and book chapters: "Territory Cults and Power in the Eastern Shan State of Myanmar," in *Stone Masters: Power Encounters in Mainland Southeast Asia*, ed. Holly High (Singapore: NUS Press, 2022), 242–67; "Visual Culture and Identity: Ethnic and Religious Diversity in the Eastern Shan State," in *Ethnic and Religious Diversity in Myanmar: Contested Identities*, ed. Perry Schmidt-Leukel, Hans-Peter Grosshans, and Madlen Krueger (London: Bloomsbury Academic, 2022), 73–91; "A Place of Belonging in Myths and Memories: The Origin and Early History of the Imagined Tai Khuen Nation (Chiang Tung /

Kyaingtong, Myanmar)," *Southeast Asian Studies (SEAS)* 9, no. 2 (2020): 181–201; "The Songkran Festival in Chiang Tung: A Symbolic Performance of Domination and Subordination between Lowland Tai and Hill Tai," *Tai Culture* 23 (2013): 50–62; "Material Religion and Ethnic Identity: Buddhist Visual Culture and the Burmanization of the Eastern Shan State," in *The Spirit of Things: Materiality in the Age of Religious Diversity in Southeast Asia*, ed. Julius Bautista (Ithaca, NY: Cornell Southeast Asia Program Publications, 2012), 61–77; "Shan Ethnic-Religious Identity: Objects, Art, and Material Religion in the Eastern Shan State," in *Shan and Beyond*, ed. Montira Rato and Khanidtha Kanthavichai (Bangkok: Institute of Asian Studies, Chulalongkorn University, 2011), 79–95; and "Tai Khun Buddhism and Ethnic-Religious Identity," *Contemporary Buddhism* 10, no. 1 (2009): 75–83.

Abbreviations

In the text and the endnotes, frequently cited works, along with the edition consulted, are identified by the following abbreviations:

CMC *The Chiang Mai Chronicle.* 2nd ed. Translated by David K. Wyatt and Aroonrut Wichienkeeo. Chiang Mai: Silkworm Books, 1998.

CSP *Chronicle of Sipsong Panna: History and Society of a Tai Lü Kingdom, Twelfth to Twentieth Century.* Edited and translated by Foon Ming Liew-Herres, Volker Grabowsky, and Renoo Wichasin. Chiang Mai: Mekong, 2012.

CTC *Chiang Tung Chronicle.* In Sao Saimong Mangrai, *The Padaeng Chronicle and the Jengtung State Chronicle Translated*, pp. 209–91. Ann Arbor: University of Michigan, Center for South and Southeast Asian Studies, 1981.

EHS Prasert Na Nagara and A. B. Griswold. *Epigraphic and Historical Studies.* Bangkok: Historical Society under the Royal Patronage of H.R.H. Princess Maha Chakri Sirindhorn, 1992. Papers 1–24, originally published in the *Journal of the Siam Society*, 1968–1979.

FACE *Frontier Areas Committee of Enquiry 1947: Report Presented to His Majesty's Government in the United Kingdom and the Government of Burma*, part 2. Rangoon: Superintendent, Government Printing and Stationery, 1947.

JKM *The Sheaf of Garlands of the Epochs of the Conqueror: Being a Translation of Jinakālamālīpakaraṇaṁ of Ratannapañña Thera of Thailand* by N. A. Jauyawickrama. London: Pali Text Society, 1978.

TMWPD Sommai Premchit and Donald K. Swearer. "A Translation of *Tamnan Mūlasāsanā Wat Pa Daeng*: The Chronicle of the Founding of Buddhism of the Wat Pa Daeng Tradition." *Journal of Siam Society* 65, no. 2 (1977): 73–110.

WPDC *Wat Pa Daeng Chronicle.* In Sao Saimong Mangrai, *The Padaeng Chronicle and the Jengtung State Chronicle Translated*, pp. 99–180. Ann Arbor: University of Michigan, Center for South and Southeast Asian Studies, 1981.

A Note on Names, Places, and Ethnonyms

How to name places, persons, and groups of people in Southeast Asia presents difficulties. It is a place with many languages and where identities are unstable. Names have changed or are changing, and a place can have many names during its long history. I have tried to avoid using modern names when talking about places in historical times. For instance, I use "island of Lanka" instead of Sri Lanka when talking about precolonial times.

In this study I have used "Myanmar" for the country from the year 1989, when the military government officially changed the English translation of the name of the country from Burma to Myanmar. For the colonial times until 1989 I have used the English word, Burma. For the sake of simplicity, I have used "Burmese" for the ethnic majority people and the language, not "Bamar." For Thailand I have used the name "Thailand" for events after the Second World War and "Siam" from the fall of Ayuthaya until the Second World War. I use "Thai" to refer to people living within the geographic area of the present-day nation of Thailand, and "Tai" to denote Tai-speaking peoples outside Thailand. In Myanmar it is common to name all Tai-speaking peoples as Shan. In this study I have used the name "Western Shan" (Tai Yai) for the Tai-speaking people in Myanmar, except Khuen. The name "Shan" has been used for all Tai-speaking peoples in Myanmar, including Khuen.

For precolonial times I have used names of dynasties, kingdoms, or cities: Toungoo, Konbaung, Ayuthaya, Sukhothai, Lan Na, Sipsong Panna, etc. For names of people and places I have tried to use the most common in academic literature, hence there are inconsistencies: sometimes Tai/Thai and sometimes Pāli or Sanskrit.

Transliteration of Khuen, Burmese, and Thai also need to be explained. Romanization of the Khuen language creates difficulties. There is no standard transliteration. For the sake of simplicity, I have tried to reproduce as closely as possible the Khuen pronunciation, and, if it was possible, to use the corresponding words in modern Thai. Many places and temples have both Khuen and Burmese names. I have avoided Burmese names if possible. I write Chiang Tung, not Keng Tung, Kengtong, or Kyiangtong. For Thai language, I have used a modified version of the Thai romanization outlined by the Royal Institute. I write *saopha*, not *chao fa* or *jaopha*, and *mueang*, not *muang* or *müng*. Pāli and Sanskrit transliteration follow the standard international conventions with diacritics.

A SENSE OF PLACE AND BELONGING

INTRODUCTION
The Place, the People, and the Borderland

The city of Chiang Tung, in the Eastern Shan State of Myanmar and approximately 160 kilometers north of Thailand's northernmost border town, Mae Sai, sits at the historic borderland of Myanmar, China, Laos, and Thailand (map 1). This borderland is known as the Golden Triangle, marked by the drug trade, human trafficking, and a seemingly never-ending civil war. Chiang Tung, or Keng Tung, as it is also called, is surrounded by high mountains at the crossroads of trade routes in the heart of northern Southeast Asia. In many ways, the city has a turbulent and violent history; at the same time, it is home to a long and flourishing Buddhist culture. The majority of residents in Chiang Tung call themselves Tai Khuen or simply Khuen, an ethnic group within the larger group of Tai-speaking peoples.

The first few times I visited Chiang Tung, everyone told me to come back in April to see the Songkran festival. I imagined a typical water festival, with splashing and drinking beer. April would bring extremely hot weather, making it not the best time for a visit. But they insisted, promising that the six hundredth Songkran celebration in 2011 would be particularly spectacular. I went for the first time that year, and I was not disappointed.

The day before the traditional start of the festival, I attended a cultural performance by young girls from various ethnic groups, who were dressed in traditional clothes. They participated in a parade, dancing traditional dances. It was beautiful to watch but nothing spectacular. The main event started the next day before lunch, as I arrived at the festival's center. A large, colorful statue, which I later realized was a representation of the Hindu God Indra, was already in place,

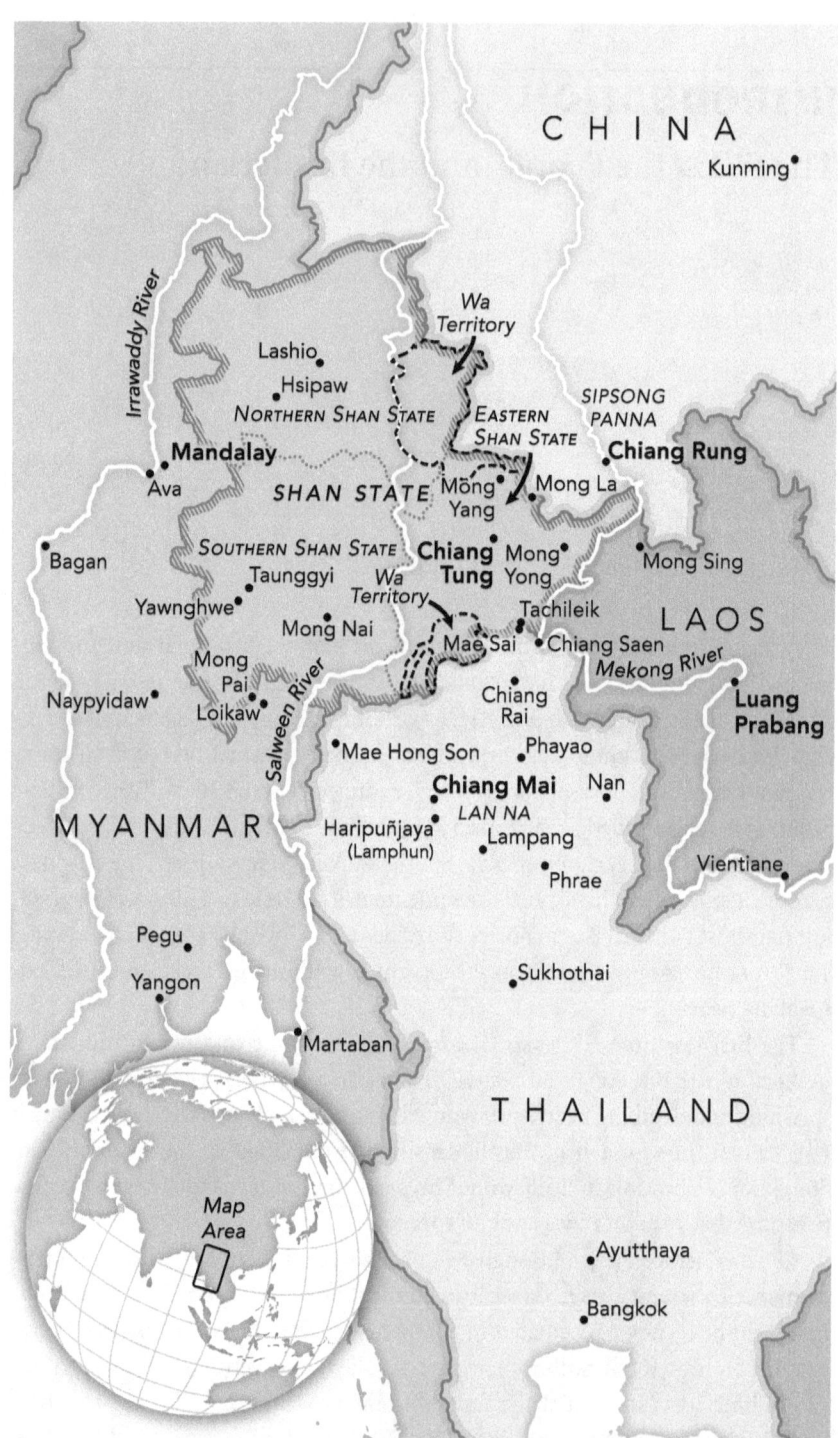

MAP 1. Chiang Tung in the borderland of northern Southeast Asia

and a couple of men were lifting a large drum onto a stand. The most sensational event this day was when a group of young men, dressed in red, beat a drum while water was constantly splashed. This lasted throughout the whole day and night, and it did not stop until noon the next day. Later, I understood that the young men belonged to the Lua ethnic group who are the indigenous people of Chiang Tung, today called Tai Loi, or hill Tai. Tai Loi (Lua) people have played a significant role in the origin and history of Chiang Tung. They belong to the larger group of Palaungic Mon-Khmer-speaking people but have lived a long time now in close relations with Tai people and converted to Buddhism. Their participation in the Songkran festivities testifies to the dependence and loyalty between the Khuen and the Tai Loi (Lua) relating to ownership and rights to land. Before the drumming began, there were blessings and readings that I could not understand, but later I learned that they were about old myths and legends of the origin and history of Chiang Tung. Altogether, this day made me feel like I was part of something magic.

The next day was even more impressive. The primary activity was a procession with thousands of people who followed the drum and the statue down to the river under constant water splashing. It was impossible to participate in everything that happened over the course of those days, as several activities happened at the same time. The most apt term for the event is a cultural performance, which Milton Singer described as something between a stage play, community theatre, a festival and a religious ritual or ceremony (Singer 1972, 71). I only heard about what occurred down at the river and could not exactly understand its meaning, but I surmised it had something to do with fertility and ritual sexual intercourse. While the festival undoubtedly expresses ancient fertility traditions, it ended with a collective creation of Buddhist sand *chedis*.

My first experience at the Songkran festival made me curious, and later I learned about more things that happened, things I did not watch. How could I understand it all? My curiosity drove me to come back, hoping to uncover the secrets and mysteries of the festival. However, it is not possible to understand the present until we know the past. To understand the Songkran festival, it was essential to learn the origin and ancient history of Chiang Tung. Victor Turner writes about the dialectic between aesthetic dramatic processes and sociocultural processes. He writes that it is "necessary to do some homework on the history, social history, and cultural history of the 'worlds' which encompass the dramatic tradition we are considering. And also on the history and sociology of the 'ideas' which impregnate these dramas" (Turner 1987, 28). The history and myths and memories of the origin of Chiang Tung and the cultural background of the ancient monsoon culture of South China and northern Southeast Asia are therefore an essential part of this book, and they are at the center of chapters 2 and 7.

I have now attended the festival several times, and these experiences led to a broader interest in Chiang Tung. Several chapters in this book are connected to the Songkran festivities and the Tai Loi (Lua) ethnic group, but the description and analyses in chapters 2 and 7 are particularly important for understanding the Songkran festival and its secrets.

I have previously studied Buddhist traditions in both Myanmar and Thailand. Visiting Chiang Tung highlighted the special and exceptional tradition there, with its roots in Lan Na culture. Lan Na was an important cultural region, sometimes called a kingdom, during the fourteenth and fifteenth centuries, with many semi-independent principalities or city-states (*mueang*). Today, the geography of the remains of Lan Na culture stretches across Thailand, China, Myanmar, and a small part of northern Laos. Something that struck me early was the character of the Theravāda Buddhist tradition still present in Chiang Tung. It differs to some extent from the Buddhist traditions of both Myanmar and Thailand. It looks like a mix, and it is surely a mix. But most of all, the Buddhist tradition in Chiang Tung has its roots in the Lan Na Buddhist culture and is an important identity marker for the Buddhist people in the town and its environs.

The largest geographical part of Lan Na, today in northern Thailand, became integrated in the late nineteenth century into the nation of Siam/Thailand and thus the national Siamese/Thai Buddhist tradition. By imposing the Sangha Administration Act of 1902, the Bangkok authorities standardized the *saṅgha* (the Buddhist religious order) and incorporated Lan Na into the national *saṅgha*, under direct control of the state. The local Buddhist tradition of Lan Na was devastated, and the authorities incorporated all monks in Siam into a national structure of clerical education. Even more drastic consequences ensued for the Lan Na Buddhist tradition in Sipsong Panna, China. The ruling party oppressed Buddhism during the Great Leap Forward from 1958 to 1960 and again during the Cultural Revolution from 1966 to 1976. They disrobed those monks who did not escape to Burma. After 1978, the Buddhist practice recovered, but today it is under the guidance of the Communist Party, administered by the Ethnic and Religious Affairs Commission and the Buddhist Association.

Today, Buddhism in Chiang Tung seems to have remained an independent, decentralized tradition, largely not controlled by any state organization. The monks in Chiang Tung belong officially to the Myanmar Sudhamma Nikāya or Shwegiyn Nikāya, but in practice they are more or less independent of official government control. This is due to the cultural characteristics of Chiang Tung Buddhism, which the government in Myanmar cannot control. The distinctiveness of Chiang Tung Buddhism can be characterized in short by an independent Buddhist *saṅgha*, a hierarchy built on seniority, an old Buddhist calendar, Buddhist rituals and literature in Khuen and Pāli languages written in the old *tham* script, a tradition of charismatic holy monks, and a specific Buddhist visual culture.

During their long history under the more dominant cultures of the Burmese, the Chinese, and the Siamese, the Khuen people of Chiang Tung have experienced both cultural proliferation and disaster. In the historical parts of this book, it becomes apparent that Chiang Tung, in several phases during its history, could have been incorporated into Siam/Thailand or China instead of Burma/Myanmar. The area even could have been recognized as an independent state, as was modern Laos. Several times throughout history, political decisions or accidental events affected the political future of Chiang Tung.

The ruler Sao Mahakhanan made one of these political decisions in the early nineteenth century when he escaped from the Siamese invaders, who deported the inhabitants, together with monks, and the ruler and his court, to Chiang Mai. Sao Mahakhanan was the only one from the court who escaped, and later he rebuilt and repopulated Chiang Tung. Another such decision was made nearly eighty years later by the British when, driven by their mistrust of the French who had settled on the other side of the Mekong, they overran Chiang Tung and integrated it into the rest of the Shan States and the British Empire, even though they considered the Salween River as a natural border and initially had halted their advance at the river. The British had sent a spy to Chiang Tung, who pointed out that it would be best to hand it over to the Chinese. Later, in April 1947 during the second Panglong Conference, Chiang Tung had the option to choose if it wished to remain in the Shan States Federation or be annexed as a part of Thailand. During the conference, a representative of the ruler decided that Chiang Tung wanted to stay among the Federation of Shan States. These snapshots back in history make visible the vulnerability of Chiang Tung, nestled between more dominant nations.

History records the exposure of Chiang Tung to surrounding political forces. Yet history is written from different angles, from different national perspectives, and for different purposes. There might be one colonial history of Chiang Tung, seen through the eyes of the British administration, and there might be another history written by international missionaries with a slightly different perspective. These differ from the myths and memories told by the people of Chiang Tung, which we will consider in chapter 2.

History also exercises power, and it can be used ideologically to persuade and mobilize groups in society. This can be seen in the differing Burmese and Tai history traditions of Chiang Tung. There is another perspective on the history of Chiang Tung written by the Thai leaders of the pan-Thai nationalism movement in the 1930s and 1940s. They considered Chiang Tung as a lost territory of the so-called Thai race. With approval from the Japanese, they bombed Chiang Tung and incorporated it as a province (Saharat Thai Doem) in the nation-state of Siam/Thailand. During the Second World War, Siam/Thailand saw itself as taking back one of its lost territories and thus rewrote the history of Chiang Tung. In the eyes of its leaders Phibun and Wichit, Chiang Tung, with its "Tai" population, was part of a Thai nation that was reunited.

The Burmese military, on the other hand, wanted to establish Chiang Tung as a natural part of Myanmar and changed its official name to Kyiangtong. To rewrite the history of Chiang Tung and position it more closely in the nation-state of Myanmar, they used Burmese religious visual culture. The big standing Buddha, built by the military in the late 1990s, is a good example of how they tried to connect the origin and early history of Chiang Tung with Bagan, the first Burmese dynasty. The Burmese military realized, particularly in the 1990s, that culture and religion could be used in minority regions to rewrite history and establish Burmese authority and power.

The words "We are not Shan, we are *Khuen*," spoken to me with determination by an old gentleman, point to the idea that the unique culture is still a living tradition among the locals, even though they have been more or less under the political and economic dominance of the British or Burmese powers since the middle of the eighteenth century. With this exclamation by the Khuen gentleman in mind, I will demonstrate in the chapters that follow how this culture kept its place in people's memories and hearts for such a long time.

Chapter 1 gives a theoretical background to this book, grounded in the geographic place of Chiang Tung and its connection to local belonging and identity. In chapter 2 I show how myths and memories narrate a common origin of the Khuen people and the place of Chiang Tung. The history of Chiang Tung as located between more powerful neighbors is described in chapters 3 and 4, highlighting its exposed location. Chapter 5 is called "Sacred Space" and describes the visual and material culture inside the assembly hall (*vihan*) of a Buddhist monastery, as well as the rituals and literature that are practiced there; and in chapter 6, about the religious culture of Chiang Tung, I focus on the ancient cult of spirits and the distinctiveness of Buddhist culture with roots in Lan Na and the island of Lanka (Sri Lanka). Finally, chapter 7 ties together myths and memories of the origin and ancient history, described in chapter 2, with the unique performance of the Songkran festival, still seen today in Chiang Tung.

Basic Facts about *Mueang* Chiang Tung

Chiang Tung (also transcribed as Keng Tung, Kengtong, and Xieng Tong; its official name today is Kyiangtong) is in the Eastern Shan State of Myanmar, but it has not always been under Burmese sovereignty. It is a historic borderland, struggling for independence. Tai people, under the leadership of King Mangrai, established Chiang Tung as a frontier state against the Mongols of China (Yuan dynasty) during the late thirteenth century. They conquered the region from a Mon-Khmer people called Lua or Lawa. Chiang Tung was, from that time, part of the loosely connected cultural network called Lan Na, which comprised several, more or less independent Tai *mueang*—principalities or city-states. The toponym Lan Na is today often used by Thai scholars to refer to the eight provinces of today's Northern Thailand.[1] However, the term Lan Na can also be used for a larger area, comprising not only the eight northern provinces of Thailand but also the whole region north of the border between Thailand and Myanmar, east of the Salween River. This includes Chiang Tung in Myanmar and Chiang Rung in Sipsong Panna, Yunnan, China, but also parts of northwestern Laos. The classical names of Chiang Tung state and city are Khemaraṭṭha and Tuṅgapurī.

Mueang is the Tai word for a principality or city-state,[2] which encompasses a city or town with the surrounding countryside. In traditional Lan Na, the most important city-states were Chiang Mai, Chiang Rai, Lampang, Lamphun, Phayao, Chiang Rung, Chiang Tung, Chiang Saen, Phrae, and Nan. However, this is a generalization that avoids historical changes, such as Nan was long independent and Phrae dependent on Sukhothai. These city-states were semi-independent and loosely connected with one another, with Chiang Mai as the most important. Each *mueang* had a ruler (*saopha*), and these rulers were often related to one another. Thongchai Winichakul has called traditional Lan Na a nonbounded kingdom with "a border without boundary line." Small city-states paid tribute to bigger ones, and it was not uncommon to give tribute to two competing ones (Thongchai 1994, 75, 97). A *mueang* settlement was physically clustered around a ruler's house and situated amid a rice plain that it ruled. In addition to the ruler's house, a *mueang* included a spirit shrine (*sao mueang*) (O'Connor 2000, 432). *Mueang* is an indigenous word that makes no distinction between a city, town, and a state. Every *mueang* was a self-governing community but not necessarily an independent state (O'Connor 2000, 432). Instead, lesser states existed within larger ones, connected via intricately knitted relationships with one another and with the central and most important city-state, Chiang Mai. Two or more *mueang* could overlap, which resulted in multiple loyalties and identities (Grabowsky 2005, 4). This vaguely definable geographical area without fixed boundaries, where smaller centers looked in all directions for security, has in academic literature been called a *mandala*.

The historic Eastern Shan State was about 31,000 square kilometers, which is approximately the same size as Belgium. High mountain ranges and deep valleys cover a large part of Chiang Tung's landscape. According to J. George Scott, the state was called "the thirty-two cities of the Khuen" (Scott and Hardiman 1901, 1:373).[3]

The *mueang* of Chiang Tung is between the Salween and Mekong Rivers. The Salween is one of the longest free-flowing rivers in the world at about 2,815 kilometers, stretching from the Tibetan Plateau into the Andaman Sea in lower Myanmar.[4] Seven mountain ranges extending from north to south limit the accessibility between the Salween and Chiang Tung. Today, several dams have been planned on the Salween by the Chinese, though they are located on Myanmar territory; but all projects have been in abeyance so far because of massive protests. The Mekong River to the east of Chiang Tung also flows from the Tibetan Plateau, and it runs through China, Myanmar, Laos, Thailand, and Cambodia, down to the Mekong Delta in Vietnam. The estimated length of the river is 4,350 kilometers, and it has long been a major trade route between Yunnan and Southeast Asia. Many dams have been built on the Mekong River and its tributaries, and many more are planned or under construction.

The town of Chiang Tung is in a fertile valley covering 117 square kilometers, and the cultivation of rice plays an important role in its economy. In the middle of the town there is a small lake called Nong Tung. Winding around the Old Town is also an eight-kilometer-long, irregular, old defensive wall with twelve gates. The wall was first constructed in the late fourteenth century and the first half of the fifteenth century, but it has been reconstructed several times. In the beginning of the nineteenth century, Sao Mahakhanan reconstructed the wall when he rebuilt and repopulated Chiang Tung. Inside the wall there are many small villages (*baan*), which number altogether around forty or fifty. Every village has a Buddhist monastery (*wat*) and a spirit shrine (*sao baan*). In total, there are forty-two traditional Buddhist monasteries in the historic town of Chiang Tung (Kreangkrai 2008, 149) and many more in the countryside. The town has no straight, planned streets nor rectangular moats, as in Chiang Mai or Mandalay. Instead, its narrow streets and paths wind up and down small hills. The wall around the city is not rectangular but circular in outline, probably representing the old Lua city plan.

It is interesting to consider the city plan of Chiang Tung in contrast with the city plan of Chiang Mai. The city plan of Chiang Mai, as well as that of Wian Kum Kam, was rectangular, an indirect Khmer influence via Sukhothai, in contrast to upper Tai towns like Chiang Rai and Chiang Sean, where the layout of the city, its moats and city walls, normally followed geographical contours (Easum 2023, 36, 49). The twelve gates and irregular shape of Chiang Tung's city walls, following the contours of the natural landscape, testify to Lua/Lawa and early Tai city formations.

The location between more powerful dynasties has made the whole Chiang Tung area a borderland, especially from a historical point of view. Since ancient times, it has been a crossroads and an important junction for trade, which brings a vital source of income. William Clifton Dodd wrote, "Kengtung is the crossroads of the nations. The long caravans come and go constantly during the dry season, down from Talifu and Yunnan fu, and nearer points in China; and up from Rangoon, Maulmein, and Bangkok; they meet and pass each other at Kengtung, leaving salt, Chinese crockery, brass pots, and iron brasiers, from the north; and other foreign goods from the south and west" (Dodd [1923] 1996, 210).

For a long time, horses or mules brought trade along the winding caravan routes. Even elephants have trod these roads. It took trade convoys and armies weeks to walk across the high mountains. Caravan routes went south from China and Kunming toward Chiang Rung and then over the mountains to Chiang Tung. Traders also came from the south, west, and east. From the west, they came from Mandalay and Taunggyi, crossing the Salween before entering Chiang Tung. To the south, people traveled to and from Chiang Saen, Chiang Rai, and Chiang Mai in Thailand. From Chiang Mai, the road continued south to the port city of Moulmein at the Salween River, or farther south all the way to Bangkok. To the east was the path to the Mekong River, and from there it was possible to reach Luang Prabang in Laos by boat. The 470-kilometer trip from Chiang Mai to Chiang Tung took thirteen days in 1887 for Lieutenant Younghusband, who explored the area before the decision was made as to whether to incorporate it into British Burma (Younghusband [1888] 2005).

Interestingly, the history of Siam before the 1920s was written as one of dynasties and rulers, not the history of the Siamese, Tai, or Thai people. The notion of the Tai people as an ethnic group with a history of its own came from Western writers. *The Tai Race* by William Clifton Dodd ([1923] 1996) described Tai people living in different countries from India to Vietnam as an ethnic group, or people, for the first time, with a unique history and national character. Dodd writes in the foreword that "Tai is not the name of any political division or country of the world. It is the name of a race" (xxi). He argues that the Tai as an ethnic group has had a long, uniting history: "And so, by looking up the Tai in history, we learn that the modern Tai people including the western Shan and southern Siamese ... have had organized governments for more than 4,000 years" (339). His writing is based on a nationalistic idea that an ethnic group of people has a national unitary character throughout history.

A few years later (1928), Khun Wichitmatra published a history book in the Thai language called *Lak Thai* (Origins of the Thai), which was highly influenced by *The Tai Race* by Dodd. This new history centered on the Thai as a race, not just the dynasties that figured in works by Prince Damrong (Baker and Pasuk 2014,

112, 130). These books invented the concept of the Thai not simply as the citizen of a certain state but as a people with a history and a national character. During 1935–36, the Ministry of Defense published a series of maps that depicted Wichitmatra's story of Thai migrations and indicated the imaginary boundaries of Thai kingdoms from the Nanchao era to Bangkok. This old-fashioned nationalistic idea must, of course, be challenged, because the dynasties and kingdoms of Sukhathai, Chiang Mai, Ayutthaya, and Bangkok all comprised many different groups of people. The Thai nationalists in the 1930s shifted the meaning of a nation from the people confined within the national territory to a community defined by ethnic origins, a long and unique history, and a common language (Baker and Pasuk 2014, 112).

Myanmar is divided into seven states and seven regions. Chiang Tung is part of the Shan State, the largest of the seven states, which covers 155,800 square kilometers. The Shan State is traditionally divided into three substates, Northern Shan State, Eastern Shan State, and Southern Shan State, but it is today officially divided into eleven districts, with Kyaingtong, as Chiang Tung is officially called, as one of these. According to the *2014 Myanmar Population and Housing Census*, the population of the Kyaingtong district is 366,861. The population of the township is 171,720, and the town is 44,289.

The borders between the nation states in the northern parts of Southeast Asia today owe much of their existence to colonial state-making, and they divide people who share much of the same culture and language. After the British took control of Burma in the late nineteenth century, Chiang Tung acquired a certain measure of self-government, together with the rest of the so-called Frontier Areas of Burma. The history of Chiang Tung and its location in northern Southeast Asia are essential in understanding the city, its people, and its culture.

Basic Facts about the Tai Khuen People

The majority of residents in Chiang Tung call themselves Tai Khuen, or simply Khuen, and are an ethnic group within the larger group of Tai-speaking peoples that includes Tai Yuan, Tai Lue, Tai Dam, and others. The traditional language spoken by local people in the town of Chiang Tung is Khuen. Khuen is a sister language of Tai Yuan and Tai Lue, spoken in north Thailand as well as in Sipsong Panna, Yunnan. The exposed geographical and political location of Chiang Tung in the world of northern Southeast Asia, sandwiched between the more significant cultures of the Burmese, the Chinese, and the Siamese, has created an awareness of its unique identity. Today almost everyone in Chiang Tung also speaks Burmese. It is the official language in Myanmar and is the language spoken in schools. Shan (Tai Yai), the language spoken in the rest of the Shan state, is also today widely spoken in Chiang Tung and is probably the most common language heard on the streets of Chiang Tung.

In Thailand, all the different Tai groups living outside Thailand are called Tai Yai, the big Thais. In Myanmar, the Khuen people may sometimes be called Gon or Gon Shan but more often are merely classified as belonging to the larger Shan ethnic group; today many of them consider themselves as part of that larger Shan ethnic group as well. The Shan people traditionally living west of the Salween River have a long and close connection with the Burmese. They were already living in the country by the middle of the twelfth century, mainly in the highlands north and northeast of the Dry Zone (Aung-Thwin and Aung-Thwin 2012, 48). They can be divided as Tai Mao (northern Shan) and Tai Long (southern Shan), but for simplicity reasons this book will use the term Western Shan.[5]

Among the Shan people west of the Salween River there are legends about an ancient kingdom or principality called Mueang Mao (Mong Mao) and a legendary ruler called Chao Sua Khan Fa. Some of these legends go back as far as the sixth century CE, but most date back to the twelfth or thirteenth centuries. The legends appear in Shan chronicles but also in Burmese and Chinese records (Yos 2001, 3–7). However, I have found no reference to Mueang Mao in chronicles from Chiang Tung, nor in inscriptions or local oral traditions. There appear to be no traces of traditions about the ancient Mueang Mao kingdom among the Khuen people of Chiang Tung. This shows an old division between the Shan culture on the western side of Salween River and Chiang Tung on the east, likely related to the rapid Salween River and many mountain ranges extending from north to south, which historically limited the accessibility between the Shan plateau and Chiang Tung.

Volker Grabowsky (1999, 61, 67; 2005, 3) calls the region the "Yuan-Khün-Lü cultural zone" because the Yuan people in Northern Thailand, the Khuen people in Chiang Tung, and the Lue people in Sipsong Panna are close, speak mutually understandable dialects, and used similar systems of writing. Earlier in the century, Søren Egerod (1959) mentioned that these peoples are closely related to one another in language and writing systems. However, Yuan writing in Northern Thailand is no longer in use. It has been replaced with the modern Thai script. In Chiang Tung and Sipsong Panna, the traditional *tham* script is still in use, with small differences. This script has been used in Chiang Tung from the middle of the fifteenth century on stone inscriptions (Griswold and Prasert Na Nagara 1978; Panpen Kruathai and Silao Ketphrom 2013) and in Khuen religious and secular literature in the form of palm-leaf manuscripts and folder books.

I will use the word Shan for all Tai people in the Shan State of Myanmar, including Tai Khuen. However, I have several times been informed by locals in Chiang Tung that they are not Shan but Khuen. During one spirit offering, I sat beside and shared a meal with an old gentleman who had gone to a missionary school when he was young. He told me with strong determination in English, "We are not Shan. We are *Khuen*. Shan and Khuen are not the same. We have different languages." Today the concept Khuen is still very much alive in the minds of older local people, but it is possible that the imagined Khuen nation soon will finally disappear in popular consciousness and be succeeded by the more political concept of Shan and the Shan State. The Shan people in Myanmar and most of Tai-speaking people outside Thailand and Laos just speak of themselves as Tai.

The Khuen people are the majority in Chiang Tung, but they do not live there alone. Tai Loi (Lua) is an ethnic group of Palaungic Mon-Khmer-speaking people who today live mostly in the mountains northeast of Chiang Tung. They have an important place in the history of Chiang Tung that we will consider more closely later in this chapter and in chapter 2. There are also three more Tai groups living in Chiang Tung: the Western Shan (Tai Yai), the Tai Lue, and the Tai Neua (Shan Chinese, or Dehong Dai). J. George Scott (Scott and Hardiman 1901, 1:417; Scott 1932, 258) describes these Tai groups living in Chiang Tung during the late nineteenth and early twentieth century as the Tai or Western Shan living near the Salween and the Tai Lue in the valleys east of Chiang Tung. Scott also mentions a Tai group that he calls Shan Chinese, who form an important community just outside the eastern wall of the city. He mentions that these people are butchers, poultry sellers, and liquor makers for the town. Most Shan Chinese still live in Yunnan, China, but many immigrated into Southeast Asia during the nineteenth century. Some villages in Chiang Tung are a majority Tai Nuea, especially around Wat Pa Daeng. Scott continues that "in the capital town the population is, as expected, very mixed. Hkön [Khuen] preponderate, but there are considerable numbers of Lü and Western Shans, as well as some Lao [Tai Yuan]. The races intermarry freely, and it is probably the mixed offspring goes to recruit the dominant people of the town and valley" (Scott and Hardiman 1901, 1:417). Susan Conway (2006, 15–16) mentions that there was no ethnic purity among the Shan courts, as intermarriage between groups was common. Tai royal families intermarried with other Tai from Lan Na, from Sipsong Panna, and from Laos, but sometimes also with Kachin, Paluang, and Burmese. Today many people are born from intermarriages or from parents who moved to Chiang Tung last century from some Western Shan states or from Tai populations (Tai Lue or Tai Neua) in China.

Basic Facts about the Palaungic Mon-Khmer People

The original inhabitants of the Chiang Tung valley were an ethnic group of Palaungic Mon-Khmer origin called Lua or Lawa in the chronicles.[6] Many Mon-Khmer-speaking peoples lived all over northern Southeast Asia before Tai people entered the area. Legends about the relationship between these indigenous (autochthonous) people and the newly arrived Tai are also present in the city-states of Chiang Mai, Lamphun, Luang Prabang, and Chiang Rung, and they probably exist elsewhere also. Shigeharu Tanabe describes how these indigenous people have been represented within Tai traditional political systems. They are "ambivalently and contra-distinctively represented, as barbarous, cannibal, uncivilized, and non-Buddhist on the one hand, and on the other hand as original land-holders, and therefore ritually superior to the Tai conquerors, particularly in relation to the tutelary spirits of domains" (Tanabe 2000, 298).

A mutual dependence developed between the newly arrived lowland people and the indigenous highland people. The lowland people needed forest products, and the highland people needed products from the lowland. Grabowsky and other scholars believe the highland people "held a strong economic position as they controlled access to precious forest products, such as ivory, rhinoceros' horn, incense, honey, opium, and cardamom, which were then sent as tribute to royal courts in exchange for cloth, knives, pottery, and other consumer goods" (Grabowsky 2003, 113–14; Liew-Herres, Grabowsky, and Renoo 2012, 17).

As early as its third paragraph, the *Chiang Tung Chronicle* describes Chiang Tung as Dammilap, the land of the Damilas. Damila is derived from the Pāli language and refers to the Tamils of south India or Sri Lanka. The Lua seem to be compared to the Tamils because of their darker skin and because they were not Buddhists. Lan Na chronicles regarded the non-Buddhist Lua, also called Kha, as "uncivilised" (Sarassawadee 2005, 31; Grabowsky 2003, 113–14). The origin of the term "Kha" is unknown but indicates the non-Tai: "although speaking sometimes unrelated languages and practicing divergent cultures, they were united by living in the forest surrounding Tai *müang*, with which they were linked ritually" (Renard 2000, 66). The Lua possessed ritual functions as lords of the territorial guardian spirits, and they held a strong economic position, controlling precious forest products (Grabowsky 2003, 113–17). According to the diary of Captain McLeod (February 3, 1837) the Lua, or Lawa as he named them, extracted iron from the hills and made muskets at the same time as the Shans (Tai); McLeod consider them uncivilized and brutes (Grabowsky and Turton 2003, 327). Small subgroups of Lua still maintain their traditional lives in longhouses in remote areas of the Shan State at the China-Myanmar border and in Northern Thailand, but many of them have been assimilated into the majority Tai/Thai/Siamese populations. Lua, Wa, and Eng are the ethnic groups of the Palaungic Mon-Khmer-speaking people, who today live in the hills and mountains around Chiang Tung.

Over a long period living on the periphery of the Khuen people, the Lua people have changed their cultural, religious, and ethnic identities in such a way that they are now considered a Tai subgroup and members of the same political-economic system as the majority Khuen. During their long relationship with the Khuen, they have also adopted Buddhism. They are called Tai Loi, meaning "Hill Tai," but they are also called Wa Kut (Scott and Hardiman 1900, 1:517–18) and Kut Wa (Telford 1937, 89), meaning "those Wa who were left behind," as the Shan word *kut* means to be left behind, because the Lua are regarded as a subgroup of the Wa. Therefore I will name them throughout this book as Tai Loi (Lua), indicating their Lua/Lawa origin.

Today, most Tai Loi (Lua) live in mountain villages northeast of Chiang Tung near the Chinese border. Many of these villages base their incomes on green tea cultivation, with some selling high-quality tea to China. Some villages were destroyed during the long conflict between the Burmese military and guerrillas, and groups of Tai Loi (Lua) are at present living on the outskirts of Chiang Tung.[7]

The Lua, here called Milakkha, had also an important role in the legends of the origin of Haripuñjaya (known today as Lamphun). In *Cāmadevīvaṃsa*, the origin of the city-state of Haripuñjaya is described as a union between culture and nature, symbolized by the Mon culture of Queen Cāmadevī and the nature of the Lua king Vilanga. The myth describes the marriage alliance between the Mon queen Cāmadevī's twin sons and the twin daughters of the Lua king Vilanga. Cāmadevī herself was brought up as a stepdaughter of the Lua *rishi* Vasudeva, a hermit from Doi Suthep (Condominas [1974] 1990; Swearer and Sommai 1998).

The Lua people who escaped from the Tai conquerors are considered related to, or part of the Wa people living to the north, on both sides of the border between China and Myanmar. Whether the Lua of Chiang Tung actually are ancestors of the present Wa people is difficult to establish with certainty, but J. George Scott was of the opinion that "it is certain that at one time they [Wa people] occupied the whole state of Kengtung" (Scott 1932, 299–300). People in Chiang Tung widely believed that the Wa people originated from the region of Chiang Tung, and the Lua people were defeated by King Mangrai. Further, the United Wa State Army (UWSA), the most powerful ethnic armed group in Myanmar, has control of the northern part of Eastern Shan State along the Chinese border, as well as a smaller zone farther south on the border with Thailand, and this group claims the right to Chiang Tung and the whole of Eastern Shan State as the original inhabitants of the area (see Wa territory in map 1). In 2019,

I heard such rumors from some of my informants. After the February 2021 coup, there have actually been some negotiations between the military and UWSA, but it would be surprising if the Myanmar military moved out of the Eastern Shan State and let UWSA take control. For the history, culture, and current political development of the Wa people at the Myanmar-China border see Magnus Fiskesjö (2021) and Bertil Lintner (2021).

1

LOCAL BELONGING

A place is a territory of significance, distinguished from adjacent and from larger or smaller areas by its name, by its particular environmental qualities, by the stories and shared memories connected to it and by the intensity of the meanings people give to it or derive from it.

—Edward Relph, *A Pragmatic Sense of Place*, 2008

The first time I visited the Songkran festival in Chiang Tung, I realized that if I wanted to understand the significance of the festival, I needed to do more than just participate and observe. I needed more knowledge, and the knowledge I was seeking was buried in myths and memories of the origin and early history of Chiang Tung. These myths and memories, told by local people from generation to generation and written in old chronicles, helped me understand that Songkran narrates the place itself.

This book is primarily an interdisciplinary inquiry about Chiang Tung as a sense of place and belonging for the Khuen people. Longing for community and group identity is one of the deepest urges of humanity, the urge to belong to a group of people sharing common experiences. Identity is part of our common everyday life and is shaped by family, neighborhood, work, group affiliation, and engagement in collective tasks or hobbies. It is also part of local or world politics when groups of people with a common ideology, religion, ethnicity, and nationality engage in confrontations with other groups of people. Identity and community are shaped everywhere, through the local and the larger world, in cities as well as in countryside.

A Sense of Place

A feeling of belonging to a specific geographic place is essential for engendering a sense of identity for many people. When I entered into the myths and memories of the people of Chiang Tung, I realized that the place itself was, and is, to a great extent, of special importance. Identity is a complex and multilayered phenomenon, almost beyond definition, and across the world, people see their identities through many different lenses. Ethnicity can be an important part of group identity, though for some people it is not very important. For some people, religious identity does not matter. They do not hold religious beliefs, or they consider their religious faith up to themselves, unattached to a religious group community. But for others, religious faith is an integral part of their lives, and they consider religious belonging to be an important part of their identity. The same can be said about local belonging and identity. Some consider themselves global citizens and do not connect with local or national belonging. But for others, a sense of belonging to a specific geographic place and to a group of people who share the same place is essential in engendering a sense of their own unique identity.

Ethnicity is not a permanent and unchanging identity, and ethnic belonging can change for a person during a lifetime. Ethnic groups also change because of many external circumstances. Those Khuen who settled in Chiang Tung more than seven hundred years ago have very little in common with the people who live in Chiang Tung today and call themselves Khuen, especially if we consider the forced resettlements of people during this time. Therefore, ethnicity cannot be treated as inherent. On the contrary, ethnic groups everywhere constantly redefine themselves and are similarly redefined by others. Southeast Asia is a region of constantly shifting ethnic boundaries, with many external factors affecting the way people consider their ethnic identity. According to Ashley South, "the nature and significance of ethnicity, and other categories of identity, have changed over the centuries—often according to political and economic circumstances" (South 2008, 4). Edmund Leach argues that ethnic groups transferred themselves from one language group to another, showing that "large sections of the peoples we now know as Shans are descendants of hill tribesmen who have in the recent past been assimilated into the more sophisticated ways of Buddhist-Shan culture" (Leach 1954, 39).

The control of human power, not the conquest of land, was the crucial factor for establishing, consolidating, and strengthening state power in precolonial Southeast Asia. Strong rulers sought to expand the numbers of subjects under their direct control. This could mean that ethnic differences were of less importance, as various ethnic groups lived closely together as subjects of the same state power. With examples from eighteenth-century Burma, Lieberman (1978, 2003) emphasizes that Shan and Burmese cultural and ethnic features served as ways to recognize political loyalty and prestige. There was a strong tendency in the mid-eighteenth century for "populations subject to the same political center to use cultural traits as a badge of their common identity, particularly in periods of transition and uncertainty" (Lieberman 1978, 480). But the boundaries between ethnic groups were not strict, and people were accepted into other communities by adopting their language, dress, religious practices, and customs. The debate about ethnic identity ignored the complex history of migration, integration, intermarriage, and forced resettlements that affected all levels of society. Susan Conway has emphasized that the concept of a correct form of dress and textiles for each ethnic group and subgroup, frozen in a lengthy time frame, thus cannot be applied to the Shan states, as people were constantly altering and adapting their dress and textiles to suit political, economic, and social conditions (Conway 2008, 124). Indeed, any discussion of ethnic relationships during this early period raises problems. Shifts in identity markers changed over time, and the sources frequently refer to groups that cannot be identified today (Andaya and Andaya 2015, 46). It is not possible to find exact records of ethnic belonging in precolonial Southeast Asia, but we will draw some conclusions later in the study of Chiang Tung.

The concept of ethnicity has long been questioned as an analytical tool. How can we use a concept if it reflects only a moment in an ongoing cultural process? At the same time that ethnicity has partly become outdated in academia, it has gained importance in the real world. In Myanmar, a country with 135 officially recognized ethnic groups as well as over fifty years of armed struggle between the Burmese military and a great number of ethnic rebel groups and armies, it is not possible to disregard how people consider themselves as belonging to a particular ethnic group. Instead of dismissing these people, "we must evaluate what ethnicity signifies for those who claim it" (Shneiderman 2015, 6). Sara Shneiderman proposes that "we must investigate anew how such forms of consciousness are produced by all kinds of individuals—not only by self-proclaimed ethnic activists—who see themselves as members of a collectivity and seek recognition as such from others. Acknowledging that ethnicity is inevitably constructed is not the end of the story but rather the beginning of understanding the ongoing life of such constructions" (6).

People may see themselves as members of an ethnic group, but these groups are, through time, constantly redefining themselves and are likewise redefined by others. People select their own history in the context of others, and every social entity should be viewed as part of a larger system, where the self-identification of a people includes attributions from its neighbors. An ethnic group is a socially constructed community that often defines itself by its origin or language, and thus a chosen history is one of the main elements in creating a self-identification for the group and prescribing its boundaries to others.

Therefore, the main analytical tool in this book is not ethnicity or ethnolinguistics. François Robinne and Mandy Sadan have suggested that ethnic categories should be treated as one cultural marker among others, not "to be an *a priori* determinant of identity and social coherency" (Robinne and Sadan 2007, 307). In this book we see that people identify themselves as belonging to a specific location, territory, or place, not just to a specific ethnic group. At the same time that individuals can be ethnic Tai, they can also naturally identify as Buddhist as well as distinguish themselves as belonging to a specific place, as Chiang Tung citizens. Belonging to a place can be as important as ethnic identity.

This book focuses on a specific geographic place, a social space, and its connection to people and identity. People from Chiang Tung can express their identity in various ways, identifying as Khon Chiang Tung, Khuen, Tai, Shan, or a Myanmar citizen. As I dove deeper into researching the Songkran festival, one purpose of this book was to understand the connection between the geographic place of Chiang Tung and the Khuen people. It seeks to understand the identity of a place, or more specifically, identification of the location as a place of belonging. This book focuses on the community and group identity of the Khuen people and the place where they belong. Myths and memories in the *Chiang Tung Chronicle* as well as those expressed orally by local people tell us about how the Khuen people imagine the origin and early history of the place where they live. The origin and early history of Chiang Tung also narrates the origin of the Khuen people. It becomes clear in chapter 2 that ethnic belonging and territorial belonging are closely connected among the Khuen people.

In discussing the Lue ethnic group from Sipsong Panna, now living in both Northern Thailand and Laos, Charles Keyes and Paul T. Cohen emphasize national cultures as important for the identity of ethnic groups. Cohen writes, "Lue ethnic identification in Thailand is, in part, a reflection of the way national culture constructs Lue identity" (Cohen 1998, 57). The identity of the Tai Lue is also constructed in quite different ways in each of these countries, China, Thailand, and Laos, because their ethnicity has been shaped by quite distinctive national cultures (Keyes 1992, 5). The concept *localized ethnic identity*, coined by Keyes (1992) and also used by Cohen (1998, 50), suggests that the names of the city-states and of ethnic entities exhibit parallel variations. Cohen argues that those who identify themselves as Lue may also identify themselves according to the place where they are living, such as Lue Mueang La or Lue Mueang Sing (50). Also, J. George Scott argues it was not uncommon for a man to deny being Tai, Khuen, or Lue and to describe himself by the name of his district, as a Yawng (Yong), native of Mong Yawng (Mong Yong) (Scott and Hardiman 1901, 1:417). Localized ethnic identity is a good term for the connection of identity to both local place and ethnic identity, and we see that it captures ideas of identity for the Khuen people of Chiang Tung.

The concept of *place* can be difficult to define. A place can be rather small and consist of a house, a village, a glade, or a chair. A place can also be as large as a landscape, a city, or a district. A place is not only a territory, it is a narrative. The sense of belonging to a place is deeply rooted inside the human mind. Abstractly, it is possible to say that a place has an identity, such as when we refer to a beach town, an industrial town, a trade town, or a mountain village. In these cases, it is the geography or the main economic activity that characterizes the specific locations. But these descriptions are rough and undefined aspects of the identity of a place and a territory. Chiang Tung can be described as a border town or a trade town. However, this book will dig deeper into the identity of Chiang Tung, looking at the place as a social space in the mind of the people. Therefore, this book focuses not just on the identity of the physical place, but, more particularly, on the way people identify themselves as belonging to the specific place.

This suggests what Edward Relph (2008) calls a *sense of place*, as opposed to the *spirit of place*. A sense of place is, according to him, what lies primarily inside humans as a synesthetic faculty that combines sight, hearing, smell, movement, touch, imagination, purpose, and anticipation. In contrast, spirit of place exists primarily in the territory itself. This book will attempt to capture the identity of people as belonging to a specific location, territory, or place—Chiang Tung. According to Relph, a place is a territory of significance, distinguished from adjacent and from larger or smaller areas by its name, its particular environmental qualities, the stories and shared memories connected to it, and the intensity of the meanings people give to it or derive from it.

A *sense of place* is a concept used across different disciplines in different ways, and it is impossible to provide a definition that works for all contexts. However, the relationship between people and place is important for individual and community identity. Place provides a profound center of human existence, to which people have deep emotional and psychological ties and are part of the complex processes through which individuals and groups define themselves (Convery, Corsane, and Davis 2012, 1). There is no clear consensus about the concept of *sense of place*, but in this book it refers to the physical place and how people connect to the place. It is about the meanings people attribute to their surroundings, including cultural, religious, and historical aspects of their place.

In the influential writings of Benedict Anderson (2006) and others, a nation is a socially constructed community, imagined by the people who perceive themselves as part of that group: "It is imagined because the members of even the smallest nation will never know most of their fellow members, meet them, or even hear of them, yet in the minds of each lives the image of their communion" (Anderson 2006, 6). Important for a common, imagined community is a myth of common ancestry. The defeat of the Lua people and the establishment of Chiang

Tung by Mangrai as a place for the Tai Khuen people is a myth of common Khuen ancestry and a chosen history, a myth that has been repeated during their long history and is still repeated today.

Shared memories of a chosen history are important for a sense of place and belonging. A chosen history is the history told by the people represented in that history. The story in the minds of the people living in that particular place may be more interesting than the straight facts and historical truths, and it may be named memory or collective memory. The places are often connected to memories, which Pierre Nora calls *sites of memory* (*lieux de mémoire*). He writes about the differences between history and memory. Memory only accommodates those facts that suit it. It is blind to all but the group it binds. He mentions that memory takes root in the concrete, in spaces, gestures, images, and objects (Nora 1989, 9). We can describe Chiang Tung as a site of memory. Buildings, images, and objects in the sacred space of Chiang Tung have memories shared by the people and contribute to the self-identification of Khuen as belonging to the place Chiang Tung. Collective memory refers to a group's remembrance of their past. It refers to the distribution throughout society of what individuals know, believe, and feel about the past, how they judge the past morally, how closely they identify with it, and how much they are inspired by it as a model for their conduct and identity (Schwartz 2016, 10). Chiang Tung memories take place in the concrete, in sacred spaces, gestures, images, and objects.

Given these ideas about a sense of place and memories, the concepts of myths and memories in this book include both myths without direct historical background and shared memories about local historical events that are essential for self-identification and common identity. To separate myth from history is both difficult and pointless. Instead, both myths and a chosen local history give a commentary on what people have held and hold to be of lasting value. Memories are a group of people's imagination of their common history and identity, with chosen glories and tragedies.

Memories of meaningful places are loaded with legends, myths, and narratives of the past. These often narrate a chosen glory or chosen trauma. The history of a chosen glory or a chosen trauma (concepts borrowed from Catarina Kinnvall 2004, 755–57) has been used for the purpose of demonstrating differences and hostilities between groups. Of course, there are dangers in bonds based on intergroup strife. As we can see throughout history, nationalism in extreme forms can lead to intolerance, war, and ethnic cleansing. Still, all humans use stories to generate meaning and identity, and those who find themselves marginalized are likely to do so. For a vulnerable minority living in an exposed position, myths and memories of an ancient past may be a way to fight for cultural coherence and survival. Myths and memories of an ancient past are realities for the Khuen people of Chiang Tung. They tell of how Chiang Tung was inhabited and became a Buddhist city and also narrate the origin of the Khuen people as an ethnic group.

Chronicles such as the *Chiang Tung Chronicle* are not written as literary texts nor as historical documents. Rather, they are a compilation of myths, legends, and historical events, and various parts probably have ancient oral roots. These myths and memories are of central interest to us in this book. Donald K. Swearer (1976, 4) holds that the permanent significance of myths and legends lies in the fact that they transcend history. He holds that "myths and legends may be used to tell us something about the history of a people, but, more significantly, they give a commentary on what a people has held and holds to be of lasting value." The myths and memories in Chiang Tung tell us about what the Khuen people understand and believe about the origin and early history of the place where they live—their common ancestry.

Local History

If the Songkran festival is about the place Chiang Tung itself, then other aspects of the culture may similarly point to the place itself. The history of Chiang Tung has convinced me that a sense of shared origin and identity in a place can be as important as a religious or ethnic-linguistic identity. The Tai Khuen consider themselves an ethnic group, along with the Tai Yuan, Tai Lue, Tai Dam, and others within the larger group of Tai-speaking peoples. The more I study the violent and dramatic history of Chiang Tung, with forced resettlements, hardships, and wars, the more I realize that events in history point to a common identity between the Khuen people and the place Chiang Tung—the place itself as a sense of place and belonging. As a borderland between more powerful neighbors, Chiang Tung's exposed place has shaped a self-image of the Khuen people.

There is a tendency in academic studies to see the geographical world as based on a pattern composed of regions, nations, and continents. National and regional borders prevent us from understanding broader patterns. Chiang Tung, at the regional border between East Asia and Southeast Asia, has to be seen from a cross-border perspective. Much has been written about Southeast Asia, often divided into categories such as Thai, Lao, Burmese, or Khmer studies. Area studies in Western universities are very nation-state- and language-centric. Erik de Maaker and Monica Janowski discuss the way modern nation-states have, for a long time, been the basis of academic area studies: "Most studies of society, culture, and history in Asia continue to accept national territories as the natural building blocks of academic enquiry.... They imply that borders between states are not only of a political and administrative nature but also create separate social, economic, and cultural realms" (de Maaker and Janowski 2020, 153). This so-called methodological nationalism, a term coined by Andreas Wimmer and Nina Glick Schiller (2002), is a logical consequence of colonial state-making, which results in borders, borderlands, and marginal societies having long been neglected in academic studies. Chiang Tung, however, has very little in common with the rest of Myanmar and is obviously not part of contemporary Thailand. Nation-state-centric research in a cross-cultural borderland like Chiang Tung has to tackle a great number of choices and presumptions based on national academic boundaries.

Not much attention has been focused on local history from marginalized societies. Sunait Chutintaranond (2002) offers an alternative way of writing history. He wants to write history from a peripheral viewpoint, emphasizing the history of autonomous centers, which in theory were in the domain of a particular king but in reality exercised autonomy. Chiang Tung is one such peripheral community with much autonomy as a mainly independent principality, though still connected to one of the more important powers in the region. Sunait suggests that the history of premodern Southeast Asia in general "should be written in the context of autonomous history, in contrast to the centralist ideology's frame of reference which emphasizes the role of a few ruling centres" (12). In writing history from the peripheral viewpoint, the first matter a historian has to keep in mind is that the idea of power of a premodern ruler was not the same as that of a ruler in the colonial period. The idea of power of a modernizing king of Siam, like that of the British colonial rulers, was based on the Western concept of centralization (Sunait 2002, 13). Mainland Southeast Asia was a mosaic of small, independent principalities, loosely grouped together at various times into larger political entities. This general pattern continued until the arrival of the colonial powers (13). Sandwiched between more dominant cultures, local history is important for the people of Chiang Tung and, arguably, for most lowland and highland people in the mountain territory of northern Southeast Asia.

Thongchai (2005, 122–26) has indicated that there are two alternative traditions of knowledge production in Thailand, which can be compared to the Western-style area studies. There are the imperial discourses of the Thai state and the local knowledge of the people themselves. Academic studies about the history of Chiang Tung will hopefully, in the future, be written by residents from Chiang Tung, with a combination of traditional academic studies and local knowledge. Thongchai has argued for local knowledge as a complement to Western-style area studies. He writes,

> People have been mingling along the borders of Thailand and its neighbors for hundreds of years as members of various ethnic groups.... [They have] inherited local knowledge about their homelands on both sides of the borders and about their pre-nation-state

neighbors. Many of them share with the people on the other side of present-day boundary lines the same myths, folklore, and other stories and knowledge. (125)

This is certainly true about the people in northern Southeast Asia, with a long tradition of crossing borders. In Chiang Tung, there is an old tradition of transmitting local history by the locals themselves. In contrast to nation-state-centric studies, this book will tell the origin and early history of Chiang Tung from the knowledge of the local people themselves. Local history, with its myths and legends, is an important part of a people's self-identification. It is a powerful force for binding people together in a sense of shared origins. It is what people believe about themselves that makes history a living reality in the present.

During its long period of isolation since the military coup in Burma in 1962, the country has lived under strict censorship, and it has been almost impossible for locals to write and publish local history. This is one of the reasons that I, as a Western outsider, am writing this history. In a country with such limitations on historical work, there is a danger for Chiang Tung to be left behind or represented as a remote geographic part in the national history of Myanmar or Thailand. I hope I can represent views from inside. Hopefully, in the future, it will be possible for local people to write and publish local history; one of my aims for this book is to inspire people to do this.

This book centers a local community in a historical borderland and as part of a global mountain territory. However, to fully understand Chiang Tung, it is not enough to conduct field studies on the micro-level. Chiang Tung is part of a large region, referred to as Monsoon Asia by the French scholar Paul Mus, and it is defined in his essay *India Seen from the East* (*L'Inde vue de l'est. Cultes indiens et indigènes au Champa*) (Mus [1933] 2011). For Mus, Monsoon Asia includes the large geographical area "with a certain unity of culture . . . in which India, Indo-China, Indonesia, a Pacific islands fringe and doubtless southern China are to be united" (22). His theory has been challenged, however, because of its oversimplification. It is a grand theory covering a large part of Asian cultures, without taking into consideration the existence of rich local traditions. It is my conviction that it is important to view Chiang Tung in the context of the culture of Monsoon Asia. The writings of Mus will therefore be important, especially in chapters 6 and 7, about the religious culture of Chiang Tung and the Songkran festival.

Buddhism in the Borderland

The heart of the Tai Khuen people of Chiang Tung is truly filled with Buddhist beliefs and practices; it is not just an echo of foreign Buddhist texts and doctrines.

Buddhist traditions constantly underwent transformation and became adopted in local traditions and practices. According to Rajeshwari Ghose, "each culture transformed Buddhist teachings and iconography into forms closer to its own heart, which led to the creation of beliefs, ideas and art forms that were neither purely Indian, nor indigenous and not even a fusion of the two, but were governed by a completely new aesthetic and world view" (Ghose 1998, 1).

The Buddhist religious culture is diverse, consisting of sacred literature, rituals, visual and material culture, monastic discipline, festivals, and other elements, and all these elements are part of a broader social and political history. It is impossible to understand Buddhism only through texts and doctrines, without an appreciation of the ways it takes form in artistic expressions. Khuen literature is a cultural treasure that embodies the great creativity of the Khuen people. The great stories of Khuen literature have their origin in the Tai Yuan-Khuen-Lue culture, written, rewritten, and embedded in material reality. Tangible manifestations such as visual art, architecture, and craft, passed from generation to generation, are of the same importance as spoken or written words. Literature, rituals, and visual and material expressions are closely connected. What we usually call a religion does not exist without material expressions and social activities. Religious buildings and objects such as sculptures and paintings tell something religious texts and stories cannot convey.

This book will attempt to capture the complex connection between tradition and change in religious culture when divided between national borders, and to understand the relationship between Buddhism and the cult of territory spirits. In the case of Chiang Tung, it is not only important to see the local Buddhist tradition as a part of the Tai Yuan-Khuen-Lue culture area, with its roots from the island of Lanka, but it is also important to see it as part of the larger geographic area of Monsoon Asia, centering on wet rice agriculture and the ancient cult of territory spirits. The local Buddhist tradition is also connected to the political history of South China and northern Southeast Asia, and it can be traced in the differences between the lowland Tai Khuen culture and the indigenous highland Paluang Mon-Khmer Lua culture.

Especially in chapters 5 and 6 of this book, it becomes apparent how well the traditional Buddhist culture of Chiang Tung has been maintained during the long and troublesome history of Chiang Tung. Buddhist beliefs and practices are an important part of shared meaning and myths for people in Chiang Tung, but they should be seen as part of a broader social, cultural, and historical context. Although I am trained in religious studies, this is an interdisciplinary inquiry into Chiang Tung as a sense of place and belonging for the Khuen people, connecting the local with the global, the present with the past, and tradition with change and transformation.

Sources

In this book, three specific sources have been used in addition to academic writings on the history and religion of Southeast Asia. First, I have done on-site research in Chiang Tung and its surroundings, including interviews and participant observations. Second, I have looked at old regional chronicles and inscriptions. The third source used is writings from Western visitors from the early nineteenth century to World War II. These three separate sources have formed the basis of this book.

Interviews and Participant Observations

Interviews and participant observations made up my days during my visits to Chiang Tung. Walking about, asking questions, and observing were important for understand Chiang Tung and its people. During my first visits, I spent many days strolling along the winding streets, visiting various monasteries. Monasteries in Chiang Tung are public spaces where everyone is always welcome, and the assembly hall (*vihan*) is almost always open. If it is accidentally closed, there are always some young novices to ask for the key. They were around five to twelve years old and spoke Khuen and Burmese along with a bit of Thai. I found that these novices were often curious and liked to chat. Some monks spoke English well, but most didn't. But it was possible to communicate in Thai, especially the northern Thai dialect. Most of the time, however, I had to use interpreters and translators when talking, for example with monks. In Chiang Tung, it was possible to find a few tourist guides, but most of them were young men from ethnic groups like the Akkha and the Lahu, and their knowledge and experiences mostly center on hiking in the mountains. Unfortunately, they have less knowledge about Khuen culture, religion, and history. Therefore, I had to spend some time during the first visits to find ethnic Tai Khuen people knowledgeable in the traditional culture of Chiang Tung. Importantly, I found a few middle-aged Khuen men and women with deep knowledge about traditional culture, with a large network of contacts and good knowledge of the English language. These were my emissaries, but they also helped me with translation during interviews. Therefore, important sources have been local people, sometimes directly, but often through translators and interpreters. These contacts followed me to temples and spirit shrines and helped me meet people. They also told me myths and history about Chiang Tung and were helpful when I was talking and listening to others.

Chronicles and Inscriptions

This book used written local chronicles from different city-states in Lan Na. The early history of Chiang Tung is narrated in local historical documents. Foremost among these is the *Chiang Tung Chronicle* (*CTC*), but local chronicles from other city-states also convey insights about Lan Na and Chiang Tung. Chronicles contain a mixture of folk legends and historical events of a political, military, and religious nature. The *CTC* is a historical chronicle, usually referred to as *phongsavadan*; it is secular and contains numerous legends and myths. The mythical legends and stories in the *CTC* about the origin and early history of Chiang Tung are of special value for this book.[1] The first part of the *CTC*, from the beginning to paragraph 99, is filled with legends, and from there on is a more historic section. The legends focus on historical accounts that are interspersed with various tales and events that belong to a Buddhist worldview. Many of the historical accounts, even in the legend section, most likely have a historical basis. The historic section, beginning at paragraph 99, starts in the year 1134 and ends in 1935.

Chronicles like the *CTC* were inscribed by hand on palm leaves and tied into bundles or were folded manuscripts written on paper produced from the bark of the *sa* tree. They were often copied from earlier manuscripts, so various versions of a manuscript can exist. The historiographic importance of these chronicles is controversial, as they were not composed for purely historiographical purposes. They were recopied numerous times over long periods of time, and many of the stories were probably handed down orally over many generations. Political chronicles like the *CTC* have a strong hagiographic character, imagining the golden history of a specific dynasty.

The *CTC* is not only about the Khuen people; other ethnic groups are also important, including the Chinese, the Tai Loi (Lua), and the Tai Yuan. Another important focus of the *CTC* is how Chiang Tung was established as a future Buddhist center through a visit by the Buddha himself. The main theme in the first half of the *CTC* is the place itself and how it became a place for the Khuen ethnic group to live. It covers the origin and early history of Chiang Tung. This theme—the origins of the place and of the Khuen people—is also a central focus in the annual Songkran festival in April.

In addition to these chronicles, *tamnan* are a kind of religious chronicle that are important sources in Lan Na. Knowledge of the religious history of northern Southeast Asia comes from these chronicles and from inscriptions. One important chronicle is the Pāli *Jinakālamālīpakaraṇam* (*JKM*) written in the early sixteenth century. Also important are two versions of a Tai chronicle from the Buddhist tradition of Wat Pa Daeng: the *Wat Pa Daeng Chronicle* (*WPDC*) and the *Tamnan Mūlasāsanā Wat Pa Daeng* (*TMWPD*). The *WPDC* is translated from the Khuen language from a copy that Sai Saimong Mangrai borrowed from the abbot of Wat Pa Daeng in Chiang Tung. It is not dated, and the different parts were almost certainly written at different times and by different hands. The whole chronicle has been copied and recopied countless times, as was usually the case among the Buddhist cultures before the time of printed books. As usual in Buddhist chronicles, the history begins with a short description of the life of the Buddha and how Buddhism reached the island of Lanka and Southeast Asia. The main part of the manuscript is about the two different orders, the Flower Garden (Suan Dok or Pupphārām) and the Red Forest (Pa Daeng), brought from Lanka to Southeast Asia during the fourteenth and fifteenth centuries, and the controversy between them.

Another version of the *WPDC* was translated by Sommai Premchit and Donald K. Swearer (1977) under the name *Tamnan Mūlasāsanā Wat Pa Daeng* (*TMWPD*) (Sommai and Swearer 1977). This version also discusses Wat Pa Daeng in Chiang Tung but is not nearly as detailed as the *WPDC* regarding events relating to the larger world. These two manuscripts, the *WPDC* and the *TMWPD*, do not follow the same structure, but the main content is the same. However, there are more complex and richer details in the *WPDC*, such as a long part containing proper pronunciation of Pāli ritual texts, and, similar to the *CTC*, part of the history of Chiang Tung.

Several local chronicles recount historical events around Lan Na. For example, chronicles from Chiang Mai, Chiang Khaeng, Nan, and Chiang Rung act as complements to Chiang Tung's own chronicles. These also mention Chiang Tung several times. Chiang Tung's early history is described here based on the chronicles, without putting too much emphasis on separating reliable historical events from mythical legends. Instead, the focus is to tell the history of Chiang Tung as the people of Chiang Tung have told it throughout the centuries.

Inscriptions are also valuable sources for early history. These are often written at the same time or shortly after the event they document. But, just like the chronicles, they are also tendentious texts with a specific purpose. Therefore, when reading chronicles and inscriptions, one must proceed with caution. There is a very interesting inscription at the monastery of Wat Pa Daeng in Chiang Tung, written in the year 1451. From this inscription, we get important information and dates that can confirm in more detail events from the written chronicles. It is important, however, to recognize that inscriptions are also written for specific purposes that do not always prioritize historical facts.

Foreign Visitors

Foreign travelers, missionaries, and colonial administrators visiting Chiang Tung in the nineteenth and twentieth centuries are key sources for the colonial and precolonial period. Sources from the British colonial administration are preserved in British archives and libraries, and documents and reports from missionaries who lived and worked in Chiang Tung are preserved at the Payap University

Archive in Chiang Mai. The writings from these foreign visitors are important, as they are the only ones we have. However, readers must be aware that they see the area through a colonial lens.

Western travelers reached Southeast Asia's coastal areas after the Portuguese found the sea route to India in the late fifteenth century. The Portuguese established a trade agreement with Ayutthaya in the early sixteenth century, but it took a while before the Dutch and the Spanish arrived in the same area, because the Portuguese tried to keep the route secret. Foreign ships also came from the east to Southeast Asia's coastline, both from China and from Japan. The Japanese sailed to Southeast Asia with a merchant navy for a short time in the seventeenth century. Yamada Nagamasa (1590–1630) was a Japanese explorer and businessperson who gained considerable influence in Ayutthaya at the beginning of the seventeenth century. He eventually became a governor of Nakhon Si Thammarat in present-day Southern Thailand. Some Japanese, if we are to believe local tradition, ended up as far as Chiang Tung.

The merchant Ralph Fitch was the first of the British who came all the way up to Chiang Mai. He made this trip in 1587, but he did not continue all the way to Chiang Tung. During the seventeenth and eighteenth centuries, many Westerners traveled to China, Burma, Vietnam, and Siam, but their travels did not extend to Chiang Tung. It was not until 250 years later that the first known Western traveler, Captain William C. McLeod, set foot in Chiang Tung. He arrived in February 1837 and stayed for nine days, and during his visit he met the ruler Sao Mahakhanan. Ernest de Lagrée was the second Westerner who visited Chiang Tung, during the French Mekong Exploration Commission expedition up the Mekong River. He made a detour from the Mekong and traveled overland to Chiang Tung in 1867. The British secretly sent out Lieutenant G. J. Younghusband to Chiang Tung in 1887 to explore the area before deciding whether to incorporate it into British Burma. Two more Westerners who visited Chiang Tung were the missionary William Clifton Dodd and his wife. They were stationed in 1886 at the Presbyterian church in Chiang Mai, and over the next thirty years they traveled widely and visited various Tai-speaking people throughout Southeast Asia. After the death of William Clifton Dodd, his wife edited and published the writings he left behind, to which she most likely contributed.

Probably the most important early Western source is the writings of J. George Scott (1851–1935). The British sent him to Chiang Tung in 1890, and he worked as a colonial administrator and traveled all over the different Shan states, collecting information and documents. He wrote and published an abundant amount of information from his time in Burma and the Shan states; his most important publication containing information on Chiang Tung is the *Gazetteer of Upper Burma and the Shan States*, published in 1900 and 1901 in five volumes.

Several travelers visited Chiang Tung between 1890 and World War II. Colonel R. G. Woodthorpe visited in March 1893, only a short time after the British conquest of Chiang Tung. He recounted his journey at the Royal Geographical Society in London on March 9, 1896, and his account was printed in the society's *Geographical Journal* in June 1896. Colin Metcalfe Enriquez traveled widely in Asia. He married a Burmese woman and settled in Mogok in Upper Burma. He traveled to Chiang Tung from Mandalay and reached it on August 10, 1915. Enriquez's book *The Burmese Loneliness* is less of a travel narrative and more a description of Chiang Tung and its people. His writings describe temples, markets, religious festivals, and some politics of his day.

In the 1930s, both Maurice Collis and Hugo Adolf Bernatzik traveled to Chiang Tung. Collis, who was a functionary in the British administration in Burma, traveled to the Shan states in 1937 and also visited Chiang Tung. He was in Chiang Tung shortly after the murder of the ruler Sao Kawn Tai, which occurred on October 22, 1937. At around the same time, the Austrian anthropologist Hugo Bernatzik traveled to Southeast Asia. In his book *The Spirits of the Yellow Leaves* he recounts his visit to Chiang Tung. He criticizes the Christian evangelism that, in his opinion, only split the ethnic groups. All these visitors have been valuable sources for my study.

2
MYTHS AND MEMORIES

> Myths and legends may be used to tell us something about the history of a people, but more significantly, they give a commentary on what a people has held and holds to be of lasting value.
>
> —Donald K. Swearer, *Wat Haripunjaya*, 1976

Myths and memories are powerful forces that can bind people together with a sense of shared origins. They may indicate what a people should hold to be of lasting value. A sense of belonging to a specific geographic place can engender a sense of unique identity for a group of people. Benedict Anderson (2006) has posited that a nation is a socially constructed community, imagined by the people who perceive themselves to be part of that group. Central to an imagined community is, arguably, a myth of common ancestry. Considering Chiang Tung's vulnerability as a historical borderland between the larger and more powerful nations of the Chinese, the Burmese, and the Siamese, it is no surprise that myths and memories of the origin and early history of Chiang Tung evoke a sense of place and belonging for the Khuen people.

As detailed in chapter 1, understanding the reasons behind the way the people of Chiang Tung celebrate the Songkran festival is central for this book. This chapter will focus on the myths and memories about the origin and early history of the place that became and still is the home of the Khuen people. The sections that follow reveal secrets about the Songkran festival, but they also illustrate how these myths and memories create a sense of place and belonging essential for self-identification and common identity for the Khuen people. These myths and memories narrate not only the origin of Chiang Tung but also the origin of the Khuen people themselves, bringing the people and the place together in a shared ancestry.

In addition, the myths and memories recount a prophecy expressed by the Buddha himself that the area would be a prosperous Buddhist site at a future time. They also narrate how Chinese hermits established the place as habitable, but the spirits of the place hindered them from living there. Instead, it was the Lua people, who were born from the soil of the place, who lived there until the Tai people conquered the area. These myths and memories are a living oral tradition told by local people, but to a large extent they are also written in the *Chiang Tung Chronicle* and the *Wat Pa Daeng Chronicle*.

The Mythical Origin of Chiang Tung

Buddhist traditions about how the Buddha visited places in South and Southeast Asia established these places as a sacred landscape. Chiang Tung became one such sacred site because it is told that the Buddha, together with his followers, visited the place that later would become Chiang Tung, and he predicted that this area would be a prosperous Buddhist city in the future. However, the myths and memories about Chiang Tung's beginnings start before the visit by the Buddha.

When the Buddha visited the location that would become Chiang Tung, it was nothing but a large lake with seven islands, which today are the seven hills in Chiang Tung. The *Chiang Tung Chronicle* (*CTC* §1–9) narrates how the lake came to be and how a cowherd, with the assistance of a flock of crows, acquired power and became a king named Gopala. Driven by greed, the king forgot his debt to the crows, so they took him to an uninhabited island. Not long after the departure of the king, a torrential rain occurred, creating landslides that blocked rivers, and the rising waters flooded the country. The people had nowhere to stay, so they migrated to faraway lands. The king died of sorrow on the island, and his soul returned as a spirit and took birth in the womb of a crab. He was reborn as an overlord of all the crabs in that lake for a long time until a son of the Chinese emperor by the name of Tuṅga Rasī came down and drained the lake. The spirit of the crab king became a guardian spirit, burrowed into the foot of a mountain.

Therefore, at the time of the Buddha's recorded visit, the place consisted only of a large lake, Dammilap, with seven islands (*CTC* §11). According to the story (§12), the Buddha came to one island together with forty-nine of his disciples, left eight hairs from his head, and was given food and honey. The Buddha's disciple Ananda took the Buddha's walking stick and planted it in the ground, and the Buddha told Ananda a prophecy: that there will be a hermit named Tuṅga Rasī who would come from the north and drain the water, and thereafter it would be a good place to live. He also said that 629 years after nirvana of the Buddha, a king will bring the Buddhist teachings and establish a prosperous Buddhist city at the location. "May there always be prosperity and abundance of food in the region; may there be crops everywhere; may there be victory for the Khema king"

(§12). This king and the prosperous Buddhist city refer to King Mangrai and Chiang Tung. As the story is told, the eight hairs became enshrined as relics in the golden *chedi* of Wat Chom Kham, which still towers over the city. These myths and memories of a visit by the Buddha and the prophecy he made established a Buddhist sacred landscape where the Khuen people have a sense of belonging.

The hermit from the north, whom the Buddha prophesied would come and drain the lake, is identified as a prince of the Chinese emperor, incorporating the Chinese into the origin story of Chiang Tung. The *CTC* describes how Chinese hermits drained Dammilap Lake and made the place habitable. However, there is a sense of ambivalence about the Chinese in the chronicle. They created a place to live, but as we will explore, the Chinese could not settle there because the guardian spirits of the place were not pleased with them and told them to leave. Later, when the Tai people had conquered the area, the Chinese tried to invade and reclaim the area.

The *CTC* (§14) tells this story in detail. One hundred and fifty years after the nirvana of the Buddha, the Chinese emperor had 1,004 wives and 1,004 sons. All the sons except four were well versed in the Vedas and the arts of war. The remaining four were instead interested in living their lives as hermits. They practiced meditation and attained supernatural powers. When the four princes said farewell to the emperor, he asked them to let him know if they found any suitable places for settlement. After they had been to several places, they came to Comsak Hill and found the walking stick and the writing about the hermit who would come from the north and drain the lake (§22).[1]

The story continues that the four hermits stayed and drained the lake until only enough water for a small lake was left, which still exists today in the middle of the town. The legends also tell that there was a female water spirit (*nāgī*) living close to the lake. One hermit told the *nāgī* about the prophecy and said she must guard this place and let no harm come to it so that it would become a prosperous state for five thousand years (§28). After the spirit received the instructions, she went to live on the Phāyang Hill. The people of Chiang Tung worshipped this female spirit in times of disorder, and according to Saimong Mangrai (1981, 282), this worship continued until the 1930s.

The hermits realized that the place was suitable for the construction of a city and returned home to tell their father, the emperor. He gave orders for one of his chiefs to move and build a city there. The chief took families to this new place, but the Chinese had difficulty cultivating the soil. The rice plants produced no grain, and the Chinese people starved, and many died. After three years, the guardian spirits of the site, through a medium, told the people that they were not pleased; the Chinese people should leave. The spirits wanted to construct a city themselves in the future (§31).

This text establishes a complex relationship between the Chinese and the place where Chiang Tung later was built. On the one hand, Chinese princes emptied the lake and made the area possible to live in. On the other hand, the Chinese had difficulty cultivating the soil because their rice plants produced no grain. The text states that the spirit of the place did not want the Chinese to be there. This ambivalence can be understood when we consider that Chiang Tung was built as a frontier state against the Mongols of China (Yuan dynasty) during the late thirteenth century. According to the text, the Chinese later tried to invade the country when Mangrai and the Khuen people had established themselves in Chiang Tung. The defense against this invasion from the Mongols of China is alive in myths and memories and contributes to the ambivalent view of the Chinese.

King Mangrai and the Lua People

Perhaps the most important event in the myths and memories is how the Tai people, under the leadership of Mangrai from Chiang Rai, defeated the Lua people.

The *CTC* describes the Lua people as the original inhabitants, the people born from the soil of Chiang Tung. After the Chinese left the place, the legend tells of how the seed of a striped gourd took root and bore many fruits. Out of these fruits, the Lua people were born. The *CTC* relates how the Lua people constructed villages and towns all over the region and chose Mangyoy as their leader. He settled in Jengkaeu, the location that is now Chiang Tung. "The [seeds of the] gourds scattered and fell into the footprints of oxen, buffaloes, elephants and rhinoceroses, and [from them] are born the Lvas who inhabit the whole country" (§32).

How King Mangrai conquered the Lua people and established Chiang Tung is described in detail in the chronicle. Mangrai was led by the gods to the place where he later would establish Chiang Tung. There he chased a golden stag, which the gods created to lure the king into the wilderness and fulfill the prophecy that a sacred Buddhist city would be established at this site. The story narrates how the king was close to catching the stag but failed again and again. Every place where the king failed to catch it was given a name. This legend establishes names for places that later would become the homeland of the Khuen people (*CTC* §61).

The golden stag finally disappeared, and the king gave up the chase, though he found that the places he had traveled to were good locations to settle.[2] He therefore told his ministers and officials, "We shall take our forces to fight [the Lvas] and drive them all away and will create villages and towns" (§62). Thus King Mangrai wanted to conquer the original inhabitants (§67–70). Myths and memories tell that he sent his two sons with armies to fight against the Lua people. However, the two brothers could not work together, and this attempt failed.

To capture the place called Jengkaeu, Mangrai changed tactics. He chose two Lua leaders loyal to him and sent them as infiltrators to create division in the Lua court of Mangyoy. After three years, they were trusted and had been promoted to important positions by the ruler. They sent a message to Mangrai that it was time for him to act, and so he sent an army north to the Lua city. The two spies at the Lua court convinced the king that Mangrai had a huge army that was impossible to defeat. The Lua king tried to escape but was captured.

The *CTC* thus tells of how Mangrai defeated the Lua people and established the city-state of Chiang Tung. According to legends, most of the Lua people moved northward, but some escaped up into the mountains around Chiang Tung. The Lua people who moved to the north are considered to be the Wa people, who live farther north on both sides of the border between China and Myanmar (see Wa territory on map 1), and the Lua people who escaped up into the mountains around Chiang Tung are today called Tai Loi.

After the conquest, Mangrai searched for a good place to build his new *mueang* with villages and a palace. After much searching, astrologers determined that the best place was the same spot where the Lua ruler Mangyoy had his palace. The astrologers said this was an auspicious place, and worship should be offered to the female spirit (*nāgī*) to whom Tuṅga Rasī had given instructions to guard the *mueang*.

The Origin of the Khuen People

Issues of confrontation and coexistence between two ethnic groups in Southeast Asia are often solved in legends with a marriage between the two groups. For example, when a Tai prince married an indigenous (Mon-Khmer) woman, a new political entity came into being, grounded in this marriage (Évrard and Chanthaphilith 2013, 65–66). However, in the *CTC*'s origin story of the Khuen ethnic group, there was in the beginning no coexistence, only a confrontation, with the victors settling in the same place from which the indigenous Lua people had fled. According to the chronicle, the conquerors did not integrate with the indigenous people. Instead, a new group of inhabitants of Chiang Tung was formed through what seems to be a political decision. Later, a symbolic agreement between the conquerors and the defeated Lua people was established.

Mangrai and his son Namthum wanted to populate the area with loyal people from their hometown, Chiang Rai, to establish a frontier state against the Mongols of China. Mangrai also chose a group of Tai people living nearby the new settlement. These people, named the Great Khuen, lived south of the newly conquered place and joined with soldiers from Chiang Rai. The Tai group was given cowrie shells as payment to persuade them to move to the new town. The men were dressed in black-and-white jackets, and their hair was cut at the hairline (§81). The chronicle relates that the soldiers from Chiang Rai had to "give up the Yon dress and to cut their hair in the manner of the great Khüns" (§81).

Interestingly, the *CTC* mentions that the new inhabitants had to use similar ethnic markers in clothing and hairstyle to ease the integration of the two people. This assimilation was necessary because it was important to fortify the town quickly before Chinese troops could enter from the north. Thus, it appeared to be a political decision to establish a new *mueang* and bring together two Tai groups to settle in villages close to the newly built palace.

Myths and memories of the origin of the Khuen people and the origin of Chiang Tung have much in common. Ethnic belonging and territorial belonging are closely related in Chiang Tung. These elements help to establish a sense of place and belonging for the Khuen people. This suggests a *localized ethnic identity*, a concept coined by Charles Keyes (1992) and Paul T. Cohen (1998, 50), as the Khuen seem to consider Chiang Tung as the place where the origin of themselves as a people and an ethnic group came into being.

Dependence and Loyalty between Tai Khuen and Tai Loi (Lua)

It is likely that some of the Lua ethnic group chose to remain among the new inhabitants and integrate with them, but others fled or were allowed to move up into the mountains outside Chiang Tung, together with their leader. "Those Lvas who could not run away came and submitted, saying: We beg to be the humble subjects of the kingdom's hills" (§69). Those Lua who moved into the mountains are today called Tai Loi, meaning Tai people living in the hills. They have, through a long period living on the periphery of the Khuen people, changed their cultural, religious, and ethnic identity in such a way that they are now considered a Tai subgroup and members of the same political-economic system as the majority Khuen. Tai Loi (Lua) now live in Chiang Tung or in mountain villages northeast of the town, and they practice Buddhism and make offerings to the spirit of the earth, like the Khuen. Historically, an economic division arose between the wet-rice-cultivating Tai people in the plains and the Lua who practice slash-and-burn agriculture on the slopes of the mountains. J. George Scott (Scott and Hardiman 1900, 1:517) suggests that the Tai Loi (Lua) influenced Khuen culture, and not just the other way around. The Tai Loi (Lua) have become Buddhists, with monasteries closely related to those of the Khuen, and in several places they share a common monastery with Khuen neighbors. There is a passus in the *Wat Pa Daeng Chronicle* recounting how hill people came down to Chiang Tung, adopted the written language of the Khuen (*tham* script), and took it back to the mountains: "Some of them came down to study and learn correctly and thoroughly the letters of the alphabet, Pāli grammar, all, and returned home to teach pupils and disciples" (*WPDC* §100).

It was probably a long and slow process for the Lua to convert to Buddhism and adopt Khuen culture, but the passus above records that the process happened in the middle of the fifteenth century. Cholthira Satyawadhna (1991, 361) establishes that an ethnic group can change its everyday language in very few generations under social, political, or military pressure. This happened to those Lua who were left behind. According to Cholthira (364), "the assimilation of Lua with Tai/Thai is the product of a long economic, sociological and political history." During the hundreds of years they lived amid the majority Tai people, their ethnic identity changed, and this group now see themselves as a Buddhist Tai people with a Lua origin (364). Among some Tai Loi (Lua) communities there is an oral tradition concerning their origin and history, but I found it impossible to establish if this has its origin in a Tai Loi (Lua) long-lived oral tradition or if it comes from the Khuen traditional history.[3]

After the Tai Khuen established Chiang Tung as a frontier state against the Mongols of China, they created a symbolic agreement with the earthborn Tai Loi (Lua) people. The relationship was characterized by domination and subordination, with ownership and rights to land at the center. However, we could also describe the relationship as mutual dependence between the newly arrived lowland people and the indigenous people, who were forced to move up into the highlands. The lowland people needed forest products, and the highland people needed products from the lowland. Though the power relationship was uneven, the agreement may have benefited both parties.

The relation between the two groups was established with a symbolic agreement, a kind of informal political contract. The coronation ceremony in the Chiang Tung palace included a symbolic banishing of the Tai Loi (Lua) people. A group of Tai Loi (Lua) chiefs were called down from the mountains to the palace when a new Khuen ruler was installed. The Tai Loi (Lua) chiefs sat on the throne to symbolize the previous rulers. They were given a meal to eat, but before they could finish their meal, they were pushed off the throne, and the new Khuen ruler ascended the throne and finished the meal.

The *CTC* narrates the first symbolic takeover:

> The brayā had a palace built at Jengkaeu at the old site of Mangyoy's house there. When the golden palace had been built, the Lvas living in Bangung and Bangham were brought down [from their hills] to sit and

eat their food on the gem-studded throne in the palace. While they were eating, the Lvas were driven out and the brayā took their place. (§80)

The coronation ceremony was an informal political contract of interdependence between two people, but it also represents a symbolic establishment of a change of ownership and rights to the land. Interesting similarities to this coronation ceremony are also present in both Luang Prabang[4] and Chiang Mai.[5]

A symbolic consolidation of the relationship between the Buddhist *saṅgha* and the state was also a part of the coronation ceremony. When the old ruler died, the state was handed over to the *saṅgha* for a short period (Scott and Hardiman 1901, 1:400; Scott 1932, 320) until a new ruler was installed through the coronation ceremony, attended by the Tai Loi (Lua). Three groups—the royal court, the Buddhist *saṅgha*, and the Tai Loi (Lua) people—had the responsibility to establish the continuity of the Mangrai dynasty when the old ruler died and a new ruler (*saopha*) had to be installed in the Chiang Tung palace.

The symbolic banishing of Tai Loi (Lua) people in Chiang Tung was conducted during every known installation of a new ruler from the thirteenth century until the late nineteenth century. The last of these symbolic takeovers occurred when Sao Intaleng was installed as *saopha* in 1897 at Chiang Tung palace (Saimong Mangrai 1981, 284n45), but the coronation as a symbolic banishing is alive in oral tradition today and was told to me by locals. Some early Western visitors, such as J. George Scott, also retold this tradition. The Austrian anthropologist Hugo Adolf Bernatzik, who traveled to Chiang Tung in the 1930s, mentioned this ritual briefly, but he regarded the ritual as held annually, not solely during the coronation ceremony (Bernatzik 1938). A possible explanation is that this symbolic banishing of the Tai Loi (Lua) people during the coronation ceremony transitioned to the annual Songkran festival sometime between 1915, after William Clifton Dodd and C. M. Enriquez participated in Songkran, and 1930, when Bernatzik mentioned it as an annual event. But soon thereafter, the symbolic reenactment of the relationship between the two peoples was transformed from a coronation ceremony to a drumming ceremony during the Songkran festival. It was told to me that Sao Intaleng chose a group of Tai Loi (Lua) from a village north of Chiang Tung to perform the drumming ceremony. The informal political contract between the Tai Loi (Lua) and the Tai Khuen about the symbolic ownership of land is today performed at the annual Songkran festival, where the Tai Loi (Lua) people drum wealth and prosperity to Chiang Tung and the Khuen people.

Fifteen kilometers outside Chiang Tung, the octagonal temple of Wat Zom Loi (Wat Jom Doi) also bears witness to the relationship between the Tai Khuen people and the Tai Loi (Lua). I was told a legend about a Lua couple who lived on the hill where the temple now stands. In return for good deeds they had done, a dragon gave them a hair relic of the Buddha. One day, when they were building a *chedi* to enshrine the relic, they were ordered by the ruler to come down from the mountain and take part in the construction of the defensive wall.[6] The Lua couple ignored the order and refused to help build the wall, as they were engaged in building the *chedi* in memory of the Buddha. When the ruler heard about their refusal, he sent his men to catch and kill the couple. They fled north and escaped to another mountain but left a spell on the temple so that no one in the royal entourage could visit and worship there without suffering bad luck. At the new mountain, they established the Wan Zai village and built a new pagoda. Today, there are small *chedi* enclosed in the octagonal pagodas at both Zom Loi and Wan Zai, but there are also spirit shrines dedicated to the couple. Wat Zom Loi remains as a beautiful octagonal temple, and it is a popular place for both Khuen and Tai Loi (Lua) locals to visit.

The Wat Zom Loi legend may be a paraphrase of the defeat of the Lua people by King Mangrai during the late thirteenth century, recalling how the Lua people had to flee north. The story may also offer another interpretation of how the Lua couple put a spell on the place to prevent the ruler and members of his royal court from entering. The story seems to speak of places of refuge, Zom Loi and Wan Zai, for the Tai Loi (Lua) people. The area where Wat Zom Loi stands is still today a controversial area important for Tai Loi (Lua) people, especially as a Buddhist Tai Loi (Lua) novice (Sao Boon Tip) has built a temple compound there where he educates young Tai Loi (Lua) boys from the mountains. This is not viewed positively by the military. Details about this Buddhist novice are included in chapter 6.

Invasion by the Mongols of China

The *CTC* dramatically portrays how Chiang Tung prevented the invasion by the Mongols from the Chinese Yuan dynasty. Not long after Chiang Tung was established, the Chinese emperor became aware of the new settlements. He knew that his people had drained the lake to establish it as habitable and therefore requested tribute in the form of rice and elephant tusks. "If that is not possible, give ten elephants and one hundred thousand silver [coins?]" (*CTC* §82).

The *CTC* relates how the ruler of Chiang Tung, Namthum, ordered the elders to negotiate with the Chinese. But the negotiation failed, and the Chinese besieged the town. They could not take the city with a frontal attack, so they instead proceeded to dig a tunnel to force an entry, with the Chinese commander sitting on a chair to supervise. Namthum had a crossbow, which he aimed at the commander. If this state is not destined to be a vassal of the Chinese, may the gods, Indra and Brahmas, who stand guard over this kingdom guide this missile so that it will strike to death the Chinese commander (§85).

The arrow shot the commander dead. However, the siege did not end, though the death prompted the Chinese to change tactics. Instead of their failed tunnel construction, they dammed up the river "to create a lake as of old" (*CTC* §83) and flood the valley, forcing the people out. The Chinese, who had made the Chiang Tung valley habitable far in the past by draining most of the water, were now filling the valley with water again. Namthum responded by means of a raft. "The raft was floated down the river until it stopped at the place where they [the Chinese] were damming the river. Lightning struck that place, and many Chinese died; [the rest] could not stay and all fled. Henceforth the state became happy, prosperous, and stable without a break" (§86).

By supernatural means, the raft hit the Chinese soldiers with lightning. This story conveys a sense of pride for the ancient past, with the city's successful defense against the powerful nation in the north.

The *CTC* also recounts a further attempt shortly afterward to make Chiang Tung a vassal of the Chinese. The emperor ordered an army to march south to defeat the forces of Chiang Tung. But in Chiang Tung there was a renowned warrior by the name Aysaengto. He had discovered a jewel in a hornets' nest and became famous because he fought with the assistance of an army of hornets. He defeated the Chinese invaders and chased them all the way back to the emperor, then filled the palace with hornets. The emperor was terrified and invited Aysaengto to stay at the palace, marry his daughter, and succeed the emperor. The myths and memories continue, recounting how Prince Aysaengto and his Chinese wife had three sons, who became rulers of Alawi (Chiang Rung), Bolaem (Mueang Laem), and Chiang Tung. This legend, told in *CTC* §89–98, retold by J. George Scott (Scott and Hardiman 1901, 1:398–99), and communicated orally to me by local people, ends with the formation of an alliance among these three city-states, two of them in Sipsong Panna, Yunnan. Aysaengto's third son, who became ruler in Chiang Tung, succeeded King Mangrai and his son. Once again, the Chinese played a crucial role in the struggle for power.

Chiang Tung and Chiang Rung were in the northern frontier zone of Lan Na during the late thirteenth century, and they had to resist aggressive attacks from the Chinese emperor. The Chinese considered Lan Na to be a vassal state called Babai-xifu or later Babai-dadian, shortened to Babai, and Chiang Tung was called Menggen (Grabowsky 2010, 205; Liew-Herres and Grabowsky 2008, xiii, 20–21). It is interesting to note that important Lan Na chronicles, such as *Jinakālamālī* and the *Chiang Mai Chronicle*, only mention the Chinese sporadically (Liew-Herres and Grabowsky 2008, 23), but in the *Chiang Tung Chronicle* (§82–86) the Chinese played an important role.[7]

The contradictory role of the Chinese as both creators and destroyers is noteworthy. They create the place by digging out the water and later try to destroy the same place by filling the valley with water to defeat the Khuen people. These myths and memories demonstrate that the defense against a powerful ancient dynasty can play a potent role in constructing an imagined community and nation.

The myths and memories written in the *CTC* represent a living tradition, important in the lives of the Khuen people today. However, this living tradition of the origin and early history of Chiang Tung is, as far as I know, preserved and transmitted only by several elderly gentlemen with a particular interest in history and tradition. These are more or less the same individuals who organize the annual Songkran festival in Chiang Tung. Should we see these elderly gentlemen as representative? Both interest in the stories and the ability to remember and transmit them may depend on class, education, gender, and age. The fact that mainly older males transmit these myths and memories does not mean that the younger generation lacks knowledge of them, but I believe that these myths and memories are losing their importance.

Japanese Samurai Soldiers

One last story that gives important context to the Tai Khuen and the integration of cultures in Chiang Tung is set around the beginning of the seventeenth century. It is a strange story about sixty-two Japanese samurai soldiers who went all the way to Chiang Tung, married local woman, and became part of the local community. No chronicles mention it, nor is it mentioned by Scott, and to my knowledge no other early travelers refer to it. But the story may not be as strange as it first sounds, because of a Japanese trading colony during the Ayuttaha period. A Japanese merchant, sailor, and adventurer by the name Yamada Nagamasa settled on the coast of Ayuttaha in 1612 with King Songtham's permission. His trading colony operated numerous "red seal" armed merchant ships (*Shuinsen*) and conducted business in Southeast Asia for a short period. Nagamasa brought with him many samurai warriors, who at times served under the king of Ayutthaya as a more or less regular army. The number of Japanese grew, and the settlement developed into a substantial colony called Baan Yipun, with nearly one thousand inhabitants. They exported deer skins to Japan in exchange for silver and swords. After 1635, the Japanese ceased trade in Southeast Asia. Still, Yamada Nagamasa had a brilliant career in Ayutthaya's court and was appointed governor of Nakhon Si Thammarat, with the important title Okya Senaphimuk. After the death of Nagamasa, the colony was attacked, and the Japanese were driven away. It is told that they went to the Khmer territory, but after a while the Japanese colony reemerged for a limited time (Iwamoto Yoshiteru 2007).

There are reliable historical sources about the trading colony of Baan Yipun, such as from the Dutch, who also traded in the area. It is unclear, however, whether the asserted arrival of the Japanese in Chiang Tung is only an imagined story or if it has some factual background. According to other legends, after the attack, several samurai took refuge in Cambodia and then continued to the north. Several died during the flight, but according to a local legend, sixty-two of the samurai went all the way to Chiang Tung and stayed there as refugees. The event occurred during the reign in Chiang Tung of the ruler Sao Nam Toom. The story goes that he welcomed the samurai, appointed them to roles in the court, and married them to local women. They became part of the local community and influenced life and culture. The craft of manufacturing swords in Chiang Tung is said to originate from the influence of these samurai. Also, hairstyles, food recipes, and traditional Japanese clothing such as wooden slippers are believed to have been integrated into Chiang Tung's local culture from these immigrants. This story of the sixty-two samurai soldiers is still told with much seriousness by some of the elderly local people. They seem to be proud of this Japanese lineage in Chiang Tung. There is also a story that a phallic object, once part of the Songkran festival, was of Japanese origin, possibly referring to the Honen fertility festival at the Tagata shrine in Nagoya. Regardless of the historical truth of this story, it is told with great seriousness by elderly local people, and it fits into the story of the Songkran festival, as we will see in chapter 7.

This is, of course, not the end of myths and memories dealing with early Chiang Tung. Some of the history of the golden age of Lan Na and early Buddhism was passed down as myths and memories, but the historical documentation of this time period is much more reliable and will be featured in the next chapter.

In this chapter about myths and memories, shared memories of a chosen history told by the people in Chiang Tung generate a collective memory of a shared ancestry. These myths and memories create a sense of feeling about the place and the past. Countless generations have retained, recovered, and transmitted memories of the past to succeeding generations. Shared memories of a chosen history are important for a sense of place and belonging to the place that is the home of the Khuen people. The shared memories of a visit by the Buddha and the prophecy made by him about a king who would come and lay the foundations of a prosperous Buddhist city established a sacred Buddhist landscape.

These shared memories address the Khuen people's relationship with the Chinese and the Tai Loi (Lua) people. The Chinese are described both as the creators of the place and those who later wanted to conquer it. The Tai Loi (Lua) are described as the original inhabitants of the place, the earthborn (autochthonous) and indigenous people. King Mangrai, with his soldiers from Chiang Rai, defeated the Lua people with the help of spies and established the city-state of Chiang Tung. The Lua people were displaced and fled north, some of them escaping into the mountains around Chiang Tung. They changed their cultural, religious, and ethnic identity in such a way that they are now considered a Tai subgroup and are called Tai Loi, Tai people from the mountains. The Tai Loi (Lua) have adopted the Tai Buddhist culture, but they also influenced Khuen culture in various ways.

It appears to have been a political decision to establish a new *mueang* and integrate two groups of Tai people to form a new ethnic group called Tai Khuen. The new inhabitants had to use similar ethnic markers in clothing and hairstyle to ease the integration of the two people. They settled in the same place as the earthborn Lua and built their palace on the same site as the old Lua palace. Especially interesting is the symbolic banishing of the Tai Loi (Lua) people during the coronation ceremony in the Chiang Tung palace. This can be seen as an informal political contract of domination and subordination or as mutual dependence between the newly arrived lowland Khuen people and the indigenous Tai Loi (Lua) highland people. This dynamic can explain many of the events during the Songkran festival. The myths and memories told here also highlight the close relationship the Khuen people have with the place where they live. Chiang Tung and the Khuen people have a common origin, which expresses a sense of place and belonging for the Khuen people.

3
PRECOLONIAL TIMES

> Collecting vegetables for baskets and collecting people for towns
> —Proverb from the time of Kawila of Chiang Mai

While the historical record from the thirteenth century until colonial times may offer a more reliable view of events than that found in the myths and memories recounted in the previous chapter, myths and memories can also be traced to this period.

When King Mangrai in the thirteenth century united the region and expanded his territory, he adopted Buddhism as a legitimation of universal power. The Indic Hindu-Buddhist worldview had already been in place in Southeast Asia for several centuries, and the Indianization of Southeast Asia is therefore a good starting point for this chapter. The Golden Age of Lan Na has been a chosen glory for the Buddhist people of Chiang Tung, but this chapter will also explore the vulnerability that Chiang Tung experienced as a borderland between more powerful neighbors at this time.

The Indianization of Southeast Asia

The cult of spirits, and especially territory spirits, in northern Southeast Asia is an ancient cult with close connections to agriculture and the monsoon climate. More elaborate and refined than indigenous belief systems, the divinities of the new Indic religions were universal rather than locally grounded and thus created a model by which Southeast Asian rulers could aspire to a status that reached beyond their specific locality (Andaya and Andaya 2015, 54). Examples from Bagan, Angkor, Sukhothai, and Lan Na testified to a very successful social construction. As for Chiang Tung, we can establish that the indigenous cult of the local territory spirit was, and still is, interwoven with beliefs and practices from a Hindu-Buddhist worldview.

The thoughts of Paul Mus are important when we explore the origin of the cult of territory spirits. However, Mus's focus was not mainly the origin of the spirit cult but rather the so-called Indianization of Southeast Asia. He pushes back against theories of the time that gave prominence to colonization or trade, which both share the assumption that Indians were dominant partners in the relationship. His special contribution, according to Chandler and Mabbet (2011, 3), was to "see clearly, at the beginning of the 1930s, the strengths both of indigenous traditions and of those that came from India, and how they interacted." In his explanation of the Indianization of Southeast Asia, Mus believed that the indigenous cult of the local earth god was interwoven with the imported beliefs and practices from the Hindu-Buddhist worldview. This process of interweaving worked fairly smoothly, according to Mus, because the same sort of cult already existed in India when the Hindu and Buddhist religions emerged (Mus [1933] 2011, 43–52). He believed that "pre-Aryan religions had arranged themselves ... in a kind of religious map, each district being identified by the cult of one of those tutelary divinities" (44). I agree that early Buddhism has its roots in the ancient sacred culture of the Ganges Valley, but it is an oversimplification to rely on this in understanding the Indianization of Southeast Asia.

The influence of an ancient Indian culture of spirit worship on early Buddhism is in line with what I have found in previous studies. The origin of early Buddhist art in India, the so-called aniconic Buddhist art, emerged out of a shared pre-Buddhist, pan-Indian culture of auspicious signs (trees, wheels, tridents, swastikas, etc.), mythological creatures (*yakṣa, yakṣiṇī, vṛkṣadevatā*, etc.), and local deities (Karlsson 1999, 2006). The use of auspicious signs, mythological creatures, and local deities must have been a way to popularize and strengthen the Buddhist movement, but it was also a way for the Buddhists to protect themselves. This art shows a close connection between an old popular fertility cult and the emergence of Buddhist communities.

Early Buddhism, however, was not solely the child of local spirits. It also emerged out of an urbanized culture, with the growth of a class of merchants, artisans, and craft workers. Donative inscriptions show that the early Buddhist *saṅgha* was intertwined with the merchant class, whereas the old Brahmanical culture, with its ritualistic priestly codes and caste regulations, was apparently not adapted for a more flexible urban society. Approximately seven hundred donative inscriptions have been found in Sāñcī from ordinary laypeople, such as householders, merchants, bankers, and weavers, but also from Buddhist monks and nuns. An intimate relationship between merchants and

Buddhist communities gave rise to a symbiotic association that not only helped the long-distance spread of Buddhist ideas but also created a mechanism through which religious paraphernalia could be easily supplied to the emerging centers of Buddhism (Sen 2015, 447). The same may be argued in relation to the acceptance of a new Hindu-Buddhist worldview by social and political elites in emerging Southeast Asian societies. The cult of territory spirits was not adapted for a more expansive universal society.

The origin of Buddhism as interwoven with the indigenous cult of local earth gods cannot alone explain, as Mus seems to believe, what he describes as a fairly smoothly conducted Indianization of Southeast Asia. The religion of pre-Aryan India cannot serve as a sufficient explanation for the Indianization of Southeast Asia. Of equal importance behind the Indianization of Southeast Asia is that the imported Indic worldview, with gods like Viṣṇu and Śiva as well as Buddhist universal rulers (*cakkavattin*) and Bodhisattvas, was universal, in contrast to the locally grounded territory cult. The Indic worldview created a model by which Southeast Asia rulers could aspire to a universal status that reached beyond their specific locality. When the Buddhist tradition came to Southeast Asia, it did not come as a true religion, in opposition to the local tradition of spiritual cults. The imported Hindu-Buddhist worldview was a contrast to the locally grounded territory cults. This was also true when Buddhist tradition came to the Tai people of northern Southeast Asia. Narratives written in Lan Na describe travels by the Buddha to many places in the region. These narratives were inspired by Lanka legends describing the Buddha traveling to the island of Lanka, and the narratives connect places in Lan Na with the international Buddhist world. Leaders adopted the Indic worldview to consolidate political authority. Different chronicles tell how early rulers of Chiang Tung and other city-states in Lan Na used Buddhism to legitimize themselves, but they met little resistance because local territory cults were not in direct conflict with the new tradition. The cult of local spirits had already made a sacred landscape of places connected to groups of peoples, which was easily absorbed by a coming Buddhist community.

The Indianization of Southeast Asia is described by John Guy (2014) as a fundamentally shaped cultural development providing a conceptual and linguistic framework for new ideals of kingship, state, and religious order. Indian influences were selectively adapted into multicentered, mandala-like political systems in which authority was extended through the declared allegiance of vassal states to the center (3). For this reason, Southeast Asian city-states in which social, religious, and cosmological orders were integrally connected have in academic literature been called *mandala*. O. W. Wolters was one of the first to introduce the concept of mandala in the discussion about the political system of precolonial Southeast Asia. He describes it as a patchwork of often overlapping mandalas, or "circles of kings." In each of these mandalas, one king, identified with divine and universal authority, claimed personal hegemony over the other rulers in his mandala, who in theory were his obedient allies and vassals (Wolters 1982, 16). Originally, the Sanskrit noun *maṇḍala*, in Hindu, Jainist, and Buddhist traditions, is described as a kind of cosmic plan, representing the manifestation of a specific deity, or groups of deities, in the cosmos and as the cosmos (Leidy 2004, 508). The word *mandala* has been used in Indian manuals of government, conceptualized as a series of concentric circles where a great ruler could maintain hegemony by building up a system of alliances with surrounding kings (Andaya and Andaya 2015, 46). Using *mandala* to conceptualize the political geography did not, of course, come from Southeast Asia indigenous culture. But likewise, it cannot be explained in terms of only Indic influences. The political geography of semiautonomous principalities or city-states as self-governing communities in Southeast Asia has a much more ancient origin than Indic Hindu-Buddhist influences. Rather than as a result of Indic influences, the political geography of city-states (*mueang*) has its origin in the indigenous geography and agricultural traditions of wet-rice cultivation in the highland river valleys of South China and northern Southeast Asia. Indic influences did not create the political geography of Southeast Asian city-states, but they fit perfectly. A prototype to the mandala-like city-state must have already been in place before the Indianization of Southeast Asia.

Stanley J. Tambiah also expresses a similar opinion when discussing the impact of Indian cosmological sources in Southeast Asia but uses the term *galactic policy*. He believes that the concept of mandala "could have taken root in Southeast Asia only because indigenous condition and social practices favored [its] incorporation or because [it] represented a 'literate' culture's formalisation of images already experienced and emergent in local conditions, a convergence that makes the quick and ready borrowing of classical Hindu-Buddhist charters readily understandable" (Tambiah 1976, 103). He has described the galactic policy of early Southeast Asia society as a "central planet surrounded by differentiated satellites, which are more or less 'autonomous' entities held in orbit and within the sphere of influence of the center" (113). Chiang Tung was an important *mueang* with many less significant *mueangs* in its sphere of interest. This may be called a mandala-like structure, but Chiang Tung cannot be called a royal center of a fully fledged mandala. Chiang Tung was never independent of larger, more important *mueangs* like Chiang Mai, Pegu, Ava, or Mandalay, except for the eight years of independence between the time the ruler Sao Kawng Tai executed the officer sent by King Thibaw in 1882 until the takeover by the British. Therefore, it is most useful to see Chiang Tung as a *mueang*, so I will use this indigenous word instead of *mandala*.

The adaptation of Indic culture in Southeast Asia from the first half of the first millennium was a long process. Indic culture, with its architecture, religious art, and rituals, could spread powerful ideologies that gave prestige and power to local rulers. The integration of Indian concepts was neither so deep nor so pervasive as was once thought; instead, there is a long and subtle interplay in which the flow was not entirely in one direction (Kerlogue 2004, 12–13). The indigenous religious culture was not a passive one in relation to the Indic Hindu-Buddhist worldview. Indic influences corresponded with various indigenous beliefs.

The states of Pyu in central Myanmar, Funan/Zhenla in southern Vietnam and Cambodia, Cham of coastal Vietnam, Dvāravatī in Thailand, Śrīvijaya in Sumatra, and Śailendra in Java were the earliest Indianized states of Southeast Asia. They flourished in the latter part of the first millennium at the same time as indigenous traditions still lived on. Many Mon-Khmer people like the Lua/Lawa in northern Southeast Asia were still mostly unaffected by Indic culture many centuries later. When Mangrai united small Tai city-states in the thirteenth century, he adopted Buddhism from the Dvāravatī culture of Haripuñjaya as a legitimation of universal power. This was brought to Chiang Tung after the Tai people had conquered the Lua people, who previously had their capital at the same place. But it was the Buddhist tradition from the island of Lanka that had the greatest significance for Lan Na and Chiang Tung.

The Golden Age of Lan Na Culture

From the eighth century, the Tai people immigrated into the region and established many small city-states in lowland valleys. In the thirteenth century, the great empires of Bagan in the west and Angkor in the east declined. In the absence of these major empires, the political landscape was fractured into many smaller states. In the vacuum left by these large and expansive dynasties, and for fear of the Mongols from China, who also tried to expand into Southeast Asia, a ruler, later known as Phaya Mangrai, tried to unify the region and expand his territory. With arms and alliances, he could rule a larger region. This period is a kind of chosen glory and a cultural highpoint that unifies the Buddhist people of Chiang Tung and Chiang Mai.

The accuracy of dating the events of Mangrai's ascendancy is not completely reliable. However, I will follow Sarassawadee Ongsakul (2005) regarding the timeline of important events during his regime.

Fearing a Mongol invasion from China, Mangrai moved his capital from Chiang Saen south to Chiang Rai in 1262 CE, and only several years later, in 1267, he conquered the Lua people and established Chiang Tung. He not only used armed forces to strengthen his power, but he also created alliances by a friendship pact with Phayao and Sukhothai in 1287. In 1292 he made a strategic decision to conquer the Mon city-state of Haripuñjaya (today's Lamphun). With this move, he linked the small Tai city-states in northern Southeast Asia with the ancient Buddhist tradition of Mon Dvāravatī culture. Finally, he founded his capital at Wiang Kum Kam in 1296 by the Ping River. Because of a major flood, he moved it shortly after to the present site of Chiang Mai, at the foot of the Doi Suthep mountain.

Mangrai was born to a minor ruler in Ngoen Yang (later known as Chiang Saen). There are different opinions of his origin as Tai or Lua (Sarassawadee 2005, 21–22), but he probably is of both Tai and Lua descent. In the *Chiang Mai Chronicle* he is described as belonging to the Lawachangkarat dynasty, but confirming his Lua/Lawa origin is difficult, as the legends in the chronicles are not written as historiography in the modern sense. Mangrai's close connection to the Lua can also be seen in his conquest of Chiang Tung. As we saw in chapter 2, he used Lua men as infiltrators before he attacked the city. This indicates that he had close contact with the Lua and probably spoke the same language. According to Wyatt (2003, 34), his mother was Tai Lue, a daughter of the ruler of Chiang Rung. His father was probably Lua, which would imply a union between Tai and Lua. After Mangrai's death, his successors could not regain stability, and Lan Na suffered both politically and culturally until Phaya Kuena (also transliterated as Ku Na) could consolidate the kingdom in 1355 (Veidlinger 2006, 42).

The historical development of early Lan Na can be divided into three periods: the formative period (1296–1335), the period of prosperity (1335–1525), and the period of decline (1525–1558) (Sarassawadee 2005, 53). Loyalty and alliances were important prerequisites for a small exposed community in precolonial Southeast Asia. Chiang Tung was under the influence of Chiang Mai but exercised power over certain smaller cities on its periphery. An inscription from 1451 says that the ruler Saddhamma Rāja Cuḷāmaṇi of Chiang Tung governed on the authority of the New City, Nabapurī, meaning Chiang Mai (*EHS*, 750; Griswold and Na Nagara 1978, 82; Veidlinger 2006, 66). For over 250 years, from its founding until the mid-sixteenth century, Chiang Tung had close, friendly relations with Chiang Mai and the rest of Lan Na. Chiang Tung was given full freedom to take care of its internal affairs as long as this did not interfere with Chiang Mai's concerns. Chiang Mai promised protection as long as Chiang Tung gave an annual tribute in the form of symbolic and actual gifts. Chiang Tung's relationship with Chiang Mai can be divided into two periods. From the founding of Chiang Tung in 1267 until Phaya Kuena took over Chiang Mai in 1355, the relations were very close, and the rulers of Chiang Tung had strong ties to the court of Chiang Mai. Chiang Tung rulers were often direct descendants of Chiang

Mai kings, as kings from Chiang Mai sent their sons or sons-in-law to rule in the dependent cities (Sarassawadee 2005, 100). The next period is characterized by rulers not being as personally linked to the court of Chiang Mai. Instead, local succession was followed, and the sons or brothers of the ruler became the new kings of Chiang Tung. The succession of the Mangrai dynasty in Chiang Tung continued until the military took over in Burma in 1962.

The Buddhist religion has left deep traces in the history of Lan Na. Most important were the arrivals of two different monastic orders from the island of Lanka: the Flower Garden (Suan Dok or Pupphārām) and the Red Forest (Pa Daeng). These Sinhalese Theravāda Buddhist movements had important impacts on the whole of Lan Na, which can still be seen today. After these orders were established in Chiang Mai, they proceeded to Chiang Tung and became established there as well. Chapter 6 describes the history of Buddhism in Chiang Tung, including the controversy between the two Sinhalese monastic orders and the relationship between rulers and the Buddhist community, and links these factors to the contemporary religious culture.

The history of Buddhism in Lan Na in the Golden Age reflects the close connection between Chiang Tung and Chiang Mai during this formative period. Daniel M. Veidlinger (2006, 66) mentions that Chiang Tung "was under the influence of Lan Na for some time." This understates the importance of Chiang Tung during this period. Chiang Tung was an important city-state in Lan Na from the middle of the fourteenth century until the beginning of the sixteenth century, but secondary to the most important city-state Chiang Mai. Chapter 6 establishes that Chiang Tung was a natural part of the religious and political culture of Lan Na during this time.

The Golden Age of an independent Lan Na began in the middle of the fourteenth century during the reign of Phaya Kuena, who ruled from 1355 until 1385. This period continued for approximately two hundred years, until the middle of the sixteenth century, when the country was invaded by the Burmese army under the direction of King Bayinnaung. This period of flourishing culture was not completely peaceful, however. War broke out against Ayutthaya frequently, and attacks from China in 1404 and 1405 were carried out during the reign of Phaya Sam Fang Kaen (1402–1441).

This Golden Age of Lan Na began to fizzle out in the first half of the sixteenth century. Following the death of Chiang Tung's ruler Si Wichai in 1523, a dispute arose between his two sons, Thao Chiang Khong and Phraya Hin. The former fled and requested assistance from the ruler of Chiang Mai, Phaya Kaeo. The second appealed to the Shan state for help (*CMC*, 164). Kaeo sent troops, led by Yi Phing Chai, to attack Chiang Tung, but they were defeated and suffered great losses. Interestingly, the *Chiang Tung Chronicle* (§136) mentions that the invading army was as large as 130,000 men. After the failed invasion, Kaeo executed Yi Phing Chai, and Thao Chiang Khong was installed as ruler of the small Mueang Phrao (*CMC*, 165). Losing many people during the war affected the stability of Chiang Mai, and soon after the fighting, a large flood drowned numerous inhabitants (*CMC*, 165). In the end, this dynastic dispute in Chiang Tung led to a strengthening of the relations with the Shan states and weakened the relations with Chiang Mai (Ratanaporn 1988, 307; Sarassawadee 2005, 82–83).

Between the Burmese, the Chinese, and the Siamese

Chiang Tung was very closely related to Chiang Mai until the middle of the sixteenth century. But there were few political or religious ties between Chiang Tung and the Shan states west of the Salween River, nor were the ties strong with the Burmese in the Irrawaddy River's fertile plains. However, this changed dramatically beginning in the sixteenth century when Burmese and Mon traders were circulating as far east as Chiang Tung (Lieberman 2003, 207).

All the hardships that afflicted Chiang Tung and its people left deep traces in the history and culture of Chiang Tung. To understand the situation of Chiang Tung in northern Southeast Asia, it is important to look at the wars and privation that it experienced as a borderland between more powerful neighbors. Chiang Tung was, more than ever, in the hands of foreign powers during the time of the second and third Burmese dynasties, the Toungoo and Konbaung.

Today, when passing the national border between Thailand and Myanmar, from Mae Sai to Tachileik, one of the first sites is a reminder of Burmese power in the shape of a gigantic golden statue of the king of the Toungoo dynasty, Bayinnaung. It was Bayinnaung who conquered Lan Na in the middle of the sixteenth century, but his greatest military achievement was the capture of Ayutthaya, the Siamese capital, in 1564. As a reminder of these military conquests, the Burmese military regime made this statue during the 1990s, pointing out to every visitor the strong Burmese military force, both in history and in present times. Chiang Tung and Lan Na were pawns in the struggles between the Burmese, Chinese, and Siamese dynasties during their long-standing rivalries.

The Toungoo dynasty, founded by King Bayinnaung (ruled 1551–1581), was probably the largest dynasty in the history of Southeast Asia (Lieberman 2003, 152). After Bayinnaung took power in both Upper and Lower Burma, he led a military expedition to the Shan states. In 1556, the Burmese army occupied Hsipaw in the northern Shan states, and afterward it continued to Lan Na and took control of Chiang Mai in 1558. From Chiang Mai, Bayinnaung could control all the city-states of Lan Na, including Chiang Tung and Chiang Rung (Sarasssawadee 2005, 112). However, Bayinnaung implemented no effective administrative control through centralized bureaucratic rule. Instead, the Toungoo kings either appointed indigenous leaders or assigned their trusted subjects to rule them, with no attempt to intervene in major affairs such as taxation, judicature, or administration (Sunait 2002, 14).

To understand the history of Chiang Tung during these years, it is necessary to look at the relationship between the two warring dynasties, the Toungoo and the Ayutthaya. Thai history books describe the years between 1558 and 1774 as the Dark Age, when Lan Na was conquered by the Toungoo dynasty. It has since been questioned, however, if these years really were as dark as previously believed (McDaniel 2007; Kirigaya 2014, 2015). The origin of the idea of the Dark Age comes from the construction of the Burmese people as the archenemy. The destruction of the capital of Ayutthaya in 1767 can be called a chosen trauma for Thailand. In historical writing from the early Bangkok period, the demonization of its western neighbors has been a key element in creating national unity and pride.

The Thai historical description is based on the nation-state of contemporary Thailand, with the area of Lan Na as a part. However, the northern part of Thailand was not part of Ayutthaya or Siam before the twentieth century. For the people of Lan Na, Ayutthaya in the south was as much a foreign country as the Burmese in Pegu or Ava. Also, soldiers from the various provinces of Lan Na were involved in attacks against Ayutthaya during the sixteenth century and later during the destruction of Ayutthaya in 1767. This is often ignored.

The concept of the more than two hundred dark years for Lan Na assumes that since the city of Ayutthaya was destroyed by the Burmese, who then ruled the region for more than two hundred years, this must have been a time of terror for the inhabitants. But the foreign power had little effect on the daily lives of people living throughout Lan Na. Most people worked their fields as before and gathered in the temples on Buddhist sacred days. Life continued mostly as usual under the local rulers, even though they ruled on the mandate of a foreign power. Buddhist traditions were still maintained, with local rulers sponsoring Buddhism as before, and the Burmese did not have any great artistic influence over Lan Na. Several Buddha images and *chedis* in Lan Na style were made during the Burmese period. Offerings to the spirits of city-states were also held according to old Lan Na customs during this time (Sarassawadee 2005, 116).

The two-hundred-plus years of Burmese rule over Lan Na are divided into two separate periods. During the first period, between 1558 and 1664, Lan Na was a semiautonomous region and only indirectly controlled by the Toungoo dynasty in Pegu. During the second period, from 1664 until 1774, Lan Na was fully integrated with Burma. In the latter period, direct government was introduced by sending officials and princes to control the various towns of Lan Na.

The kingdom of Ayutthaya, with the capital of the same name, had been one of Bayinnaung's most powerful neighbors. It had access to shipping and, thus, modern weapons from the West. One of Bayinnaung's goals was to defeat Ayutthaya. As a Buddhist ruler, he justified his conquest with his wish to possess a white elephant, a sacred Buddhist symbol of righteous royal power, as there were four of them in the court of Ayutthaya. Therefore, he sent a request to Ayutthaya's King Maha Chakkraphat for one of the white elephants. The king refused to submit to Bayinnaung, who used this as a pretext to launch an attack, and in 1564, Bayinnaung's armies defeated and took Ayutthaya. It was through his defeat of Chiang Mai that Bayinnaung was able to march all the way to Ayutthaya. After the Shan states and Lan Na were incorporated under Bayinnaung's rule, Bayinnaung's armies incorporated large numbers of soldiers from these borderlands between Toungoo and Ayutthaya. The king and the queen of Ayutthaya were taken as prisoners of war and brought to Pegu with the four white elephants. The defeated king was allowed to become a monk upon his arrival at Pegu.

Chiang Tung was loyal to Bayinnaung during his reign, and the *CTC* (§159) describes how forces from Chiang Tung and Chiang Rung helped the Burmese fight against Ayutthaya. The kingdom that Bayinnaung built on military conquests and alliances had been maintained through personal relationships with local rulers. This soon broke apart. His successor Nanda had difficulty maintaining power over this vast area. He spent much of his reign fighting against Ayutthaya. During this time, Lan Na and Chiang Tung were sandwiched between the two rival powers, Toungoo in the west and Ayutthaya in the south.

The time between Bayinnaung's death in 1581 and 1664 is characterized by the weakness of the Burmese power in Lan Na. The various towns of Lan Na tried to enforce autonomy but lacked coordination. Chiang Saen, for example, broke with Chiang Mai around the year 1600. King Naresuan of Ayutthaya claimed his reign over both and attempted to mediate between them (Sarassawadee 2005, 119–20). Bayinnuang's grandson Anaukhpetlun tried to restore the Burmese dynasty, and in 1614 he attacked Chiang Mai and took back power.

The first half of the seventeenth century seems to have been a relatively stable period in Chiang Tung. The chronicle (*CTC* §174–75) describes a time of peace and happiness, where both the free people and the slaves could trade, and there was plenty of rice and fish. It was also a time of relatively long reigns. For example, Mahā Dhammikarājā ruled for twenty-four years, and the chronicle describes this time as one of prosperity for the people and the Buddhist order. Mahā Dhammikarājā also built a monastery called Suvaṇṇarāma before he died in 1620. According to the chronicles (*CTC* §174), Chiang Tung was independent during this time.

Ayutthaya failed in its attempt to recapture Chiang Mai in 1664. This also changed how Lan Na came to be governed. Previously this had been an area of several relatively free city-states that had to pay tribute to the Burmese, but after the attack, all of Lan Na became an integral part of the Burmese kingdom. The central unified role Chiang Mai had had for a long time disappeared. Lan Na was divided into a southwestern part, with the center in Chiang Mai, and a northeastern part, with the center in Chiang Saen. The towns of Nan, Phrae, Chiang Rai, Lampang, and Phayao were more or less independently ruled by the Burmese. Local rebellions were common, but there was no collective resistance against the Burmese. The Toungoo dynasty ended in the early part of the eighteenth century with an uprising by the Mon people. In 1740, the Mon formed a short-lived kingdom called Hanthawaddy.

The Konbaung dynasty was founded in 1752 by King Alaunghpaya. It is referred to as the third Burmese dynasty and was an expansive militant regime with its capital in Ava. First, the Burmese defeated the Mon in Pegu, and, as a result, they also wiped out most of the Mon ethnic group from Southern Burma. In 1760, they attacked Ayutthaya but failed to conquer the city before Alaungpaya died.

Hsinbyushin (also named Mangra) headed the Konbaung dynasty from 1763 to 1776. A successful rebellion in Chiang Mai against the ruling Burmese only resulted in a new major attack from the Burmese. An army of thirty thousand, many from the Shan states, invaded the region of Lan Na and captured Chiang Mai in 1763, displacing the entire population. The result was a destroyed and devastated city. A large part of the population was recruited by force as soldiers in the Burmese army or deported to the Burmese capital, Ava. When Chiang Mai later was restored, Chiang Tung was painfully drawn into the conflict when Chiang Mai needed to repopulate the city.

Chiang Mai and Lan Na were only the first step toward a final victory over Ayutthaya. With large numbers of troops in Chiang Mai, the Burmese could now attack Ayutthaya from three directions, north, west, and south. The Burmese attack was massive, and Ayutthaya was poorly prepared. The Burmese army finally broke through the walls of the city in April 1767. They destroyed the entire city and deported thousands of residents to Burma. The defeat is still a historic event that stirs strong feelings in Thailand. After the fall of Ayutthaya, several regional centers took up the reconstruction of the country. The most successful was led by the charismatic Taksin in Chantaburi, who built a new capital in Thonburi. The Konbaung dynasty had ruled Chiang Mai for only eleven years, from 1763 until 1774, when local leaders in Lan Na swore allegiance to the Siamese king Taksin (Sarassawadee 2005, 127–29).

The expansion of the Konbaung into the Shan states and Chiang Tung had provoked China. At the same time as Hsinbyushin waged war against Ayutthaya, he also had to fight against the Qing empire of China. The Burmese had captured Chiang Tung and pressured Chiang Rung in Sipsong Panna for tribute. This escalated into frontier wars between 1765 and 1769. After several failed attempts, the Qing troops attacked and occupied Chiang Rung and Chiang Tung, even though the Qing recognized the latter as Burmese sovereign territory. The court of Chiang Tung was divided, and the Qing exploited this division by allying with the anti-Burma faction (Giersch 2006, 100–101). It was not long before the Burmese regained Chiang Tung. Another Qing invasion followed, but in the end, the Burmese-backed Sao Muang Sam recaptured Chiang Tung. According to the *CTC* (§204–5), Sao Muang Sam was assisted by troops from Chiang Rai and Chiang Saen, but the war brutally affected Chiang Tung with a great famine in 1766.

Siam's new ruler, Taksin of Thonburi, realized the importance of preventing the Burmese from repeating their invasion. Therefore, he tried to seize the areas from which the invasion was launched and sent troops to Chiang Mai. The Burmese were prepared and ordered the forces of Chiang Mai and Lampang to launch a counterattack. The forces of Lan Na changed sides, however; they joined the Taksin troops and helped drive out the Burmese.

The so-called Dynasty of the Seven Rulers, Chao Chat Ton, was the name of the reconstruction of Lan Na. It was started by the rulers of Chiang Mai, Lampang, and Lamphun after the Burmese had been expelled from the area. The name refers to Kawila and his brothers, who ruled the three cities. After the help from the Siamese king Taksin, they turned south for an alliance with Siam. Kawila was appointed ruler of Chiang Mai in 1782, while the city was still deserted. Initially, he ruled from Lampang with the support from Siam but moved to the outskirts of Chiang Mai, Wiang Pa Sang, in 1782.

Localized Ethnic Identity

The control of manpower, not the conquest of land, was the crucial factor for establishing, consolidating, and strengthening state power in precolonial Southeast Asia. The losers suffered severely from massive depopulations. Control over manpower was strength and status, since labor, rather than land, was considered a scarce resource (Reid 1988, 129–36; Grabowsky 1999, 45; Liew-Herres, Grabowsky, and Renoo Wichasin 2012, 63–67). It was common to take war captives back to the victorious city-state and let them settle there as workers.[1]

Chiang Mai was abandoned for almost twenty years. The new king, Kawila, started to repopulate and revive the city as the cultural and political metropolis it once was. He started several military campaigns, beginning in 1782 and ending with his death in 1816. He attacked Chiang Saen, Chiang Tung, and many other smaller *mueang* to take prisoners of war and repopulate Chiang Mai. The Yong people, now living in Lamphun, were brought there as war captives from Mong Yong in the early nineteenth century. Today, the place of origin has been used to define the Yong people now living in Lamphun.

Forced resettlement and displaced people were realities in Chiang Tung. During the early nineteenth century, Chiang Tung suffered at the hands of its more powerful neighbors. Forces from Chiang Mai, Lamphun, and Lampang invaded Chiang Tung in 1802 and defeated the Burmese forces that were stationed there.

Large parts of the population in Chiang Tung and other cities in the north were forced or persuaded to move south and populate Chiang Mai, which greatly needed a growing population. According to the *CTC* (§214) the population movement was forced, but the *Chiang Mai Chronicle* (Wyatt and Aroonrut 1998, 250) describes it as voluntary. This relocation of the royal family, nobles, monks, and commoners helped Chiang Mai to develop rapidly, but Chiang Tung was left deserted and defenseless. Today there are many ancestors of these displaced people living in Baan Haiya, just outside the southern gate of Chiang Mai.

A younger brother to the Chiang Tung ruler, Sao Mahakhanan, together with his family and followers (*CTC* §214–15), escaped the deportation to Chiang Mai. He had once fought with the forces of Chiang Mai against the Burmese, but this time he headed north and established himself in the small city-state of Mong Yang. Sao Mahakhanan and his followers remained independent from both Burmese and Siamese powers from 1804 until 1812. However, confrontations between forces from Burma and Lan Na meant Sao Mahakhanan had to flee several times. He probably wanted to establish an independent city-state between the Burmese and Siamese powers, but in the end he had to choose a side. Realizing that opposition to the superior Burmese forces was useless, Sao Mahakhanan changed sides and joined the Burmese in fighting against Kawila's forces. This decision was momentous for the future of Chiang Tung.

Sao Mahakhanan ruled until his death in 1857. He is the first person from Chiang Tung for whom we have some personal information, because Captain William C. McLeod, who was the first Westerner to visit Chiang Tung, met the ruler in 1837. On February 20, 1837, after a thirty-six-day trip by horse, elephant, and on foot through Lamphun, Chiang Mai, Chiang Rai, and Mae Sai, McLeod entered Chiang Tung from the south. He stayed for nine days, meeting with Sao Mahakhanan several times (Grabowsky and Turton 2003, 342–60).[2] From Chiang Tung, he continued the journey to Chiang Rung in Sipsong Panna, Yunnan.

Interestingly, McLeod compared Chiang Tung with Chiang Mai and concluded that the monasteries in Chiang Tung were much better looking and that the monks were much stricter in their religious duties (66–67, 208).

Sao Mahakhanan told McLeod that Chiang Mai was hostile to Chiang Tung and to the British and did not allow any communication or trade with Chiang Tung. He regretted he could not have any contact with his relatives who had been sent to Chiang Mai. Chiang Tung and Chiang Mai were trapped in power politics, and the relationship between them mainly depended on the relationship between Siam and Ava. Sao Mahakhanan sought friendship with Chiang Mai, but the Siamese in Bangkok did not allow any contact with Chiang Tung. They tried to strengthen their protection against the Burmese and therefore did not want Chiang Mai to have friendly relations with Chiang Tung.

During the reign of Sao Mahakhanan, Chiang Tung experienced a peaceful period lasting thirty-five years (1813–1848). Sao Mahakhanan consolidated the area's power through alliances with both Chiang Rung and Chiang Khaeng. He also strengthened his position by donating to the monks. The *CTC* (§231) describes that in 1822 he donated clothes to one hundred monks and sponsored the production of one hundred Buddhist texts. The chronicle also tells that he held a rocket festival. He wanted to establish himself as a protector of Buddhism and a good regent. During his reign he also prepared for future conflicts by repopulating the city and started a major restoration project of the city wall. The wall, with its twelve gates around the city, was finished in 1816, and remnants of these walls and the gates still exist today.

According to local legends, a Tai Loi (Lua) couple was living at the location outside Chiang Tung where Wat Zom Loi still stands, as mentioned in chapter 2. The ruler wanted everyone to help rebuild the defensive wall. However, the Tai Loi (Lua) couple refused to come to the city to be part of the construction work and instead built a *chedi* to contain a relic of the Buddha. The ruler sent soldiers to capture them, but the couple escaped. This story indicates that non-Tai people were also involved in the repopulation of Chiang Tung. The same was true for Chiang Mai during Kawila's repopulation, when he sent out for non-Tai people and paid them to settle in Chiang Mai. Andrew Alan Johnson claims that "the more ethnically diverse the city, and the more various the nations that paid tribute to the monarch, the greater his status" (Johnson 2014, 36). In any case, it is undeniable that the repopulation of Chiang Tung and probably many other city-states comprised a large number of different ethnic groups.

Artisans and craft workers were especially coveted when war captives were taken. According to the Burmese chronicle *Hmannan Yazawin Dawgyi*, after the conquest of Chiang Mai in 1558, whole families of skilled artisans and craft workers, such as painters, lathe workers, gold and silversmiths, blacksmiths, bronze workers, masons, lacquer workers, dyers, embroiderers, perfumers, and men skilled in the training and care of elephants and ponies, as well as those skilled in the culinary arts, were sent to settle in the Burmese capital Pegu ("Burmese Invasions of Siam" 1959, 19).

Cultural and artistic exchanges between different powers were to some extent related to forced resettlements of captured populations. Skilled craft workers were forced to settle in the capital close to the royal palace. Those who had to resettle in the new country after slave-gathering warfare had, of course, no choice, but there was a tendency to incorporate slaves into the social structure of society, since labor was a scarce resource.[3] In the early nineteenth century, the art of lacquerware was brought from Chiang Tung to Chiang Mai with war captives. They settled just south of the Chiang Mai gate, in Nantharam and Wua Lai in the Haiya subdistrict. Lacquerware workshops with descendants from Chiang Tung can still be found in the area.

It was not only war that pushed people to relocate. According to the *Chiang Mai Chronicle*, Kawila persuaded a town entirely populated by the Karen people to move to Chiang Mai. He also tried to attract those who escaped into the mountains during the Burmese attacks. Between 1782 and 1816, Kawila led at least three important waves of resettlement campaigns (Grabowsky 1999, 53). Nevertheless, even the most organized campaigns of forced resettlement failed to depopulate the raided territories. By fleeing into the jungles and mountainous areas or retreating to safe enclaves, large parts of the population could escape (Grabowsky 1999, 59; 2019, 48). It is impossible to know how many war captives were displaced. Even when a chronicle tells us that a city was completely depopulated, there could have been many people who fled into the forest or mountains and later turned back.[4]

Khuen villagers may call themselves Khuen, but at the same time they can identify themselves as a Chiang Tung citizen and a member of a particular village. There is a deep connection between identity and territory. Schliesinger (2000, 152) states that it is a common practice among Tai peoples to derive a new group name from a location. J. George Scott mentions that it is not uncommon for a man to deny being a Tai, a Hkön (Khuen), or a Lü (Lue), and to describe himself by the name of his district as a Yawng (Yong), a native of Möng Yawng (Mong Yong) (Scott and Hardiman 1901, 1:417). A large part of the population in Lamphun Province in northern Thailand are people called Tai Yong, or simply Yong, who were forced to immigrate from Mong Yong. They are often distinguished as an ethnic group, but they are in fact very close to the Lue people who once lived in Mong Yong, near the Mekong River in the Eastern Shan State of Myanmar. Mong Yong was once part of the principality of Sipsong Panna, but later it was incorporated in Chiang Tung. The Yong people were brought as war captives in the early nineteenth century when King Kawila repopulated Chiang Mai. According to the local oral tradition, documented by Ing-Britt Trankell (1995, 33–34), it was the Yong themselves who had requested the help of Kawila to be freed from Burmese rule, but they soon discovered that they were no better off than before. Yong leaders therefore appeared before Rama I in Bangkok and were given permission to settle in Lamphun Province, where they named their settlements after their original homes. Trankell points out that locality is a basic ingredient of identity for the Yong. Locality is expressed in terms of origin and belonging, and, together with the cult of the local guardian spirits, it represents the moral community (Trankell 1995, 37).

As already noted, ethnicity is not a permanent and unchanging condition, and the case of the Yong people clearly emphasizes that locality and a common ancestry are important for people's collective identity. In fact, Leach (1954) claims that the first loyalty of the Shan (Tai) people is to a place, not to a kin group. Leach argues that a Shan cultivator is tied to his land and cannot readily switch his allegiance from one territorial chief to another as can a Kachin. The Shan identify themselves as belonging to a village, and even if circumstances compel them to live elsewhere, they will still describe themselves as belonging to their home village (Leach 1954, 213). As already pointed out in chapter 1, Charles Keyes (1992) and Paul T. Cohen (1998) have used a concept called "localized ethnic identity" when discussing the Lue ethnic group from Sipsong Panna now living in Northern Thailand and Laos. They comment on a paper by Michael Moerman (1965) and point out that those who identify themselves as Lue may also identify themselves by the place where they are living.

The Chiang Tung Wars of the Nineteenth Century

During the middle of the nineteenth century, Chiang Tung experienced many difficult years of devastating wars. The conflict, called the Chiang Tung Wars, included the city-states of Chiang Tung, Chiang Mai, Chiang Rung, and Luang Prabang, but the background of these devastating wars was the relationship between the three main powers in the area: the Qing dynasty of China, the Konbaung dynasty of Burma, and the Rattanakosin dynasty of Siam. This chaotic time peaked when Bangkok sent troops to conquer Chiang Tung three times between 1849 and 1854. Chiang Tung resisted the invaders, largely thanks to the renovated defensive walls, as well as for cultural reasons, as much of Bangkok's army consisted of soldiers from Lan Na, who had stronger emotional ties with the people of Chiang Tung than with the Siamese from the south.

The trouble began in Chiang Rung, the northeast neighbor of Chiang Tung. Chiang Rung had been loyal and paid tribute to the Chinese emperor since the fourteenth century, but from 1564, Chiang Rung paid tribute to both the Chinese and the Burmese. This lasted until the middle of the eighteenth century when the rivalry between the new, expansive Burmese Kounbang dynasty and the Chinese Qing dynasty led to conflicts. From the middle of the sixteenth century, the dual loyalty continued for almost two hundred years, and every new prince in Chiang Rung first had to be approved by both the Chinese and the Burmese rulers before he could be installed (Liew-Herres, Grabowsky, and Renoo 2012, 49–51). Later, when the conflict between the Chinese and Kounbang escalated, candidates loyal to either of them put themselves forward as rulers.

When Chiang Rung's ruler Mahawang died in 1836, a power struggle ensued over who would succeed him. Through a network of family ties and intermarriage, two different groupings at the court in Chiang Rung had crystallized. Suchawan, who was loyal to the Chinese, should have succeeded his father as the new ruler, but he had a rival, Cao No Kham, who had established his own power base and was supported by the Burmese. This hinted at the coming power struggles that would drag Chiang Tung into devastating wars. In 1837, the ruler Sao Mahakhanan of Chiang Tung related to McLeod that the state of Chiang Rung was chaotic. This was nothing compared to the chaos that was to come, as described in the *Chronicle of Sipsong Panna* (*CSP* §32).

After few years of relative calm, China withdrew its support for Suchawan, who instead turned south to the various rulers in Lan Na who were allied with Siam. Chiang Rung's finances were in poor shape, which led to increased taxes. Cao No Kham, with the support of mountain people, continued to raid the territory of Chiang Rung. He also received help from Chiang Tung troops led by Mahaphom, the son of Sao Mahakhanan. They tried to take Chiang Rung, but they failed. China and Burma wanted to put an end to the conflict in Chiang Rung, so they came to an agreement that guaranteed the safety of Cao No Kham as long he remained in exile in Chiang Tung and the rulers of Chiang Tung prevented him from causing any problems in Sipsong Panna (Smith 2013, 87).

However, the treaty collapsed in 1840 when the Burmese king became angry with Suchawan, who would not pay tribute to him in person. In his defense, Suchawan could not do this, as the Chinese had banned him from leaving Chiang Rung. Cao No Kham went to Amarapura, the new Burmese capital, and asked the king for help. Burmese forces, led by Cao No Kham, attacked Chiang Rung in 1841 with the support from Chiang Tung and other Shan states. Suchawan fled to China, and Cao No Kham took the city without resistance. In return, the Chinese sent an army of around seven thousand soldiers to attack Chiang Rung, driving Cao No Kham out of Sipsong Panna. Suchawan returned to the throne of Chiang Rung once again.

After the defeat of Cao No Kham, the Burmese withdrew their support for him, and the ministers who had supported him were arrested and executed. It was not the Burmese who had chosen Cao No Kham as their candidate; it was the rulers of Chiang Tung. The Burmese themselves had no agenda for disposing of Suchawan; however, they were supportive of Chiang Tung, which was an important strategic location east of the Salween River (Smith 2013, 88–92). The tensions between Chiang Rung and Chiang Tung remained. So far, only two of the main powers of the region, the Konbaung dynasty of Burma and the Qing dynasty of China, had been involved in this first phase of the Chiang Tung Wars. Lan Na and Siam had largely remained uninvolved. However, this would soon change. Troops from Chiang Mai attempted to invade Chiang Tung on orders from Bangkok several times between 1846 and 1854.

A riot in Chiang Rung caused the court to flee south to Luang Prabang and ask Bangkok for support. King Nangklao (Rama III) realized that there was an opportunity to control both Chiang Rung and Chiang Tung. Therefore, in 1849, Bangkok ordered the rulers of Chiang Mai, Lamphun, and Lampang to attack Chiang Tung. However, Chiang Tung successfully defended itself, partly owing to a lack of motivation from Lan Na forces; the ruler of Chiang Mai had no interest in attacking but had to act on the order from Bangkok. Bangkok had planned to send forces to assist, but this was canceled because of the death of Rama III. When King Mongkut (Rama IV) took the throne in Bangkok in 1851, he continued the war plans. The attack on Chiang Tung in 1849 caused the Burmese to prepare to defend Chiang Tung and Chiang Rung. However, when the Siamese forces did attack, in 1852, the Burmese forces were engaged with the British in the western part of the country. The British had already caused Burmese losses during the First Anglo-Burmese War in 1824–1826, in Arakan, Manipur, Assam, and Tenasserin. The whole of Southern Burma would soon fall to the British; Mongkut knew this was likely and considered it an important reason to hurry the attack before the British won.

A second invasion of Chiang Tung started in 1852 with forces from Bangkok and Siamese provinces and from Tai principalities under Siamese suzerainty. The forces were divided into two armies, one of which was composed of soldiers from Nan, Phrae, and Lomsak. The other had soldiers from Chiang Mai, Lamphun, and Lampang. When the armies met in Chiang Saen, they had swollen to about thirty thousand troops. Both armies traveled from Chiang Saen, at thirteen-day intervals, and entered the Chiang Tung valley from the south. The defending forces included only seven thousand men from Chiang Tung, with no assistance from the Burmese, who were fighting the British. This was the first time in history that Siamese forces marched north of Chiang Saen. They besieged the city and established fortifications outside all twelve city gates (Smith 2013, 112–14).

Although equipped with artillery, the Siamese could not breach the walls of the city, as the walls were on high ground, and the Siamese artillery could not shoot high enough (Smith 2013, 118). There were not enough firearms within Chiang Tung to arm all the defenders, who instead relied on guerrilla tactics, mounting a series of swift raids on the enemy fortifications and rapid retreats back within the walls of the city. They launched surprise attacks while dressed in red clothes and speaking the Lan Na language to disguise themselves as Lan Na soldiers, as there was still more likeness between the language in Chiang Tung and Chiang Mai than between Bangkok and Chiang Mai.

Chiang Tung's position between forces from Siam on the one side and forces from the Burmese Konbaung on the other shows the vulnerability of this location. The ruler Sao Mahakhanan may have considered surrendering and subjecting himself to the power of the Siamese. In 1837, he had complained to McLeod that he had no friendly relations with Chiang Mai, though his family lived there after being captured. At the same time, his children were stationed in the Burmese court in Amarapura for their education. He would never see them again if he handed over the city to Siamese patronage. The siege lasted for only twelve days in May 1852, before the two Siamese armies gave up the siege and surrendered. Smith claims that "the war was doomed from the start, and for cultural, rather than strategic, reasons" (Smith 2013, 128–29). Many people of Lan Na had their roots in Chiang Tung and the north, from the time of Kawila's repopulating projects, and had stronger emotional ties with them than with the Siamese from the south. Slave-gathering warfare and repopulation movements between the two cities had made their populations closely related.

Nevertheless, Siamese forces eventually prepared for a new attack on Chiang Tung. The Second Anglo-Burmese War was over, the British having annexed a portion of southern Burma, and King Mindon had succeeded on the throne of Amarapura. Now that the western front was calm, the Burmese prepared an attack on the Siamese forces.

The defense of Chiang Tung was handed over to Sao Mahakhanan's son, Mahaphom, who would succeed his father as ruler. Mahakhanan was seventy years old and had been blind for thirty years. At the sieges of 1849 and 1852, Chiang Tung had received no reinforcements from Burmese soldiers. The new Siamese attack began in 1854. This time, the defenders of Chiang Tung, some seven thousand soldiers, were strengthened by nine thousand Burmese and Shan troops. These sixteen thousand defended the city against the Siamese army of twenty thousand men. One reason for the active participation of Burmese in the defense of Chiang Tung was that the newly installed King Mindon wanted to demonstrate his power to defend his area of interest, unlike his predecessor; the defense of Chiang Tung could be interpreted as a defense of Burma itself.

Nevertheless, just as before, Chiang Tung was respected as a vassal state ruled by a local ruler (*saopha*).

Although the route of the Konbaung army to reach Chiang Tung was more difficult than that of the Siamese troops, the defenses were in place by the time the attacking Siamese army arrived. King Mongkut's brother, Wongsathirat, who led one of the two attacking armies, complained that the forces of Chiang Mai were war-weary and ill-prepared. After a two-month march, the Siamese troops arrived in the Chiang Tung valley at the end of April 1854. The Siamese side once again was unsuccessful, with the campaign ending in a major, bloody defeat and withdrawal of the attackers. King Mongkut explained the failure as due to the difficult terrain and the long distance to Chiang Tung (Smith 2013, 148–49). The Chiang Tung War, which started with fighting for power in Chiang Rung during the 1830s and involved forces from Burma, China, and Siam, ended with the invading Siamese troops defeated on their third attempt to take Chiang Tung. Meanwhile, the British had taken control in Lower Burma, and it would not be long until they claimed power over all Burma. The ruler Sao Mahakhanan had repopulated Chiang Tung, rebuilt the defensive wall, and reigned during the long and horrible wars. He is today remembered as a national hero, and a newly installed statue of him stands in Chiang Tung.

The Limbin Confederacy

After King Mindon's death in 1878, Mandalay turned into a chaos of power struggles. Mindon was succeeded by Thibaw, one of his sons, who was married to his own half sister, Supayalat. She gained great influence over the throne, and afterward she was blamed for much of what happened during the reign of Thibaw. The relationship between Mandalay and the Shan states worsened under the kingship of Thibaw, who had a more aggressive attitude than his predecessor and demanded greater tribute from the Shan rulers.

In 1881, a new ruler, named Sao Kawng Tai, was crowned in Chiang Tung. Both the Burmese and the British remembered him as a feared ruler. J. George Scott described him as a "distinctly murderous old ruffian" (Scott 1932, 249), although he never met him. Sao Kawng Tai had a sister who had been married to Mindon but was murdered on behalf of Thibaw shortly after Mindon's death. Sao Kawng Tai understood that King Thibaw was weak and revolted against him, proclaiming independence for Chiang Tung (Mangrai 1965, 198).

Thibaw had a high-ranking officer with thirty bodyguards stationed in Chiang Tung. By the order of Sao Kawng Tai himself, they were all brutally killed in 1882. He also sent soldiers to Chiang Rung to overthrow the ruler Sao Seng, who was loyal to Thibaw. Sao Seng was duly eliminated, and his head, packed in honey, was sent to the ruler of Chiang Tung (Mangrai 1965, 103). Nevertheless, Sao Kawng Tai's rebellion against Thibaw was apparently not a bid for complete independence but more a maneuver for increased autonomy and a protest against high taxes (Thant Myint-U 2001, 173).

The revolt against Thibaw spread to other Shan states. The next year, Sao Hkun Kyi, the ruler of the Shan state of Mong Nai, also rebelled against Thibaw. The rulers of Mong Nai and Chiang Tung, together with several Shan rulers, protested against the king's aggressive policies and plotted to remove him from his Mandalay throne. This revolt has been remembered as the Limbin Confederacy. The Shan leaders put forward a royal prince named Limbin as an alternative regent to Thibaw. Limbin had already broken with Mandalay and moved to British Lower Burma. He was a cousin of Thibaw and therefore of royal blood. Mong Nai was a significant Shan state, and one daughter of the ruler Sao Hkun Kyi had been married to Mindon. When Thibaw came to power, he had imprisoned her. In border disputes between different Shan states, Thibaw had opposed Sao Hkun Kyi. When ordered to appear at the Mandalay court, Sao Hkun Kyi refused and fled to Chiang Tung, where he had an ally in Sao Kawng Tai (*CTC* §291–94). Some rulers of smaller Shan states also joined in their rebellion against Thibaw, but it was the rulers of Mong Nai and Chiang Tung who were the leaders in the Limbin Confederacy.

Limbin arrived in Chiang Tung in December 1885, but the British had already imprisoned Thibaw. This was not known in Chiang Tung. Maybe Limbin already knew this when he arrived in Chiang Tung but chose not to tell. Prince Limbin hoped the British would restore the monarchy in Burma and choose him as successor to the throne now that Thibaw was out of the picture. However, this did not happen.

The Limbin Confederacy continued as a rebellion against the British presence, but the Shan rulers did not all see eye to eye. Some of them welcomed the British. The forces of the Limbin Confederacy crossed the Salween River to the west, joined by many of the rulers in the small southern Shan state. But some of the Shan states in the north took the British side in the conflict. After a series of negotiations between the British and various Shan rulers, the British struck a deal with the ruler of Mong Nai and Prince Limbin.

Chiang Tung was an important city-state in the Golden Age of Lan Na, from the middle of the fourteenth century until the beginning of the sixteenth century. This era is a chosen cultural highpoint for the Buddhist people of Chiang Tung and forms the basis of the culture that still exists today. The tumultuous time from the middle of the sixteenth century, when King Bayinnaung conquered Chiang Tung and the rest of Lan Na, until the British set aside the Konbaung king

Thibaw in the late nineteenth century, illustrates the exposed location of Chiang Tung in the historic borderland between major powers on all sides. It is important to recall this vulnerable situation when examining the identity and culture of the Khuen people. Important historical events for Chiang Tung during these days are the defense in the nineteenth century by Sao Mahakhanan and the Sao Kawng Tai Revolt against King Thibaw in 1882.

Two opposite tendencies during this precolonial time are actually two sides of the same coin. First, we have seen that the control of human resources, not the conquest of land, was the crucial factor for establishing, consolidating, and strengthening state power in precolonial Southeast Asia. Forced resettlement was a reality for many people. Forced resettlement and displaced people were certainly realities in Chiang Tung, as large parts of the population were forced to move south and populate Chiang Mai, which left Chiang Tung deserted and defenseless. Ethnic belonging was affected when people were compelled to move and integrate into a new society. Second, a seemingly opposite tendency is that locality and a common ancestry are important elements for people's collective identity. The Tai people often derive their names from location, as we have seen from those who were forced to immigrate from Mong Yong and today call themselves Tai Yong. These two opposite tendencies points to the close relationship between place and identity.

Repopulating Chiang Tung meant that large parts of the population were replaced by people from many places and ethnic and social groups. Despite this population exchange, the Khuen identity has been maintained through all the years. This points to the deep connection between the Khuen identity and the local place *mueang* Chiang Tung, which I see as a localized ethnic identity.

4
FOREIGN RULERS

> The Kiang Tung province in the hands of the British can never be anything but a source of weakness to the integrity of the Burmese kingdom. It will, like the Irishman's coat tails, be dragging along the ground—a constant challenge to outsiders to tread upon it.
>
> The soundest policy would appear to be to hand over the province to the Chinese; not as a possession, but as a tributary State, making certain stipulations, for trade and defence against aggression, favourable to British interests.
>
> —George J. Younghusband, *The Trans-Salwin Shan State of Kiang Tung*, 1888

The colonial period meant major structural changes throughout Southeast Asia, particularly in its northern borderlands. As we have seen in previous chapters, the area was not characterized by national borders but by a more flexible geopolitical system, borders without boundary lines (Thongchai 1994). This system changed completely with the arrival of the colonial powers to the region. The borders between the nation states in Southeast Asia today owe much of their existence to colonial state-making and have divided people who share much of the same culture and language. But as we already have seen, the struggles to define the political borders of northern Southeast Asia started during the Konbaung dynasty of the Burmese, the Qing dynasty of China, and Rattanakosin dynasty of Siam, before the colonial powers interfered.

The British Annexation of Chiang Tung

The colonial state-making had a pronounced effect on Chiang Tung, and a short background on the colonization of Burma and Chiang Tung is necessary to understand this effect. The reasons behind the British involvement in Burma can be partially found in the expansion of the Konbaung dynasty. Under the leadership of King Bodawpaya, Konbaung expanded westward and occupied Arakan in 1784, confiscating the holy Mahāmuni Buddha image, also called Arakan Buddha. Today, this statue is considered to be one of the most holy images in

Myanmar. The Burmese brought the image to Amarapura, once the capital of the Konbaung dynasty and today in the suburbs of Mandalay. In a later chapter we explore the magical power contained in this image, attributable to the belief that it was made during the time of the Buddha. During colonial times, a replica was made of it for Chiang Tung.

The expansion west meant a common border between British India and the lands of the Konbaung dynasty, which led to conflicts. King Bagyidaw, Bodawpaya's successor, spurred by his previous conquests, planned to take over Calcutta, which was the capital of British India. However, in what became known as the First Anglo-Burmese War, the British were victorious, and from 1824 to 1826 the Burmese lost Arakan, Manipur, Assam, and Tenasserim. During the Second Anglo-Burmese War, which began in 1852, the British conquered all of southern Burma. The British victory in 1852 also triggered a palace revolt against King Pagan. His half brother, Mindon, gained power, which began a new but short period of development. Mindon was reform-minded and tried to modernize the country. He founded Mandalay as a new capital and sought to maintain good relations with both the British and the French. Under his rule, the country experienced prosperity, though the British were still a latent threat. King Mindon of Mandalay had good relationships with most of the Shan states, and the Shan rulers demonstrated their respect by giving annual tribute. There were only a few small rebellions against Mindon. During this time, the relations between Chiang Tung and the other Shan states strengthened. The prosperous period lasted only until the death of Mindon in 1878, when his successor Thibaw took up the throne.

It was not a given that the British would capture all the Shan states after defeating Thibaw in 1885 and occupying Upper Burma. Two important Shan states, Hsipaw and Yawnghwe, came into conflict with the others and requested help from the British. Arthur Hedding Hildebrand and J. George Scott conducted the negotiations for the British. The British could not resist the invitation and continued into the Shan states. Within three months of the presence of British troops in the Shan hills, the whole of the southern Shan states submitted without a fight (Mitton 1936, 100–101). On May 4, 1886, the British Foreign Ministry declared that the whole of Upper Burma, including the Shan states, now was part of British India (Aung Tun 2009, 167). Chiang Tung, however, was not included. The British had only reached the Salween River, and the territory east, known as the Trans-Salween, was left at this point without intentions to intervene.

Siam also had an interest in the Trans-Salween territory. In the middle of the nineteenth century, the Siamese had tried to conquer Chiang Tung but failed. In 1884, Siam proclaimed it would send troops into the Trans-Salween territory to strengthen its holdings in the area. The British protested strongly in the form of a letter to the Siamese commissioner in Chiang Mai. The Siamese were afraid of jeopardizing their relationship with the British, so they withdrew the proclamation and wrote a new one, in which the idea of sending troops into the Salween valley was abandoned (Charan 1987, 43–44).

This marked a pivotal point for the future of Chiang Tung, when the rest of the Shan states were in the hands of the British, and Siam withdrew its ambition to claim supremacy in the region. Would Chiang Tung be independent in the future, or would France, the colonizer to the east, attempt to include it in its territory? Chiang Tung was surrounded by several strong powers and unable to defend itself against any of them. The ruler, Sao Kawng Tai, was inclined to fight for independence but knew from experience that small city-states have to pay tribute to their neighbors. However, there was no time for alliances. The British were impatient but did not know how to act. There were probably various reasons the British first hesitated at the Salween. What the British knew about Chiang Tung came mostly from rumors and from the visit of Captain William C. McLeod, one of the few Western travelers who made it all the way to Chiang Tung in the early nineteenth century. They had also heard rumors about the present ruler of Chiang Tung, Sao Kawng Tai, who disliked Europeans. The British may have been afraid to have him as an enemy. On the one hand, he was warlike and had rebelled against the Burmese king and given sanctuary to other Shan rulers who had broken with Thibaw. On the other hand, he was a bitter enemy to Thibaw, whom the British had recently deposed.

The British knew that the Frenchman Ernest Doudart de Lagrée had visited Chiang Tung twenty years earlier. He was the second Westerner to visit Chiang Tung. Two steamboats from the French Mekong Exploration Commission had started from Saigon on June 5, 1866, for an expedition up the Mekong River. The expedition set off in search of a waterway to China, but it was also an important effort against the British, aiming to establish the area along the Mekong as a French territory. Seven commission members and a crew of twenty men were on the expedition. The leader, Doudart de Lagrée, made a detour from the Mekong and went overland to Chiang Tung, and in 1867 he met Mahakhanan's son and successor, Sao Maha Hpom. McLeod was well-remembered in the court, and this was perhaps one reason they welcomed the French visitor. Doudart de Lagrée did not complete the expedition but died before it reached its destination. Francis Garnier, who took over as commander after the death of Doudart de Lagrée, recorded his colleague's memories of Chiang Tung.

The British might have been wary of the French, who were already on the other side of the Mekong, not far from Chiang Tung. For the British, Chiang Tung was a key gateway to Chiang Rung and, farther on, to Yunnan. Another reason the British stopped before they entered Chiang Tung may have been that the Salween River is very wild, with steep banks. To the east are several high mountain ranges, which make it difficult to reach Chiang Tung from the west. The British also knew that Chiang Tung was not a natural part of Burma; traditionally it had ties to Lan Na, which had close connections to Siam in those days.

Therefore, prior to deciding whether to continue their conquest on the other side of the Salween, the British sent a young lieutenant by the name of George J. Younghusband to spy on the feared Shan ruler of Chiang Tung. They wanted Younghusband to explore the area before any decisions were made on incorporating this land into British Burma. Younghusband did not travel across the Shan states to Chiang Tung but instead took the southern and less difficult road from Moulmain in southern Burma, through Siam, and across Chiang Mai, Chiang Rai, and Chiang Saen to get to Chiang Tung. From Chiang Mai he followed a Chinese-Yunnan trade caravan, hiring three small ponies to carry his belongings. This trip of 468 kilometers between Chiang Mai and Chiang Tung took thirteen days. A key reason for taking this southern road was that the Chiang Tung ruler would suppose him to be a British spy if he had arrived from the west. Entering from the south, he could pass as an American explorer or a missionary.

Younghusband was to determine if it was possible and desirable to annex this remote Shan state. His duties also included investigating the relationship between the Chiang Tung ruler and the French, as well as seeing how well fortified the city was. When Younghusband finally entered the town, he felt threatened, but he did not know how serious these threats were. He was not met with a friendly welcome and had to stay outside the city wall for several days (Younghusband [1888] 2005, 5). His life could have been more seriously in danger if he had come two months earlier. The ruler Sao Kawng Tai had just died and had been replaced by his young son, Sao Kawng Hkam Hpoo. His son was only twelve years old, so power rested in the hands of his four council members. Younghusband described the young ruler as a "thin, pale, and rather idiotic-looking youth" (14). One member of the council informed Younghusband he probably would not have survived one day in Chiang Tung if the old ruler had still been alive. Several American missionaries tried to get permission to visit Chiang Tung during the time of Sao Kawng Tai, but the ruler consistently objected to this.

Younghusband stayed in Chiang Tung for ten days in March of 1887. The city walls impressed him, and he estimated that there were roughly ten thousand troops in total—about three thousand soldiers in the city and the surrounding valley as well as seven thousand throughout the state between the Salween and the Mekong. After his stay, he sent a memorandum to his superiors, declaring that the British should not attempt to incorporate the Trans-Salween region. He wrote,

> [Chiang Tung] runs between two foreign nations, and ends on the border of a third. A province open to invasion to all three of them—to

> China from the North, to Siam from the South, and to the French from the East, and separated from the actual possessors of the country by lofty and impassable ranges of mountains, ... The Kiang Tung province in the hands of the British can never be anything but a source of weakness to the integrity of the Burmese kingdom. (13)

He recommended that "the soundest policy would appear to be to hand over the province to the Chinese; not as a possession, but as a tributary State" (14). The British had good relations with China but not with their own major rival, the French. In the end, the British did not follow the advice from Younghusband. They did not stop at the Salween but continued east toward Chiang Tung in 1890. This was four years after the British took Upper Burma and the rest of the Shan states. It had been eight years of independence for Chiang Tung since the assassination of King Thibaw's emissary in 1882.

Charles Crosthwaite, the British chief commissioner of Burma (1887–1890), also wrote that the "arguments in favour of making the Salween our eastern boundary had considerable force. The river gave a clear and definite frontier drawn from north to south. . . . There were strong reasons, therefore, for not going a yard farther than was necessary" (Crosthwaite 1912, 210–11). But he continues with a long exposition on why Chiang Tung had to be in the British domain. If the British decided not to take responsibility for the Trans-Salween states, China and Siam might absorb them, leading to a belt of territory between the British and French dominions. It was certain to be the refuge of all the discontent and lawlessness of Burma (Crosthwaite 1912, 212–13).

Why the British changed their minds is partly related to the progress of the French. The road to Chiang Tung was easier to travel from French Indo-China, compared to crossing the Salween from the west. And the British feared that the French wanted Chiang Tung to create a trade route to southern China. After all, the French had sent an expedition to find the upstream Mekong waterway to China. Also, the British wanted a trade route to Chiang Rung and farther into Yunnan. One more important reason to enter Chiang Tung was that the British did not want to appear weak in the eyes of all the Shan rulers on the west side of the Salween. They feared rebellion. It could create thoughts of resistance if the rulers believed the British were too weak to hold Chiang Tung.

The British also had the prospect of commercial interests in Chiang Tung, especially as the Salween was a timber highway. The territory east of the Salween was rich in timber, but even more important, they could transport the timber down the Salween to Moulmein in Lower Burma. And it would create various problems if they used the Salween as a boundary. Charan Chakandang (1987, 50–75) believes that the motives may have been mixed and indicates four reasons the British had for crossing the Salween River: the fear of French penetration; possible trouble from local gangs; to impress the local population with British strength; and a potential future economic advantage. Again, Chiang Tung was in the clutches of a geopolitical conflict. This time, two international colonial powers, the British and the French, amplified Chiang Tung's exposed location between larger and more powerful nations. After some hesitation, the British decided to incorporate Chiang Tung, the most eastern Shan state, into their empire. This decision by the British was momentous for the future of Chiang Tung.

J. George Scott was a Scottish journalist who became a functionary in the colonial administration in British Burma. He also worked as a teacher and headmaster at St. John's College in Rangoon (Yangon). He was fluent in Burmese, spoke Shan as well, and was knowledgeable about Burmese culture.[1] Together with Arthur Hedding Hildebrand, Scott was in negotiations with Shan rulers on the western side of the Salween when he was selected to lead a delegation to Chiang Tung. On March 14, 1890, Scott, along with a young military officer named F. J. Pink and a military medical officer named Darwin, were sent to Chiang Tung. They had twenty Indian soldiers (sepoys) and a handful of caravan mules with them. A letter was sent to the ruler to remind him that Chiang Tung used to pay tribute to the late Burmese government, which had then been replaced by the British. The British hoped he would make an announcement of his acceptance of British suzerainty, but the reply was evasive (Scott 1932, 248–49).

Scott and his wife, Geraldine Mitton, described the visit to Chiang Tung and the meeting with the ruler (Scott and Hardiman 1900, 1:307; Scott 1932, 248–58; Mitton 1936, 137–53). The journey took fifteen days altogether. Eight years of independence had elapsed since the ruler Sao Kawng Tai had executed the officer sent by King Thibaw in 1882. But Sao Kawng Tai had just recently passed away, and a new young ruler was in charge. After some misunderstanding, the ruler and his brother, the heir-apparent, came to meet the British delegation at separate parties, "riding on gorgeously caparisoned ponies and shaded by numerous gold umbrellas" (Mitton 1936, 142). Each had his own bodyguard of several hundred men, most of them armed. Half the town followed, and a half moon of two to three thousand people surrounded Scott and his men. They were formally presented with gold and silver flowers, representing tribute. The party was asked to camp at the old Burmese military camp just outside the palace gate. The ruler was only sixteen, and Scott could see that he was very nervous. Most of the chief ministers were also present. His brother, the heir-apparent who later became the next ruler, Sao Kawn Kiao Intaleng, was described by Scott as a bright little boy.

The next day, the prince and his brother met Scott and his delegation in a smaller palace building with a large golden throne bounded by a railing. The ruler and his brother sat in front of the throne on chairs. Scott and his men were allowed to sit between them. The British apparently did not impress the ruler and his brother. Initially, they resisted submitting to the British propositions. Chiang Tung had been independent for eight years since the rebellion against the last Burmese king, Thibaw. Why would they let go of independence now? The British had not come with any great, scary, or impressive army, and it was not long ago that Chiang Tung had fought off armies from Siam.

There was an intermission during the visit that possibly affected the outcome of the negotiations. A couple of mule drivers from the British group visited a theater performance (*pwe*). Then a fight broke out between them and the ruler's bodyguard. One of the mule drivers was shot and killed, and another was injured. When Scott heard about this, he was upset and wrote a letter to the ruler that same evening, requesting that he promptly hand over the men guilty of the shooting. The next morning, some of his mule drivers reported it was the ruler himself who had killed the man.

One reason for the incident may have been that the mule drivers were carrying guns in the palace yard, which was strictly forbidden. The ruler and his bodyguard may have thought this transgression an insult or a plot and acted hastily (Scott 1932, 253–55; Mitton 1936, 141–52). Scott met the ruler the next day, and after convincing arguments, the ruler accepted the takeover by the British. The event of the day before and the British reaction may have affected the ruler's willingness to accept the British. The takeover of Chiang Tung, the largest Shan state, was therefore without bloodshed, except for the unfortunate mule drivers. We do not know exactly what happened during the negotiations between Scott and the ruler of Chiang Tung. A private letter from the commissioner Charles Crosthwaite was the only recognition Scott got.

It is interesting to speculate on what actually happened during the British party's stay in Chiang Tung. Their instructions were to be discreet and see what type of man the young ruler was (Scott 1932, 249–50). The mule driver incident might have ended in disaster for the British if Scott had humiliated the ruler. Instead he solved the incident discreetly, and neither side had lost face. However, Scott mentions that at a government garden party years later, the ruler of Chiang Tung told him it was only because of the intervention of his wives that the British were not massacred (Mitton 1936, 152; Mangrai 1965, 214).

An agreement (*sanad*) was written between the British and the ruler of Chiang Tung. Sao Kawng Kham Hpoo would pay the same tribute that Chiang Tung had made to the Burmese court in Mandalay during the time of King Mindon. Sao Kawng Kham Hpoo died in April 1896, at the age of just twenty-two. He was succeeded by his younger brother, Sao Kawn Kiau Intaleng, who ruled during almost the entire colonial period.

At the same time that the British became rulers of Burma and the Shan states, Siam had strengthened its political and economic influence in Chiang Mai and the surrounding cities of Lamphun, Lampang, Phrae, and Nan. Although Siam was struggling to avoid becoming a colony of any European power, the policy that Bangkok used against Lan Na was a colonial policy. The relatively independent city-states in Lan Na could no longer exercise their traditional powers, while Bangkok gained more and more control. A rebel movement arose around 1890 when Ai Nan Techa (Phaya Phap) started a rebellion against the Siamese power in Chiang Mai. The rebels did not direct their actions at the local elite and the prince of Chiang Mai but against the powerful in Bangkok who indirectly ruled Chiang Mai.

Also around this time, an agreement was signed between Siam and France: the French had a twenty-five-kilometer-wide corridor on the western shore of the Mekong inside the territory of Siam, where they were able to trade without the intervention of Siamese authorities or the military. French trading stations were established in both Chiang Khong and Chiang Saen. This could be seen as indulgence from Siam's side to appease a colonial power, but it may have helped them avoid being colonized. The new borders of British and French territories prevented local traders from freely walking the invaded trading routes. The trade routes between China and Chiang Mai that crossed Chiang Tung were now severely restricted. Siam introduced a tax to all traders from Chiang Tung who could not show a British passport. In that way, the large trade of livestock previously driven by local merchants had been interrupted.

These difficulties for local traders were a cause of the 1902 rebellions in Phrae, commonly referred to as the Shan Rebellion of 1902–1904. Pakamong was a merchant from Chiang Tung who was in debt to a sister of Chiang Tung's ruler. He had moved to Phrae and stayed there as a local merchant. All the rules and regulations made it difficult to make a living through trade, so he resorted to life as a robber.

According to official Siamese documents, the ruler of Phrae backed Pakamong to start a revolt and drive away the Siamese administration in Phrae. Several hundred people joined the uprising and attacked the seat of the Siamese commissioner, executing twenty Siamese officials. Successes triggered the rebels to expand their rebellion, but when reinforcements came from Bangkok, the uprising was slowed (Tanabe 1984; Walker 2014). The Siamese influence over the northern provinces was a source of dissatisfaction that sparked this revolt, as the local rulers had lost much of their power. Agreements between Siam and the British gave British merchants permission to trade deep in Siam's northern parts. Trade in timber was a major source of revenue for the British.

Colonial Times

Colonial Burma was a military occupation with a racial hierarchy. A key part of colonial race thinking was skin color. At the top were Europeans, foremost the British, but also included were Germans, Frenchmen, and other western Europeans. Lower in status were the Indian, Chinese, and Burmese businesspeople, landowners, professionals, and civil servants. Lowest of all were other non-European peoples (Thant Myint-U 2020, 20–21). The British ruled and administered Burma directly as part of British India. Witness accounts of the brutal regime can be found famously in writings of George Orwell. When the British conquered Upper Burma, they imprisoned the king and abolished the entire royal court. They also effectively took away the power of the traditional ruling class in Mandalay and around the country, and they stopped Burmese traditions. Instead, Indian civil servant immigrants became the link between the British and the Burmese people.

In the mountainous border areas populated with ethnic minorities, the British chose not to overturn the existing social and political order but to harness it for their purposes. Here in the so-called Frontier Areas, the British largely did not challenge the authority of traditional headmen, chieftains, and local lords (Taylor 2007, 72–78). Governing the Shan states directly was not financially possible for the British. Securing peace at a minimum cost required cooperation with traditional Shan rulers. The formal expression of the cooperation reached between the British and local Shan rulers is found in the *sanads* and letters of appointment (Maule 1993, 91). Under the terms of these agreements, the rulers had their positions confirmed and were guaranteed noninterference in internal state administration, so long as British authority was observed. An annual tribute was remitted to the colonial government to be, and British advice was to be acted upon whenever advanced (Maule 1993, 91).

The Shan states had never been united. Each state was ruled by its *saopha*, and these states had continued to function independently of each other when they accepted the Burmese kings as their sovereigns. During colonial rule, when the British had assumed the role of the Burmese kings, the Shan rulers took for granted that the same, decentralized administration would continue. Every Shan ruler wanted his executive power undisturbed. This was the case in the beginning, and much about life in Chiang Tung and the rest of the Shan states continued as before, though under the authority of the British. The rulers and the court still had the practical and symbolic power maintained in traditional palaces (*haw*). Like the ancient Burmese kings, the British promised not to interfere with internal affairs as long as the ruler remained loyal. Every Shan ruler was in charge of administration and establishing law and order, with his own police, civilian officials, and judges—though, of course, they had no legal jurisdiction over European citizens. The rulers also had a responsibility to maintain local roads and bridges as well as provide education and health care for their subjects. They also collected taxes and were important figures during ceremonial celebrations. The British, however, took away all rights to forests and minerals.

With many self-governing Shan states, the administration was so decentralized and diverse that it would have been difficult for the British to apply a uniform system of regulations. Many of the states were tiny, and the cooperation between them was not the best. Consequently the British eventually felt the need to reform the administration of the Shan states and established a federal Shan State (Aung Tun 2009, 173–74). This federal state became active in 1922, with a northern and a southern part. Chiang Tung came to belong to the South Shan State. In this new administration the Shan rulers had to submit their cases before two British officials, the assistant superintendent and the commissioner, before they could submit them to the governor. The new federation was not popular with the Shan rulers. They thought that this was a restriction on their status and prestige. They protested several times against the new order and wrote several memorandums between 1930 and 1939, where they complained about what they saw as degradation of their status (Aung Tun 2009, 183).

The British had removed customs between the different states immediately after they assumed control. No roads used for transport with carts or cars existed between the states; trade had followed the paths where mules, ponies, and elephants could transport goods. The British built roads between the various Shan states as well as two railway lines. They completed the line to Lashio in 1897, while the one to what would become the Southern Shan State was not completed until 1915. No railway line was built to Chiang Tung because of the high mountains between the Salween River and Chiang Tung.[2] Trade between the Shan States and the rest of Burma increased markedly with access to both rail and road. Still, it was mainly Burmese and Indian merchants who brought European, Indian, and Burmese goods to the Shan States. As often is the case, local handicrafts decreased in favor of imported products.

The British attitude toward ethnic groups was to keep them separated. They didn't understand that in Burma these groups had lived in close relationships with one another for hundreds of years. The British instead saw separation as a way to resolve conflicts by removing potential enemies (Renard 1988, 117). To control the Shan States, the British tried to create good relationships with the Shan rulers. And a good British education, of course, was a way of creating good relationships. Therefore, in 1902, they instituted a school in Taunggyi for the sons of the Shan rulers (Taylor 1988, 26; Renard 1988, 119). Earlier, the rulers had sent their sons to the Burmese court for education. Now, in the colonial period, the rulers sent their sons to British schools in the country, but some rulers also sent their sons to England for education. The British awarded titles to Shans they trusted and assigned these at an annual *durbar*. Many of the Shan rulers became Anglophiles and acquired British habits. They built their palaces like British farmhouses and cultivated British crops.

The nationalist and anti-British currents that prevailed in Burma had very little support among the Shan population. Burmese nationalist leaders appealed to the Shan rulers that they should join the movement, but this idea was rejected. The British takeover did not have a big impact on ordinary Shan citizens, and the Shan rulers' status and prestige continued intact. That the British replaced the Burmese as rulers in Mandalay meant little to ordinary Shan people because it was the local rulers that had the visible power. The biggest change was possibly the introduction of health care, including smallpox vaccinations.

Sao Kawn Kiao Intaleng succeeded his brother as *saopha* of Chiang Tung in 1897. He was an influential ruler who held power for thirty-eight years during the British administration. This was a relatively stable period before the chaotic time of the Second World War. According to a *sanad* written between Sao Intaleng and the British in 1896, he was granted five free years without paying tribute to the British as a recognition of the loyalty of his representatives. It was also explicitly stated that Sao Intaleng would be in charge of managing the internal affairs of Chiang Tung (Aung Tun 2009, app. 2). For Shan rulers, it was customary to have several spouses, and Sao Intaleng followed this tradition. He married six women and had nineteen children with them.

William Clifton Dodd was a missionary at the Presbyterian church in Chiang Mai and traveled together with his wife widely throughout Southeast Asia. The couple had visited Chiang Tung and described Sao Intaleng as a calm and modest ruler. When he became shy or worried, he stuttered. Dodd, who was treated kindly, testified to a spirit of religious tolerance and had interesting discussions with monks in the city. He described a great procession held every year, in which the ruler rode out to a hot spring on his royal elephant, which took about an hour, and stayed there for five days. On most of his trip, he would be dressed in ordinary clothes and ride under a white parasol on the unadorned elephant. Before entering the city gate, however, he switched to his royal clothes, and the elephant would be outfitted in the usual royal decorations. Dodd testified that when the procession passed through the city, everyone went quiet and ceased their daily activities, even if it was a big market day (Dodd [1923] 1996).

Captain C. M. Enriquez, who visited Chiang Tung in 1915, also described Sao Intaleng as a sympathetic person, with very little interest in formalities and ceremonies. He was a father figure who knew many of his subjects by name, and they could all come into the palace as they wished. He was, Enriquez wrote, the most charming and simple Shan ruler Enriquez had ever met (Enriquez 1918, 24). Enriquez also states that the ruler had a motorcycle that he drove slowly through the city, followed by several servants and friends cycling next to him.

Six years after Sao Intaleng became the ruler of Chiang Tung, the British invited him to visit the 1903 Delhi Durbar. He went there with his wife Paduma and his sister Princess Tip Htila, along with other Shan rulers. A British photographer took a group portrait of Shan and Karen rulers dressed in ceremonial clothes (figure 1).[3] The British Empire organized the 1903 durbar as a ceremonial event for the coronation of King Edward VII and Queen Alexandra as emperor and empress of British India. In Delhi, Sao Intaleng witnessed with his own eyes a palace in British-Indian style. He was impressed and built his new palace using a similar design. With the construction completed in 1906, Sao Intaleng now had the largest of all the palaces in the Shan states (figure 2).[4]

Relations between Chiang Tung, British Burma, and the other Shan states became lively during the colonial era. The connections with Chiang Mai were not completely closed, and in general it was a time of opening up to the world for Chiang Tung.

FIGURE 1. Shan rulers in ceremonial clothes at the 1903 Delhi Durbar. Sao Intaleng is seated second to the left. *Back row:* Karen princes of Bawlakè, Gantarawadi, and Kyebogyi. *Front row:* the rulers (*saopha*) of Mong Pawn, Chiang Tung, Mong Nai, and Yawnghwe. Photo by J. George Scott; Royal Collection Trust / © His Majesty King Charles III, 2023.

FIGURE 2. The Royal Palace of Chiang Tung, built 1906 and destroyed 1991. Published with kind permission from the Chiang Mai House of Photography by the Associate Professor Kanta Poonpipat Foundation.

The protector of Buddhism in Chiang Tung had always been the local ruler, and the British respected him as long as he was loyal to the crown. When the British rose to power and deposed Thibaw, the Burmese Buddhists lost their chief protector, the king, but the Buddhist culture of Chiang Tung had never considered the Burmese king as their protector. The British administration was not seen as threatening to Buddhism in Chiang Tung because the colonial power remained neutral in religious affairs. Missionary work was entrusted to independent churches. Presbyterians, Baptists, and the Catholic Church were active in Chiang Tung, but their impact on the Tai Khuen Buddhist people was small. Christian missionaries found non-Buddhist ethnic groups like Akha and Lahu much easier to convert.[5]

In a *sanad* dated February 10, 1890, Charles Crosthwaite, the chief commissioner, had written that the ruler shall "pay tribute to the same amount and in the same form as formerly paid to the King of Burma" (Mangrai 1965, xxxiv). Otherwise, Chiang Tung and the Frontier Areas had a large degree of autonomy regarding administration and in establishing law and order. According to the *sanad* of 1896, the new ruler, Sao Intaleng, was permitted "to administer the territory of Kengtung [Chiang Tung] in all matters, whether civil, criminal, or revenue" (Mangrai 1965, app. vii–iv). Nothing special is stated in the *sanad* about religious affairs, simply because this was something that the British administration did not actively interfere with. The role of the ruler as the main protector of Buddhism in

Chiang Tung during the colonial period continued as before. Sao Intaleng sponsored the casting of a replica of one of the most venerated and famous Buddha images in Burma, the Mahāmuni Buddha, and sent monks on a pilgrimage to the island of Lanka (British Ceylon). Royal protection of Buddhism was a kind of legitimation of power, even though that power was limited by subordination to the British colonial administration. The Buddhist activities of Sao Intaleng will be described in more detail in chapter 6. Unlike in Chiang Tung, Buddhism in Chiang Mai and the rest of Lan Na increasingly became controlled by the authorities in Bangkok. The local rulers lost their role as Buddhist protectors when Bangkok integrated the Buddhist traditions of Lan Na into the national Thai *saṅgha*.

In July 1935, after thirty-eight years of rule, Sao Intaleng died. He was succeeded by Sao Kawn Tai, who didn't remain on the throne for long. During a reception in the palace garden in 1937, a man dressed in black suddenly appeared from behind a tree and emptied his two guns at the ruler. The assassin later was caught, but not the person who commissioned the murder. It was believed, however, that the ruler's half brother Sao Phrom Lue or someone in his circle of friends was behind the assassination (Simms 2017, 196–97; Collis 1938, 271–76).

The widow of Sao Kawn Tai tried to succeed her husband as ruler, but Sao Phrom Lue's power was too strong (Collis 1938, 275). After the death of Sao Kawn Tai, Captain Roberts, the British assistant superintendent, was the appointed administrator of the state until the beginning of the Second World War. Sao Sai Long was only ten years old when his father was assassinated and therefore was sent to Britain and Australia for studies. He was later installed as the forty-third ruler of Chiang Tung in 1947 at only twenty years old. He reigned until April 1959, when all the thirty-three rulers of the Shan states signed an agreement to transfer the hereditary rights and administrative powers to the Shan State government (Aung Tun 2009, 363–65). The traditional powers maintained by the *saopha* were forever lost in favor of a democratic government. But this ended with the military coup in 1962, whereupon Sao Sai Long was imprisoned for five years without trial. During his time as ruler, he had renovated and raised the *chedi* at Wat Chom Kham in a Burmese design similar to the Shwedagon Pagoda in Yangon, which still today shines throughout the city. Figure 7 shows the *chedi* at Wat Chom Kham in its traditional Tai style.

The Second World War

There was a strong resistance among the Burmese people against the British when the Second World War began. Japan was seen as an Asian brother and savior by many, and there was an expectation that that country would expel the colonial powers. Aung San was a leading independence activist and is often called the father of modern Burma. He and the resistance movement had contacts in Japan before the war and were trained by the Japanese. Those in favor of independence and in the resistance movement looked to Japan for help, and initially they took the Japanese side in the war, fighting against the British. The Burmese helped the Japanese occupy Burma and expel the British and their troops.

The Shan and Burma's other minority people, however, did not have the same negative attitude toward the British. The Karen and Kachin people continued to be loyal to the British and organized opposition to the Japanese. Skepticism toward the Burmese resistance movement grew strong among minority peoples throughout the war. The Japanese occupation, it eventually became apparent, meant no independence for Burma as the resistance movement had hoped. The new power turned out to be at least as brutal as the British had been. When they realized the Japanese were not liberators, the resistance movement changed its loyalty in the summer of 1944, allied itself with the British, and declared war against Japan.

The Second World War was a troublesome time for Chiang Tung. Before the war, in 1938, the Thai nationalist politician and military commander Phibun had become prime minister of Siam. One of his first steps was to change the name of the country from Siam to Thailand. Within Thailand's borders there were many nationalities besides Central Thais: Cambodians, Malays, Lao people, Chinese, and a wide variety of other peoples who lived in the mountains to the north. Phibun wanted to signal that it was the country of the Thai people, but the change of name was also a statement against the economically strong Chinese who lived in the country.

The Japanese ambassador in Bangkok informed the nationalist government under Phibun on the evening of December 7, 1941, that Japan had declared war against the United States and Great Britain, and that they needed to use Thailand for the transport of soldiers. The following morning, the Japanese invaded Thailand in nine places. This happened at the same time as the attack on Pearl Harbor. Phibun had no way of preventing the Japanese from using Thailand for their troop movements. He allowed this, and in return Thailand's sovereignty was guaranteed. Thailand and Japan signed an alliance agreement on December 21, 1941. Because both Japan and Thailand were Buddhist countries, the signing was performed in front of one of Thailand's national symbols, the Emerald Buddha in Wat Phra Kaeo, Bangkok. In this way, the Buddha became a witness to the alliance between the two countries, inspiring hope that it would bring success in the war. Phibun and his government did not see themselves as subjugated by the Japanese, but as allies.

Shortly after the attack on Pearl Harbor, China's Chiang Kai-shek offered the Western Allies full cooperation and suggested that the Chinese Nationalist (KMT) troops should move into northern Burma. The British accepted this offer, and units of the Ninety-Third Division of the KMT army based in Yunnan moved south. In early 1942 they arrived in Chiang Tung and encamped at the market.

During this time, Thailand was helping Japan liberate Burma and the Shan States from the British. A Thai army was sent by train to Chiang Mai and from there planned to continue overland to Chiang Tung. Many of the soldiers came from the northeast and were inadequately armed, poorly motivated, and not equipped to cope with the climate in the northern mountains (Aung Tun 2009, 196–206; Forbes 2002; Forbes and Henley 2015).

On May 3, 1942, twenty-seven Thai bombers flew over Chiang Tung and dropped bombs on the market, where they knew that the Chinese soldiers' quarters were located. The bombs killed many of the Chinese, and those who survived fled. Thai troops made their entry into Chiang Tung a few weeks later and occupied the city. In other parts of the Shan States it was the Japanese who attacked, but in Chiang Tung it was the Thai army. Phibun was delighted and visited the north in early 1943. The condition of the troops made him realize they needed support. He gave orders to Bangkok to send medicine, uniforms, and food. The British soldiers had been evacuated to India, and the Chinese were still fighting against the Japanese. Many refugees from Burma fled to India or China, and many others died either from the fighting or from various diseases such as malaria and dysentery. The KMT soldiers had withdrawn to the hills and forests surrounding Chiang Tung, occasionally clashing with Japanese forces who had followed the Thais into the Shan States (Aung Tun 2009, 196–206; Forbes 2002; Forbes and Henley 2015).

From 1942 to 1945, Sao Boon Waat, one of the nineteen children of Sao Intaleng, ruled Chiang Tung, subordinate to the administration of the Thai military. The Thai troops were not popular but met no direct resistance. The Japanese decided to divide the Shan States in August 1943. They had formally granted Burma independence, and the Shan States west of the Salween River were to be part of Burma. The region east of the Salween River, however, was given to Thailand, and Chiang Tung and Mong Pan became a province of Thailand under the name Saharat Thai Doem. It was only with the atomic bombings of Hiroshima and Nagasaki in August 1945 and the Japanese capitulation that the Thai troops left Chiang Tung. Some parts of the KMT army stayed in the mountains after the war, allying themselves with Nationalist refugees from China following the Communist seizure of power in 1949. Most of the Thai soldiers had left for the south after the Japanese capitulation, but some stayed, settled, and married in Chiang Tung (Aung Tun 2009, 196–206; Forbes 2002; Forbes and Henley 2015).

The Anti-Fascist People's Freedom League (AFPFL), with General Aung San as its leader, was the strongest Burmese organization after the war. The British prime minister Clement Attlee invited Aung San to visit London in 1947 to negotiate the conditions of Burmese independence, and the meeting ended in the Aung San–Attlee agreement, signed on January 27, 1947. Later in 1947, Aung San also met a second time with leaders of the ethnic minorities in what was called the Panglong Conference. In attendance were Shan, Kachin, and Chin leaders. The meeting concluded with the signing of the Panglong Agreement on February 12, 1947, which assigned full autonomy of internal administration to the Frontier Areas and provided that citizens should enjoy the rights and privileges that are fundamental in democratic countries (Aung Tun 2009, 226–27).

The Karen, Mon, Arakanese, Wa, Naga, and Karenni did not attend the Panglong Conference. Some were not invited, and some chose not to attend. The Karen ethnic group was not part of the meeting, as a combination of false British promises, sustained Burmese hostility toward the Karen, and the refusal of the Karen leadership to compromise when faced with the loss of British support led to the Karen rebellion, which broke out directly following independence (Walton 2008, 901). Matthew J. Walton explored the impacts that participating or not in the Panglong Conference had on various ethnic groups. He suggests that there are different versions, or myths, of the Panglong Agreement and points to three different versions coming from the main actors: the government/military, the democratic opposition, and the ethnic minorities (Walton 2008, 890). The Panglong Conference certainly had a significant impact on the future of Chiang Tung.

Another event that may have changed much of the political future of Burma happened just at the time of independence from the British. The leader of the AFPFL resistance movement, Aung San, together with eight other political leaders, were assassinated on July 19, 1947, shortly following the 1947 election to the Constituent Assembly, which AFPFL won overwhelmingly.

The Exposed Location of Chiang Tung

Several times in the course of its history, political decisions or historical accidents had direct consequences on the future of Chiang Tung. As previously mentioned, one of these political decisions was made in the early nineteenth century by the ruler Sao Mahakhanan when he escaped the deportation to Chiang Mai and fled to Mong Yang and later received help from the Burmese to rebuild and repopulate Chiang Tung. Another political decision that had crucial significance for the future of Chiang Tung was the decision by the British to conquer Chiang Tung in 1890. The British considered letting China take over all rights to Chiang Tung but changed their minds and proceeded to absorb Chiang Tung, integrating it into the rest of the Shan States and the British Empire.

These political decisions or, sometimes, historical accidents greatly affected the future of Chiang Tung. The Khuen people in Chiang Tung were aware of the *mueang*'s exposed location as a borderland between larger and more powerful neighbors. And in the nineteenth century, even as the colonial powers of the British and the French changed the regional balance of power drastically, the exposed location of Chiang Tung did not change. This vulnerability certainly contributed to defining its identity and culture.

Another political decision that affected the future of Chiang Tung was made during the second Panglong Conference in 1947, during the negotiations between ethnic groups and the Burmese under Aung San's leadership. Several meetings were held to discuss what the agreement meant and what the different nationalities really wanted. This was facilitated by the Frontier Areas Committee of Enquiry (FACE), led by the British politician D. R. Rees-Williams. At that time, Chiang Tung had the opportunity to choose if it wanted to remain in the new republic of Burma or be part of the Kingdom of Siam/Thailand. Sao Sai Long was installed as the new ruler of Chiang Tung on March 1, 1947. During the meetings with the FACE committee, Sao Zing Zai officiated as representative of the ruler, and Sai Ling Tip served as representative of the people of Chiang Tung. FACE recorded evidence heard by the committee from the town of Maymyo on April 14, 1947, and published it word for word (FACE, app. 1, 21–22):

> CHAIRMAN: Sao Sing Zai, you are the representative of the *Sawbwa* [*saopha*] State, and your colleague is a representative of the people. Is he not?
>
> SAO SING ZAI: Yes, sir.
>
> CHAIRMAN: What is the wish of the Sawbwa and the people with regard to the future association of the Kengtung State with the other Frontier Area people? In other words, does the Kengtung State wish to remain in the Shan States Federation?
>
> SAI LING TIP: Yes.
>
> CHAIRMAN: What do the people wish with reference to the future association of the Shan States and Ministerial Burma?
>
> SAI LING TIP: It depends on the decision of the Shan States Council.
>
> CHAIRMAN: Have they got any views on it at all?
>
> SAI LING TIP: We want internal autonomy and equal rights in the federation.
>
> CHAIRMAN: Is that in the Shan States Federation?

SAI LING TIP: Yes.
CHAIRMAN: Have you got any ideas as to the form of federation?
SAI LING TIP: Representatives should be sent on a population basis to the Federal Council.
CHAIRMAN: What subjects should the Federal Council deal with?
SAI LING TIP: It depends on what the internal government cannot decide.
THE HONORABLE U TIN TÜT: You mean subjects which the internal government cannot properly deal with?
SAI LING TIP: Yes, sir.
CHAIRMAN: Do you wish to send representatives to the Constituent Assembly?
SAI LING TIP: Yes.
CHAIRMAN: In what proportion?
SAI LING TIP: On the basis which is a compromise between a population basis and a racial basis.
CHAIRMAN: Does Sao Sing Zai agree with what you have said now?
SAO SING ZAI: Yes, sir.
CHAIRMAN: Sao Sing Zai, your state is very closely associated with Siam. Is it not?
SAO SING ZAI: Yes, in everything.
CHAIRMAN: In fact, it is much easier to get into Siam than to get into Burma?
SAO SING ZAI: Yes.
CHAIRMAN: Are you still anxious to remain in the Shan States Federation?
SAO SING ZAI: Yes, for the present.

This decision to remain in the Shan States Federation and not be annexed as a part of Siam must be seen in the context of Chiang Tung's recent history. During the Second World War, Siamese aircraft had dropped bombs on the city, and in 1942, Chiang Tung had become a province of Thailand. Yet the ties between Chiang Tung and the other Shan states had been strengthened during the British times. For example, the ruler Sao Kawng Tai had married a daughter of the Hsipaw ruler, and after he was assassinated in 1937 she divided her days between Chiang Tung and Taunggyi. Intermarriage and family ties were definitely one important reason for the decision to remain together with the other Shan states.

Armed Conflicts in the Shan States

In January 1948, the Union of Burma was proclaimed an independent republic. Since then, it has suffered from prolonged conflict between the state and armed ethnic organizations. This conflict has its origin in the British divide-and-rule policy during colonial rule. And after World War II, several ethnic groups were dissatisfied with the new government and wanted independence or autonomy. For example, the Karen National Union (KNU) began an armed insurgency in 1949, seeking independence for the Karen people. Not only did ethnic groups rebel, but Burmese communists also took up arms. The situation was further complicated when Chinese Nationalist Kuomintang forces fled into the Shan State in 1950, supported by the CIA. Jane Ferguson (2016, 134; 2021, 77) has categorized the warring parties operating in the Shan State into five major groups: (1) the soldiers of the Burmese state, the Tatmadaw; (2) KMT soldiers, supported by the KMT in Taiwan, the CIA, and the Thai government; (3) soldiers of the Communist Party of Burma; (4) state separatists and ethnic militias with a political desire for autonomy; and (5) the home-guard militia, organized privately but given trade concessions (and sometimes arms) by the Burmese government. On the whole, there were nearly forty independently operating militias in the 1960s and 1970s in the Shan State alone (Ferguson 2021, 77). Many of the different armed groups financed their activities via the drug trade.

In 1949, the long struggle for power in China between the Communists and the Nationalists ended, and the Nationalists, led by Chiang Kai-shek, escaped to Taiwan. But two divisions of the Nationalist forces had been stationed in southwestern China, and they crossed the border to the Shan State in early 1950. This had devastating consequences for the people in the Shan State. Rice fields were abandoned, villages and small towns were deserted, monasteries and temples were destroyed, and local people were forced to move to new settlements or flee. Women were raped, and men were recruited either as soldiers or porters. A further consequence of this invasion was the split of ethnic nationalities into various factions to classify them as either pro- or anti-Communist or Nationalist. This proved devastating for the future. The KMT forces became deeply involved in the opium trade and opened up a big narcotics enterprise across the Shan State to Thailand and around the world. Various Chinese adventurers or opium smugglers also came to join KMT troops, hoping to do illegal business across the border. Following the appearance of the KMT, the volume of the opium trade burgeoned. In particular, the Tai Neu (Chinese Shan) who had been living close to the border on the Chinese side greatly suffered from the fighting.

Even before 1949, hundreds of former Chinese National soldiers had settled in Chiang Tung city (Gibson 2011, 17). In the beginning of 1950, the number of KMT soldiers in the Shan State was about seventeen hundred, and they established their headquarters in Mong Yang, about sixty-five kilometers north of Chiang Tung. The KMT reconstructed the road between Chiang Tung and the border of Thailand at Mae Sai and Tachileik, hoping to get military supplies from

Thailand more quickly. The Shan State had suddenly become a part of world politics. The Chinese government in Beijing made accusations of US involvement in the conflict. The CIA was indeed involved, though the US government denied it. Arms made in the United States that were used by KMT soldiers probably came from private American companies in Southeast Asia. KMT troops made raids back into China, and troops from Communist China crossed the border into the Shan State to retaliate. The fighting between 1950 and 1953 was intense, and the KMT had to fight against both the Burmese military and the Communists. The KMT failed to make permanent inroads into China and changed their strategy to guerrilla warfare.

KMT leaders denied a request from the Burmese government to surrender and instead expanded their activities. The Nationalists in Taiwan supplied them arms, and the KMT troops spread through the eastern parts of the Shan State, from north to south (see map in Aung Tun 2009, 302). In May 1953 an agreement was reached in the United Nations to evacuate all foreign troops from Burma. It took several months to evacuate some fifty-five hundred KMT soldiers, but at least three thousand stayed because of their involvement in the drug trade (Aung Tun 2009, 323). Most of the fighting ended in 1953, but it was not until 1961 that all KMT soldiers were driven out of Burma with the assistance of the Chinese army. They were forced into Thailand and continued the drug trade. Descendants of KMT soldiers who entered the Shan State during the conflict in the 1950s are still living in Thailand, many with Thai citizenship.

Since the Shan rulers had signed the Panglong Conference, they cooperated with the Burmese prime minister U Nu until the late 1950s. They had been promised full autonomy after ten years, and when this time ended with no fulfillment of that promise, they launched a militant resistance. The Shan State Army (SSA) was founded in 1964 by unifying four small rebel groups. The SSA and its political branch, the Shan State Progress Party (SSA/SSPP), split in the 1970s after entering an alliance with the Communist Party of Burma (CPB), which supplied them with weapons. One reason for the split was that several older Shan leaders opposed the alliance. They resigned or were expelled.

The Burmese government had various problems uniting the country, beyond just controlling ethnic minorities. Because of the political situation in 1958, U Nu handed over power to the military, led by General Ne Win. The military ruled the union until 1960, when a new election was held, and U Nu was voted in once again as prime minister. The government continued to be chosen with democratic elections until 1962, when Ne Win seized power in a military coup d'état. He ruled the country until 1988 as a military dictator of a socialist state with the motto "Burmese Way to Socialism."

Before the Second World War there was surprisingly little poppy cultivation in the mountains of northern Southeast Asia. Small amounts of raw opium were harvested in the eighteenth and nineteenth century, but India and Afghanistan were the main producers of the drug for international trade. It was foremost the British East India Company and the French government who encouraged poppy-growing in the area, and it soon became a valuable cash crop for those hill-tribe refugees from southern China who were pushed into the region in the nineteenth and twentieth centuries (Lintner 2000). Between 1976 and 1996, Khun Sa was the dominant opium warlord, but he claimed he was fighting for independence for the Shan State. With his drug trade, he could finance an army of around twenty thousand men. Jane Ferguson argues that he was both a nationalist and a warlord, and his armies were fighting for both a political cause and to protect their trade network (Ferguson 2021, 145–46). Khun Sa surrendered to the Burmese government in 1996 and received government protection. After the fall of Khun Sa, others started a new armed group under the name SSA without consent from the SSA/SSPP. This new SSA army is often called SSA-South (SSA-S) in the media because it is based at the Thai border, in contrast to the SSA/SSPP, who are called SSA-North (SSA-N).

Also important for the eastern Shan State were the United Wa State Army (UWSA) at the border region near China north of Chiang Tung and with a smaller southern territory bordering Thailand, and the Mong La group, also at the border region near China (Special Region 4), northeast of Chiang Tung. Both these groups are remnants from the Communist Party of Burma, which surrendered to the government in 1989. The UWSA claims that the Wa people are the remnants of the indigenous Lua people and have political and military ambitions for the whole eastern Shan State (See Wa territory on map 1).

During the 1970s, the fighting between the army and ethnic armed groups was not far from the city of Chiang Tung, but the battles mainly occurred in the mountains. Many civilians were affected, and villages had to be relocated. The result was that this created many refugees and others who sought protection abroad.

Since colonial times, national borders had been established, and trade of teak and opium became largely monopolized by the state. This did not totally prevent the old tradition of cross-border trade. After independence and the 1962 coup in Burma, the flow of refugees increased dramatically at the Burmese-Thailand border. And after the August 8, 1988, antigovernment uprising (8888 Uprising), large refugee camps were established inside the Thai border. Busarin Lertchavalitsakul (2017) discusses the meeting of state border control and cross-border communities at the border between the Shan State, Myanmar, and Mae Hong Son, Thailand. She argues that state agencies, local officials, border elites, and armed ethnic rebel groups (SSA-S) all seek to consolidate their power in controlling cross-border flows of humans and commodities. The more the state aims to consolidate its power through territorialization, the more it is challenged. Shan traders and migrants continue to cross political boundaries and nation-state borders through official border checkpoints and numerous walking trails in the jungle.

The 8888 Uprising in Burma was a nationwide antigovernment protest that ended in the brutal killing of over a thousand students, monks, and other civilians. The State Law and Order Restoration Council (SLORC) was formed, and the military continued to maintain power. Until 1989, the military was fighting two interconnected civil wars, one against ethnic nationalist armies and the other against the communists. With the collapse of the CPB, the Burmese government started a divide-and-rule strategy against the ethnic armed groups. Bertil Lintner's *Burma's Path to Peace* (Lintner 2023) offers a detailed overview of Burma's civil war since independence and examines the country's past experiences of peace efforts and why they have failed to end its decades-long series of wars.

Shanland and Tai New Year

The resistance movement among the Shan people has been fought with more than weapons. During recent decades, the notion of a single, united Shan State, a Shanland, has been extensively articulated. The motivation for this is the ongoing ethnic conflict and the resistance against Burmese military oppression. SSA-S has been one of the most important armed insurgent groups claiming to represent Shan nationalism and the Shan struggle for independence. Currently, the most significant support for the envisioned Shan nation can be found online as rock music and cultural videos on YouTube. Jane Ferguson (2008a, 2008b, 2021) and Amporn Jirattikorn (2011) have highlighted that modern media and popular culture form a basis for a Shan imagined community. Amporn argues that over the past decade, video compact discs have become the dominant Shan medium (Amporn 2011, 33) and describes the contemporary Shan insurgency as "a 'virtual' insurgency, whose strategies are employed through the cultural and political realm and whose fighting is mediated by mediascapes" (38).

In November every year, a New Year celebration takes place all around the Shan State. It is called Shan New Year or Tai New Year and is celebrated as part of a common Shan nationhood. It is not the Songkran New Year festival in April, which has no political agenda. The Shan New Year, a symbolic manifestation of a cultural and virtual imagined Shanland, has increased in importance since the beginning of the 1990s. It is a manifestation of Shan culture, highlighting the Shan flag, long drums, dance performances (sword, martial arts, and Kinnari dance), and traditional sporting competitions. It is celebrated by many Tai groups in Myanmar, Thailand, and abroad, for example in the UK, the US, Australia, and Malaysia. The migration of the Shan into Northern Thailand for political or economic reasons has created a large group of young migrants, especially in Chiang Mai, who use this New Year celebration as a political manifestation of the Shan State, their homeland. The Shan New Year has been presented thousands of times through YouTube as part of a global cultural event.

Amporn Jirattikorn has argued that the idea of Shan nationhood came into being only after the Second World War when Shan chiefs agreed to join the Union of Burma but kept the right for secession after ten years if they so wished (Amporn 2011, 22). Before that time, the Shan states had no shared agenda. Burma proper was incorporated into British India under direct rule, and all the different Shan states remained relatively autonomous as protectorates. In 1922, the British brought together all the small states into a federated Shan State. The existence of this united Shan State increased the conflict between the Burmese and the Shan people during the time after independence. After independence in 1948, discrimination against minority groups increased and only became worse following the military's rise to power in 1962.

After the military coup, some Shan cultural organizations began to celebrate Shan (Tai) New Year in November. It has been argued that the Shan New Year celebration has roots back to the seventh and eighth centuries, during the Nanchao period (Khur Yearn and Loi Pang Lai 2006), though its ancestry is impossible to establish with surviving historical records. Leslie Milne briefly mentions a feast during the time she lived in Nam Kham at the beginning of the twentieth century. Toward the end of the Shan year in November, young men, approximately sixteen years of age, visited the surrounding villages, poured water on the hands and feet of elders, and asked forgiveness for any sins that they were guilty of during the past year (Milne [1910] 2001, 121).

In contemporary Myanmar, as the Shan people attempt to organize and unite themselves, the Shan New Year may play an important role, particularly because of its reach in modern media and on the internet. There are in fact recognizable differences between the celebration of the Songkran New Year in April and the Shan New Year in November. The Songkran or Tingyan New Year festival is celebrated in large parts of Southeast Asia and has no political agenda. It can best be described as a performed drama about fertility, prosperity, and a place of belonging. In contrast, an imagined Shan nation expressed in the Shan New Year celebration is a more recently constructed political and symbolic manifestation of a culturally and virtually imagined Shanland. Still, today it seems possible for the Tai Khuen people in Chiang Tung to identify themselves with an imagined Khuen community and with a Shan nation at the same time. For a more detailed analysis of the military and cultural struggle of Shanland see Jane Ferguson's book *Repossessing Shanland* (2021).

Burmanization

The 8888 Uprising ended in the killing of over a thousand students, monks, and other civilians. The May 1990 election was a landslide victory for the National League for Democracy (NLD) but was rejected by the military junta. After these events, the new Burmese military government, the State Law and Order Restoration Council (SLORC), realized that it could not win the struggle against ethnic resistance movements with weapons alone. The government began the Border Area Development Program, which later in 1992 became the Ministry for the Progress of Border Areas and National Races. Ceasefire agreements were part of this program. In 1989, Khin Nyunt, the chief of military intelligence, organized the first ceasefire between SLORC and armed rebel groups. Between 1989 and 1995, SLORC brokered arrangements with about twenty-five rebellious groups. The Border Area Development Program built road infrastructure, schools, and hospitals in rebel-occupied territories. Another important policy adopted by the military was to deploy culture and religion by including minority regions in official versions of the history of Burma/Myanmar, a trend seen clearly in Chiang Tung. Culture, religion, and history can be sources of power, and religious buildings and objects sponsored by the Burmese military were manufactured as visual representations of a Burmese Buddhist culture. The military sought nothing less than to rewrite the history of Chiang Tung and include it more centrally in the history of the Burmese dynasties. It was natural to use Buddhism to this end, as Buddhist traditions were central in the history of the Burmese rulers.

Since the fourteenth century, there have been royal palaces (*haw*) for the rulers of Chiang Tung. The last palace (figure 2), built by longtime ruler Sao Intaleng, stood until 1991, when the Burmese military regime demolished it. Despite its colonial roots, that palace was one of the most visible symbols of Chiang Tung's independence—and it had an even longer pedigree. During the late thirteenth century, when the Tai people conquered the place of the indigenous Lua people, they build a palace on the site of the old Lua palace. Most likely there was a palace standing on the same spot continuously from at least the fourteenth century until 1991, when the Burmese military ordered its demolition.

The Burmese military government understood that the palace had a deep symbolic meaning for the local people. They wanted to destroy this reminder of the time when the *saopha* ruled the city-state of Chiang Tung. And the white palace also stood as a reminder of the British colonial era, which was a time of hardship for the Burmese. The regime therefore destroyed the palace, and in the place where it stood built a large, unsightly hotel. Local people had protested against the demolition and refused to cooperate with the project. The military had to use workers from other parts of Myanmar to demolish the building. Today there is a rumor among the locals that the hotel is haunted.

During the same time, the Burmese military started a systematic "Burmanization" of Chiang Tung and other minority regions as a way of including them within Burmese culture and the history of the Burmese dynasties. The Shwedagon Pagoda in Yangon, a stupa celebrating the eight hair-relics of the Buddha, is one of the most sacred and significant buildings in Myanmar. Its origin is believed to date to the first millennium, but the first historical evidence appears much later, in the fifteenth century. In any case, it stands as a symbol of Burmese Buddhism and culture.[6] The Burmese regime built replicas of the Shwedagon Pagoda in both Buddhist and non-Buddhist minority regions to remind people of the country to which they belong. Regardless if someone enters the Shan State from China or Thailand, there is a replica of the Shwedagon Pagoda. There is one in Mong La (Special Region 4) at the Chinese border and another at the town of Tachileik, at the Thai border. The one in Tachileik includes typical Burmese stylistic elements, like the eight planetary shrines associated with the days of the week, the Hamsa bird, and an image of the Buddhist monk Upagopta. The regime has also made Shwedagon replicas throughout Shan State, including in Kunhing, Mong Yai, Mong Pan, and Panghsang.

Close to the Tachileik border checkpoint there is also a large statue of the Taungoo dynasty king Bayinnaung. This king conquered Lan Na in the middle of the sixteenth century, and all the city-states of Lan Na had to pay tribute to him. The statue is a reminder of Burmese power to all people crossing the border there. It was once blown up by a bomb and since has been protected by the military; tourists were for some time not even allowed to take photos.

The former president Thein Sein was very active in spreading Burmese culture during the time he was stationed in Chiang Tung. He was prime minister of Myanmar between 2007 and 2011, and in 2011 he became the first civilian president of Myanmar since 1962. But before that time he had served from 1997 to 2001 as the highest commander of the Triangle Region Military Command in Chiang Tung. During the years in Chiang Tung he and his wife were very active in spreading Burmese culture. They were responsible for building a twenty-meter-tall Buddha statue atop one of the Chiang Tung hills, pointing down at the town with his index finger. It is illuminated in the evenings and easily seen all over town (figure 3). The construction of the statue started in 1998 and was finished in 2000. Local people appeared very skeptical of this military-made Buddha statue, and no locals were invited to participate during the consecration ceremony. There is a rumor that the image will bring bad luck for those who look at it.

FIGURE 3. The twenty-meter-tall Buddha standing statue presides atop one of the hills in Chiang Tung. Photo by author.

The symbolism of the statue is a combination of two sources. One is a local Tai Khuen legend, and the other a story apparently constructed by the Burmese military. The local legend is about a visit by the Buddha to Chiang Tung during his lifetime. As we already have seen in chapter 2 about myths and memories, the Buddha is said to have visited the site that later would become Chiang Tung and predicted that a prosperous town would be established there. This legend is well known to the local people.

The latter story tells of an old Burmese Bagan monastery that is supposed to have been standing on the hill. Relics and *sarira* stones from the Bagan times are claimed to have been found on the hill. However, no archaeological evidence has been presented, and it is well known that Buddhism was introduced from Haripuñjaya and the island of Lanka in the thirteenth and fourteenth centuries, not from Bagan. The supposed Bagan-period monastery is, with all probability, made up to claim a Burmese origin of Buddhism in Chiang Tung. To my knowledge, there are no chronicles or inscriptions that mention Bagan monasteries or Buddhist missions from Bagan. Local people became very skeptical of this military-made Buddha statue and consider it as not properly consecrated and therefore not worthy of veneration. It is a fake, they say. This idea was reinforced when lightning hit the statue shortly after the construction was finished, and the index finger broke. Local people saw this as an omen and avoid the statue. I have been told that the famous Khruba Bunchum, during one of his visits to Chiang Tung, warned local people not to look at the statue's face. Khruba Bunchum is a charismatic *ton bun* monk who travels extensively throughout the Upper Mekong borderlands, initiating the building or renovation of religious monuments and sharing merit with the laity. (More detail about him and other *khruba* monks can be found in chapter 6.) Local residents also told Sara Davis (2005, 164–67) about the "fake" Buddha statue when she visited Chiang Tung. They said that the famous monk told them that looking directly at the statue will make one ill.

Several years after the construction of the standing Buddha, a smaller statue was constructed close to it. This statue, which no longer exists, was of the monk Shrin Araham, who converted King Anawrata and brought Theravāda Buddhism to Bagan (figure 4). The statue was thereby an additional attempt to emphasize the Burmese origin of Buddhism in Chiang Tung. This statue depicted the king on his knees, holding a manuscript in both hands in front of the standing monk; the life story of Shin Araham was written at the foot of the statue. The text said that the true faith of Theravāda Buddhism was introduced to Bagan by Shrin Araham during the reigns of the first four Bagan kings.

Clearly, this statue emphasized Burmese Buddhism and national culture in this minority region. I visited the site in April 2013 and saw the statue, but in 2015, when I visited the same spot, the image had been removed, and there was no trace of it. I was told that local people had been dissatisfied and complained about the statue. According to rumors, it was destroyed by some locals, while

FIGURE 4. Statue of Shrin Araham and King Anawrata, in Chiang Tung. Photo by author.

others suggest it was a thunderstorm that damaged the statue. In either case, someone took away the damaged statue and cleaned up the place. Superstitious beliefs by the military may be the reason they did not rebuild it.

The Shwedagon Pagoda, the standing-Buddha statue, and the statue of the Bagan king and his monk are evidence of attempts to rewrite the history of Chiang Tung to include the area more closely in a Myanmar national identity. However, there is also another image that bears witness to this Burmanization: the replica of the Mahāmuni image that the ruler Sao Intaleng cast during the colonial period (figure 5). The original Mahāmuni image is one of the most famous Buddha images in Myanmar and has a remarkable place in the history of Burma. It came from Arakan in the western part of today's Myanmar, on the Bay of Bengal, a state that had been independent until the Burmese conquered the last Kingdom of Arakan (Mrauk-U) in 1784. The presumed magic power in this image is due to the belief that it was made during the time of the Buddha. King Bodawpaya captured it as a trophy in war and brought it to the capital in central Burma during the eighteenth-century Konbaung dynasty.[7]

Therefore, even in the colonial period of the 1920s, there was a kind of Burmanization in Chiang Tung, though it was initiated by the ruler Sao Intaleng and his court. Originally, the Mahāmuni replica was connected to Sao Intaleng as a symbolic representation of royal power, and it was installed in 1926 at a newly constructed temple close to the palace (see Karlsson 2009). This royal connection

FIGURE 5. Mahāmuni Buddha image, Chiang Tung. Photo by author.

was severed by the military coup in 1962, but later the Burmese military recognized the replica's symbolic representation of power. The military custodians of the image would write the name of the military commander and his wife on a piece of blue cloth and put it at the baldachin on top of the head of the image. When local people bowed down in veneration before the Buddha, they also bowed before the Burmese commander. Merit would supposedly pass to the commander and his wife from every local visitor who worshiped the image. Each new commander shifted the names, putting the names of himself and his wife on top of the image. Before the military was in charge, it was possible for the local people to donate robes to the image as an act of merit. Today, this is not possible, as the military has taken command of the statue.

The symbolic power of the Mahāmuni Buddha, used by the kings of Arakan and the Konbaung ruler Bodawpaya, and a replica of the same image, used by Sao Intaleng of Chiang Tung and, more recently, by the Burmese military commanders in Chiang Tung, has very little to do with the Khuen people today. Today the Mahāmuni image is taken care of and venerated in a ritual performed mostly by Burmese people. Chapter 6 discusses the connection between Buddha images and political power, and chapter 7 looks at how the Burmese military took the symbolic role as rulers during the traditional Songkran festival.

The military wanted nothing less than to rewrite the history of Chiang Tung and include it more closely in the history of the Burmese dynasties. They also wanted to spread Burmese Buddhism, in contrast to Khuen Buddhism, with its roots in Lan Na culture. Military strength was apparently not effective enough in the ethnically, religiously, and culturally fragmented country of Myanmar. Expanding Burmese culture to minority areas and taking control of minority cultures became the unofficial national politics of the Myanmar government, as we have seen with Chiang Tung.

All the examples above demonstrate how religious visual culture is a symbolic language that can be used in conflicts and expresses power and sovereignty. At the same time, it may be a powerful means of imagining a common identity. Visual culture is a language quite different from written texts, as gazing upon visual objects involves different emotions than reading a text. Looking at visual objects is a social act. In the words of David Morgan (2005, 3), "Seeing is an operation that relies on an apparatus of assumptions and inclinations, habits and routines, historical associations and cultural practices." The military was aware of the uniqueness of Buddhism in Chiang Tung, especially in contrast with Burmese Buddhism, but the military also recognized the powerful impact that visual culture may have on local people. In chapter 5 we will look more closely at the exceptional Buddhist tradition of Chiang Tung visual culture with roots in the Lan Na culture.

Chiang Tung has never been as controlled by an outside power as it is today. In precolonial times, Chiang Tung was a semiautonomous principality or city-state, depending on more powerful neighbors but most of the time not directly ruled by them. The local rulers had to demonstrate their respect by giving an annual tribute of symbolic or valued objects. Northern Southeast Asia was not characterized by national borders but by a more flexible geopolitical system. Today, the borders between nation states in Southeast Asia owe much of their existence to colonial state-making. It was not a given that the British would cross the Salween River and capture the Trans-Salween and Chiang Tung, but for fear of the French, the British in 1890 took control over the whole area up to the Mekong River. During colonial times, Chiang Tung and the rest of the Frontier Areas acquired a certain measure of self-government, as long as they observed British authority.

The ruler Sao Intaleng still maintained the role of protector of Buddhism in Chiang Tung during the colonial period. The British administration did not threaten Buddhism in Chiang Tung because its policy was not to interfere with religious affairs. The British entrusted missionary work to independent churches, but these did not have much success with the Tai Khuen Buddhist people. As protector of Buddhism, Sao Intaleng sent monks on a pilgrimage to the island of British Ceylon to pay homage to the Tooth Relic and to study sacred Buddhist texts. He also sponsored the casting of a replica of one of the most venerated and famous Buddha images in Burma, the Mahāmuni Buddha. This replica of an image believed to have been created in the lifetime of the Buddha was cast in Mandalay, brought in pieces to Chiang Tung, and installed in 1926, most likely as a symbol of power, in Wat Phra Sao Luang, a temple built close to the palace solely to house the image. The 1920s were a time of increasing connections between the different Shan states and Burmese culture. In 1922, the British brought together all the small Shan states into the Federated Shan States, a development the various Shan rulers did not like. They thought that this was a restriction on their status and prestige.

After the Second World War, Chiang Tung had the opportunity to choose if it wanted to remain in the new Republic of Burma or be part of the Kingdom of Siam/Thailand. The ties between Chiang Tung and the other Shan states had strengthened during the British times, and its years under the power of the province Saharat Thai Doem of Thailand may have contributed to its decision to remain with the Shan States Federation. The independence of the new Republic of Burma was characterized by a prolonged conflict between the Burmese state and armed ethnic organizations, the Communist Party of Burma, and Chinese Kuomintang soldiers. During the Panglong Conference, the Shan States were promised full autonomy after ten years, and when this time ended with no fulfillment, they launched a militant resistance, and the Shan State Army was founded in 1964. Democratic elections ended in 1962, when General Ne Win took over with a coup d'état and ruled the country as a military dictator until 1988. Many armed groups financed their activities via the drug trade, fighting for both a political cause and to protect their drug trade network.

After the 8888 Uprising and the May 1990 election, which was a landslide victory for the National League for Democracy but rejected by the military junta, the new Burmese military government, the State Law and Order Restoration Council (SLORC), acquired power. The Communist Party of Burma surrendered in 1989, and remaining Wa soldiers formed the United Wa State Army (UWSA), with its political branch the United Wa State Party (UWSP). The UWSA is today the largest ethnic army, with twenty thousand soldiers, and functions as a virtually independent nation, with a northern territory bordering China and a smaller southern territory bordering Thailand. The UWSA claims the Wa people are the ancestors of the indigenous Lua people and consequently has political and military ambitions for the whole territory east of the Salween River. It has recently held talks with the new Burmese military government about its aims in the eastern Shan State. The UWSA has long been supported by China with weapons and military training, and the Chinese may have interests in overland connectivity between China and Thailand, across the eastern Shan State, via a new prospective Wa State. However, the people I talked to in Chiang Tung did not see this development as realistic, because no government in Naypyidaw would hand over political power in the eastern Shan State to the Chinese.

In the 1990s, the Burmese military government brokered ceasefire arrangements with about twenty-five rebellious groups and started a program to spread Burmese culture in minority regions. They built replicas of the Shwedagon Pagoda and erected statues of the Taungoo war king, Bayinnaung, to remind people which country they belong to. In Chiang Tung the Burmese military also demolished one of the most important symbols of Chiang Tung independence, the royal palace, and constructed a twenty-meter-tall, military-made, Buddha statue pointing down at the town with his index finger, a statue the local people believe will bring bad luck to those who look at it. Also in the 1990s, the Burmese military seized symbolic power over the Mahāmuni replica in Chiang Tung by writing the name of the military commander and his wife and putting it on top of the head of the image. The military aimed to demonstrate power and rewrite the history of Chiang Tung to include it more closely in the history of the Burmese dynasties.

5

SACRED SPACE

> Memory takes root in the concrete, in spaces, gestures, images, and objects.
> —Pierre Nora, *Between Memory and History*, 1989
>
> Great stories are always stolen, always adapted, and always shared.
> —Justin McDaniel, *Gathering Leaves and Lifting Words*, 2008

The Khuen Buddhist monastery, with sacred objects inside the assembly hall, is at the center of the sacred space in Chiang Tung. Ceremonies are held in the assembly hall, and literature on palm-leaf manuscripts and folder books has been collected in the monastery and forms the basis of Buddhist ceremonies. The Buddhist visual and material culture is about the production and history of sacred objects and the way people look at, talk about, and use these objects. It is a social drama around visual objects in sacred spaces that includes art, architecture, and crafts, which together make up the interior design of the monastery. Myths, rituals, and doctrines are attached to the sacred objects, and as we will see in this chapter, these objects are infused with memories of a sense of belonging, demonstrating Chiang Tung's historic connection to Lan Na.

Visual and Material Culture

As far as we know, there has never been a society without religious thoughts and practices, and there has never been a religion without visual expressions. The Buddhist visual and material culture of Chiang Tung imagines a community and group identity of the Khuen people, expressing a sense of belonging and uniqueness. "We are not Shan. We are *Khuen*," as an older man once told me with emphasis. The myths and memories we explored in chapter 2 tell us about what the Khuen people understand and believe about the origin and early history of the place where they live. These myths and memories are reflected in a feeling of affinity with Chiang Tung. Identity and affinity to the place also exist in a shared culture of religious buildings, sacred objects, literature, and religious ceremonies. Religion is not only thoughts, doctrines, and words. Visual culture, such as religious buildings and sacred objects, are important parts of religious practice. Throughout history, generations transmitted culture to succeeding generations, creating a sense of emotional connection about the sacred place and the sacred past. According to David Morgan, members of an imagined community "need symbolic forms such as songs, dance, images, and food to allow them to participate in something that is larger both spatially and temporally than their immediate environment" (Morgan 2005, 59).

Chapter 4 examines how the Burmese military focused on creating Burmese buildings and objects in Chiang Tung in order to rewrite the history of Chiang Tung and include it more closely in the history of Burmese dynasties. The military attempted to implant Burmese Buddhism, to overshadow the Buddhist culture of Chiang Tung. This chapter examines the reasons behind the military's use of Buddhist statues to spread Burmese culture and history to Chiang Tung, attesting to the idea that visual and material culture are a symbolic language that can be used in conflicts and to express sovereignty. But visual culture, such as religious buildings and sacred objects, can also express identity and be a powerful means of imagining a common identity. Looking at traditional Buddhist visual and material culture in Chiang Tung brings us closer to the identity of the Khuen people and Chiang Tung culture. To understand the sense of belonging and cultural identity of the people of Chiang Tung, it is essential to be aware of their visual and material culture. Memory takes place in the sacred spaces of Buddhist buildings and their interiors with images and objects. Therefore I look at a few objects of everyday religiosity infused with symbolic meanings that are present in almost every Khuen assembly hall. These objects reveal important parts of the Buddhist culture of Chiang Tung.

The Khuen Monastery

The first thing that one notices when coming to present-day Chiang Tung is its large number of Buddhist monasteries. Buddhist buildings, including stupas (*chedi*), assembly halls (*vihan*), ordination halls (*ubosot*), the library (*ho trai*), and the residences for monks and novices (*kuti*) are visible everywhere and are an important part of social life for the people. On temple grounds there is often a bodhi tree (*Ficus religiosa*). People gather in the sacred space during religious holidays and festivals, from the days of their childhood throughout life. In the gaze of a local Khuen resident, everything is familiar. Monasteries are the center of every village or block, and they have both a functional and a symbolic role in the way Buddhist people live their daily lives. The reciprocity between the villagers and the village monastery, with food given to the monastery and knowledge and merits given back to the villagers, occurs in these sacred spaces.

In these Buddhist buildings, architecture and rituals are closely related, and the interiors are filled with symbolic meaning. Buildings contribute to the construction of a shared worldview, or, in the words of Peter Blundell Jones, "buildings provide a mirror that reflects our world, our knowledge about it, and the way we interact with it" (Blundell Jones 2016, 3). The relationship between buildings in a Buddhist monastery and the activities that take place inside is both complex and variable. The interaction between user and building is a two-way process. The buildings are constructed traditionally to serve the activities in daily life and religious festivals. The buildings themselves define what and how to do and how to behave in them. The arrangement of buildings in a Buddhist monastery has to mesh with a set of habits, beliefs, and expectations held by persons who use the space. These habits, beliefs, and expectations have, from generation to generation, been formed in these buildings by what has taken place there. Buildings preserve old traditions and convey to their users a sense of identity, continuity, and connect the present with the past.

The archetypes of the *chedi* and *vihan* go far back in Buddhist history. The *vihan* or assembly hall has been developed from the design of early Buddhist cave temples. The *chedi* or stupa is a domelike tomb where the bones of the Buddha were collected. According to legends, the relics of the Buddha were divided into eight equal parts and distributed to the kings, acting as the Buddha's presence. They were stored as relics and spread to different parts of the Buddhist world. The relics of the Buddha and his most famous companions were sealed in reliquaries, which were enclosed in a stupa. These burial mounds became one of Buddhism's most prominent symbols. They spread widely across the Buddhist world in different designs and are called *stūpa, cetiya, dagoba, dhatu-gopas, pagoda,* or *chedi*. The spread of these relic buildings is a testament to Buddhism's emphasis on the cult of the physical Buddha. Every monastery in Chiang Tung has a centrally located *chedi*. The worship of relics of the Buddha is one of the most widespread, venerated practices in the whole Buddhist world. According to legends, six strands of hair the Buddha left when he visited the place that later became Chiang Tung became enshrined in the golden *chedi* of Wat Chom Kham. At Wat Pa Daeng, the widow Siridīghā constructed a *chedi* and enshrined the remains of her late husband, the ruler of Chiang Tung, together with three relics of the Buddha brought from Chiang Mai. A stone inscription dated 1451 (Griswold and Na Nagara 1978) reveres the former ruler, who is entombed in the same relic chamber as the Buddha.

The design of the monastery clearly shows Chiang Tung's historic connection to Lan Na, and the relationship with Northern Thailand is obvious. The architectural design of Wat Ho Khong (figure 6) and Wat Chom Kham (figure 7), seen in old photos from the beginning of the colonial period, reveals similarities with Lan Na design (Tai Yuan-Khuen-Lue) and distinct difference from the Buddhist

FIGURE 6. Wat Ho Khong, Chiang Tung, in a photo from British colonial time. Royal Geographical Society, copyright Getty Images.

FIGURE 7. Wat Chom Kham, Chiang Tung. The photograph was taken sometime between 1890 and 1906 by J. George Scott and published in his book *Burma: A Handbook of Practical Information* (London: Alexander Moring, 1911).

architecture in the rest of Myanmar, including the Shan States west of the Salween. Monasteries in Chiang Tung have been markedly renovated since what is visible in the old photos.

There are forty-two monasteries in the historic town of Chiang Tung (Kreangkrai 2008, 149) and hundreds more in the countryside outside Chiang Tung. Kreangkrai Kirdsiri (2008) distinguishes between four architectural types of assembly halls in Chiang Tung and its environs: the Tai Khuen style, the Tai Yai style, the Tai Lue style, and the Tai Yuan (Lanna) style. These distinctions are tenuous at best, but this book is not the place for a more detailed look at architectural styles. In terms of monastery design, I have chosen to concentrate on what I will call the Tai Yuan-Khuen-Lue style of Chiang Tung and how it differs from that of the western Shan states (Tai Yai style).[1] The similarities of religious architecture among Tai Yuan, Tai Lue, and Tai Khuen are easily seen by comparing the old Tai Khuen monasteries in figures 6 and 7 with Tai Yuan monasteries in Nithi Sthapitanonda (2016, 58–104) and Tai Lue monasteries in Liangwen Zhu (1992, 34–74).

One of the most obvious visual differences between the Tai Yuan-Khuen-Lue style and the Tai Yai style from western Shan is the design of the monastic buildings. Most Tai Yai monasteries comprise one large wooden building on stilts or on the ground that serves as both a residence for monks and an assembly hall. Compared to a Chiang Tung monastery, which is a monastic complex with several buildings, a Tai Yai monastery is often just a singular unit with a stupa sometimes very far from the monastery, reflecting the influence of Burmese design. The floor in a Tai Yai monastery is usually divided into three different levels, separated vertically from each other by about fifteen to twenty centimeters. The lowest level is for laypeople, and the next is for monks. In the middle of the building, on the highest level, is the central Buddha statue (Robinne 2003, 75–92; see also Murakami 2012 and Cheong 2016). A very distinctive feature is the high and complex roof.

The monastic ground of Chiang Tung monasteries includes several buildings, much like those in Northern Thailand. For this reason, I also refer to the Tai Yuan-Khuen-Lue style as the Lan Na style. The monastery grounds in Lan Na architecture are composed of three different parts: *buddhavāsa*, *saṅghāvāsa*, and *thoranisaṅgha*. *Buddhavāsa* is the most sacred area and includes important buildings with Buddha images and relics enshrined, *saṅghāvāsa* is the monastery area where the monks are living, and *thoranisaṅgha* is an area surrounding the others (Nithi 2016, 58–59). The monastic ground is a public center of a village, but also a sacred area separated by a fence from the rest of society. The low fence is not for protection but instead highlights what belongs to the sacred area.[2]

Traditional Lan Na assembly halls have several, multilayered pitched roofs, with the highest in the middle. The assembly hall is rectangular, with the entrance at one of its ends. An altar with the main Buddha image sits inside the assembly hall on the western, short side. The interior of the assembly hall has two colonnades, with pillars traditionally made of solid teakwood, extending between the two ends, which define the spacious inner temple room from the outer, lower part running along the long sides. The space between the main entrance and the principal Buddha image is empty of furniture; this is where people sit on the floor during ceremonies. On the left side from the entrance, between the pillars and the outer wall, there is a long platform for monks to sit on during ceremonies.

East is considered an auspicious direction for Buddhists, and the main Buddha image (figure 8) is placed on the west, short side facing east, toward the main entrance and incoming people. The Buddha's full image confronts the viewers and meets their gaze. Making images or venerating and offering before them are actions that allow believers to connect with the sacred and establish a sacred space and a religious environment, but the actions also establish a feeling of belonging to an imagined community, with a common identity. Almost all Buddha images in Chiang Tung depict the Buddha sitting in *bhūmisparśamudrā*, the so-called earth-touching position, with the right hand touching the ground. A variety of other images are placed, sitting or standing, around the main image. Buddha images in monasteries in Chiang Tung have a folkloristic facial appearance close

FIGURE 8. Buddha images, Wat Chiang Jan, Chiang Tung. Photo by author.

to those of images among the Tai Lue, but they differ somewhat from those of Burmese or Thai Buddha images. In chapter 6 I discuss the consecration of Buddha images and an imaginable divine presence of the Buddha embodied within the image.

Many of the more famous monasteries in Chiang Tung have existed for several hundred years, but during the colonial times many of the buildings were renovated or newly built. As a result, the monastic buildings in Chiang Tung, especially the assembly halls, do not resemble the old wooden monasteries in Chiang Mai. Christian churches in Western styles built during the colonial times affected the construction of Buddhist monastic buildings, especially the assembly halls (Kreangkrai 2008, 149). Many traditional assembly halls were renovated and rebuilt higher than before, with bricks replacing wood, and churchlike windows installed high on the walls or even behind the images of the Buddha (figure 9).

Examples of older monasteries and assembly halls in the Tai Yuan-Khuen-Lue style still exist in Tai Loi (Lua) villages far away in the mountains, mostly northeast of Chiang Tung, halfway between Chiang Tung and Mong La at the Chinese border. For example, Wat Baan Saen (figure 10) was probably built as early as the fifteenth century (Kreangkrai 2007). These Tai Loi (Lua) monasteries can help give an idea of the original shape of the early monasteries

FIGURE 9. Wat In, Chiang Tung. Notice the windows at the assembly hall. Photo by author.

FIGURE 10. Wat Baan Saen, in a Tai Loi (Lua) village in the mountains northeast of Chiang Tung. Photo by author.

in Chiang Tung. The Baan Saen monastery assembly hall is an especially interesting example of the plausible appearance of the earliest monasteries in Chiang Tung. The Tai Loi (Lua), living secluded in the mountains in traditional longhouses, without the means to rebuild their sacred buildings over the years, fortunately offer us a picture of the original features of Khuen monastic buildings.

Temple Banners

When one enters an assembly hall in Chiang Tung, among the most striking features to be seen are the colorful elongated banners (*tung*), up to three or four meters long and fifteen to thirty centimeters wide, hanging from the ceiling (figure 11). In Chiang Tung culture, the memories of relatives are above all connected to these temple banners. People in most cultures remember their past relatives and ancestors through specific objects, such as live candles, flowers, or wreaths. Often they are placed on a grave or tomb or in front of a picture. These objects are infused with memories of individual relatives and of the past, sometimes long gone. The relatives who have passed are those who could convey cultural traditions, and the memories of them form the bond of a common ancestry, connecting the present with the past.

FIGURE 11. Temple banners in the assembly hall, Chiang Tung. Photo by author.

The temple banners represent a connection between the world of human beings and the spiritual world. They are manufactured and hung as religious gifts to honor the Buddha and create good merit for deceased or ill relatives. It is a common practice by women in Chiang Tung on the annual death day of a relative to gather in the *vihan* of the local monastery and attach a banner to the ceiling to create a better next life. The banners help dead relatives leave any hellish world and instead come to a paradise in the sky and maybe meet the future Buddha Metteyya (Soangsak 2008, 110).

Banners show the close connection between the culture of Chiang Tung and the rest of Lan Na, including Northern Thailand, northwestern Laos, and Sipsong Panna in Yunnan, China. Similar banners with local characteristics can be found in this Tai Yuan-Khuen-Lue cultural region. In Chiang Mai, these banners have become popular decorations for tourists, but according to Rebecca Hall, they still have important roles in funerals, guiding the spirit of the deceased from one location to another and then on a path to heaven (Hall 2016, 51). Today in Chiang Tung the banners are often made from paper and can be purchased at the local market, but they are not made for tourists as in Chiang Mai. The design on Chiang Tung banners is less intricately crafted compared to those in Chiang Mai and Northern Thailand, but it still conveys a very significant symbolic meaning.

Rebecca Hall emphasizes two different purposes for the banners she studied in Northern Thailand and Laos. "The cloth banners used to decorate *wats* are significant means used by women to assure that they and their relatives will travel to heaven after death and the banners are also used by women to express their creativity to others in their community and produce pride in their local environment" (Hall 2008, 3).

The banners appear in various styles, sizes, and designs within the Lan Na cultural area, with many local variations. For example, Soangsak Prangwatanakun (2008, 112–18) categorizes different banners among the Tai Lue in Sipsong Panna, where there is a rich tradition of textile fabric, with beautiful banners woven in traditional colors of black and red on a white background, in a handicraft that is still practiced.

It is possible to find many different banners in Chiang Tung. Some of the most common show painted animals, such as birds, horses, elephants, monkeys, buffaloes, and cows. Horses and elephants are natural symbols of transportation and war and are important in the story of Prince Vessantara. A common motif is sixteen different animals with a horse on top, followed by two peacocks, three parrots, and up to sixteen geese. Many banners have thin strips of bamboo placed at regular intervals, as in a ladder to the heavens. Another, less common banner depicts the twenty-eight known Buddhas.

A very special banner common in Chiang Tung includes hanging needles. Sharp needles symbolize intelligence, and a banner with needles is donated not for dead ancestors but for oneself before a test or an exam. These are also common among Tai Lue and are called *tung khem* by Soangsak. It is believed that whoever gives needles as an offering will be sharp or intelligent (Soangsak 2008, 117).

Common are also banners with motifs associated with the Buddhist cosmological worldview that include life, death, and life after death, a world of the central mountain Meru and various heavens and hells. Tāvatiṃsa heaven has a special significance. It is believed that it was there that the Bodhisattva stayed before he was born into our world as the Buddha. An important motif is a religious building called *Prasad*, a tower of several levels that narrows toward the top. *Prasad* is a kind of palace believed to be found in the Tāvatiṃsa heaven.

A special banner used in funerals is called "three-tail banner" (*tung sam hang*) and is described by Hall. The form of the banner is interpreted as the Triple Gem of Buddhism (Buddha, *dhamma*, and *saṅgha*) by some and as the three characteristics of existence (*anicca*, *dukkha*, and *anatta*) by others. The banners have a distinct connection to the key Buddhist concepts central to any funeral that serves both to assist the dead and to inspire the living (Hall 2016, 44).

Banners have a long common history in the Lan Na cultural area. However, today in Northern Thailand they represent a textile craft tradition and an important identity marker for Lan Na culture more than a living religious tradition. This Lan Na textile craft tradition has become an important part of the tourist industry of Thailand, with beautifully crafted banners together with umbrellas, elephants, and numerous other items. Banners as Lan Na identity markers developed in the 1980s, inspired from the textile tradition among the Tai Lue. From that time it became popular in Chiang Mai and elsewhere to decorate shops, bars, restaurants, department stores, and everywhere else frequented by tourists with beautifully crafted banners.

However, in Chiang Tung, where the religious meaning is still immediate, the old textile tradition of making banners seems to have lost its importance.[3] Almost all banners are today made of paper and can be purchased in the market. But the religious power inherent in the banners is still present, and they hang from the ceiling in the assembly hall of most of the monasteries of Chiang Tung. Within this we can recognize that older cultural traditions evolve in different directions depending on the social, religious, political, and historical conditions in the society. In Chiang Tung, there was no prerequisite for keeping old traditions of crafts and art in the absence of a tourist industry. However, the religious tradition of banners is still vibrant.

Symbols of Kingship, Power, and Generosity

Inside almost every assembly hall in Chiang Tung there are small statues of several highly valued animals: the peacock, the elephant, the horse, and the bull. Made by skilled craft workers, these statues symbolize kingship, power, and generosity. The peacock is a royal symbol of power, masculinity, and a harbinger of rain, and the bird historically symbolized the role of the Chiang Tung ruler: the ruler was to the people as the peacock was to a group of peahens. The ruler was also polygamous, like the peacock. Sao Intaleng was the last ruler to follow in this tradition, with six wives and nineteen children.

Peacock motifs are widespread in Chiang Tung Buddhist architecture, both in paintings and as wooden statues. A wooden peacock in an assembly hall is a work of skilled craftsmanship, adorned with lacquer, gold painting, and pieces of glass depicting its extravagant feathers (figure 12). The statue is used as a screen to shield monks when they recite Buddhist texts because the words are not thought to emanate from the monks but from the Buddha himself. It is also a shield in the other direction, for monks who do not want to watch the laypeople listening. These beautifully decorated peacock statues stand in almost every assembly hall in Chiang Tung, whether or not they are used in rituals. Painted peacocks are also common on inner and outside walls, and live peacocks were only allowed in the palace garden.

The peacock is highly venerated within the Tai Yuan-Khuen-Lue cultural zone and is also an important part of the cultural traditions of Tai Lue people in Sipsong Panna. But in Sipsong Panna today, the peacock has been appropriated

FIGURE 12. A temple peacock statue in Chiang Tung. Photo by author.

by the tourist industry. The peacock dance has been reinvented, feminized, and is performed by young girls for Chinese visitors to the "exotic" borderlands of Yunnan. Sara L. M. Davis writes how the tourist industry "reinvented folktales, folk dances, ethnic dress, and even local scripts; it changed the Tai Lüe and other ethnic minorities from peoples with complex oral and written traditions into simple and romantic 'folk,' and ultimately into silenced and commodified spectacles—feminine bodies on display" (Davis 2005, 119). In Chiang Tung there is no tourist industry like that in Sipsong Panna, and the peacock has not been reinvented.

In addition to the peacock, the horse and the elephant are omnipresent and also represent kingship, power, and generosity. In almost every Khuen monastery there are two small wooden statues placed in front of the Buddha images: a white elephant and a white horse (figure 13). Elephants and horses are war animals, and political powers sought to monopolize ownership of them. For example, the *Chiang Mai Chronicle* relates that "having spoken thus, King Mangrai gathered up his troops, his elephants and horses ... and attacked a domain that lay to the south" (*CMC* 1998, 38). But above all, the crafted elephant and horse refer to the story of Prince Vessantara (Vessandorn).

The ceremony of *Dham Vessantara Jātaka* shows the life of Prince Vessantara as one focused on generosity. During this ceremony, the assembly hall is adorned with wild plants, representing the forest where the exiled prince lived. The entrance of the monastery is decorated especially for this ceremony to represent a forest gate. Beyond the forest gate and in the assembly hall are banana

FIGURE 13. Elephant and horse temple statues in Chiang Tung. Photo by author.

trees and sugarcane, as well as a thousand small, colored flags.[4] These flags are distributed to the thirteen sections of the *Dham Vessantara Jātaka* describing the story of the prince. The flags are placed in exact numbers in rows on both sides of the place where the offerings are put, according to the number of stanzas (*gatha*) in each section that will be recited. In the middle of the assembly hall is a beautiful recitation seat made of bamboo and decorated in the shape of a palace. The monk sits on this seat, facing east while reciting. Thirteen paintings are hung in the assembly hall, illustrating the thirteen sections describing the story of the prince. Two trees, one silver and one gold, are also placed in the assembly hall during the recitation.

The elephant and horse statues were traditionally painted white with attached royal regalia, with a small banner above each depicting the same animal. The animal statues are part of the celebration of *Dham Vessantara Jātaka* and represent the gift offered by the prince. According to my informants, laypeople presented them to the monks every year at the ceremony, but the statues never leave the *vihan*; they all remain on the floor below the main altar with the Buddha. In some monasteries, the elephant and horse are also made of cotton wool and decorated with royal regalia during the celebration of Prince Vessantara. These statues may be as tall as one meter and made of thousands of cotton threads, representing infinite generosity. Similarly, a bull is sometimes made of cotton wool, representing the story of Sujavaṇṇa, and is used during recitation of the *Sujavaṇṇa Wua Luang*.

The inner walls and teak pillars of the assembly hall in most Khuen monasteries are marked with gold stenciling on a red background (see book cover). Sometimes the stenciling has decorative patterns such as plants, flowers, *chedis*, and animals, but often the stenciling depicts sacred Buddhist stories. The Vessantara *Jātaka* is evidently very popular, but other *Jātaka* stories are also frequently depicted, especially the last ten lives of the Buddha. One very popular story among the Tai Khuen and Tai Loi (Lua) is the local story of Sujavaṇṇa (Peltier 1993), which, like that of Vessantara, discusses the perfection of giving. In this story, self-sacrifice is the main point. Even if Sujavaṇṇa is regarded as the hero of the story, it is Ummadanti, the daughter of the king of the bulls, who is the main figure. She is the exemplary daughter who takes care of her parents when they get old. The story says that she grew up without a father and later wanted to know who he was, so that she could take care of him in the last days of his life.

Temple Drums

A temple drum (figure 14) hangs from the ceiling inside every assembly hall of Chiang Tung. This is a ritual drum to be used in a religious context, not as a musical instrument. Drums have a prominent place in the Khuen culture, and there are close connections between the Buddhist temple drum, the drum used in the Songkran festival, bronze drums from the ancient monsoon culture, and ritual drums used by indigenous people. Chapter 7 looks more carefully at the

FIGURE 14. Temple drum, Wat Noi Naw, Chiang Tung. Photo by author.

cultural and symbolic background of drums, but here we will concentrate on the Buddhist temple drum.

The drum is made of a rough, hollowed tree trunk that can be up to one meter in diameter, with a length of up to one and a half meters. The drum is curved like a barrel and covered at both ends with taut skin. Many of the drums are stenciled with gold leaf in geometric patterns or with figures on a red background, like the decorations on the walls and pillars inside the temple. Some drums have texts written on them that tell of their production, consecration, or installation.

Every ritual in a Tai Khuen monastery begins and ends with the beating of a temple drum. These drums are highly venerated sacred objects and often hang in a corner inside the assembly hall, near the main entrance. The Khuen temple drum, or the heart drum (*gong chai*), has a body, four ears, and a heart, and before it can be used for ceremonies in the assembly hall it is treated as a living being that must be tamed with sacred rituals when it is manufactured, consecrated, and installed.

In the summer of 2015, I interviewed Sai, a local craft worker who was about thirty years old. Sai and his father are probably the only ones in Chiang Tun still making these temple drums since an elderly craft worker passed away a few years earlier. Sai told me it takes about a month to produce one drum, and the price is equivalent to about US$1,300. It provides both religious and worldly merit to donate a drum to a monastery. The drum they were making during the time of the interview had a diameter of 60–70 centimeters and a length about double that. Sai told me that previously they made the drum from one trunk of a thick

FIGURE 15. Ritual installation of a temple drum. Photo by author.

tree, but now it is impossible to get trees big enough to make a drum. Instead, drums are now made like manufactured oak barrels, such as those for wine, beer, or food. It is also difficult to get skins that are large enough for drums with a diameter of over seventy centimeters.

The temple drums are hung horizontally, just like the ancient bronze drums. Descriptions of rituals have details on how to make them. The drum has a female and a male end. It is important that the wood be correctly oriented, with the wood on the female end from the part of the tree closer to the root. The skins on the drumheads must be from two different animals (*Bos taurus*) slaughtered at different times. One must be from a female cow (heifer) and the other from a bull. There is a calendar that tells which days are for fastening the skins, but the skins have to be fastened on different days. It is also clear from the calendar that during two specific months of the year it is not possible to attach the skin.

The Khuen temple drum is equivalent to a living being, but only after its heart has been installed and the drum has been ritually consecrated. A silversmith manufactures a heart of silver and a gemstone (usually a ruby) is placed inside the heart. The silver heart is clamped inside so that it hangs in the center of the drum. When the drum is beaten, the heart vibrates. Besides the heart, the drum must also have ears: two ears made of the female skin and two ears made of the male skin. This will make a drum with a body that has four ears and a heart. Two holes are made on the body of the drum, one directed upward and one downward. The bottom hole is to allow the sound to reach the creatures that inhabit the underworld, and the top for those who inhabit the heavens.

Once all the physical parts of the temple drum are in place and a heart has been installed, it is regarded as alive and dangerous and has to be tamed; it must be installed in a monastery as soon as possible. The consecration is performed by a layperson, and on a calculated day the drum is brought to the monastery. Monks and laypeople from the monastery meet the drum and perform a ritual to install it (figure 15). A monk who has mastered the proper rituals has as his tools a metal chain, a black rod, and blacksmith pincers. The monk uses the pincers to pull the ears of the drum to see if it makes any mischief. With the chain, the monk draws the drum into the monastery. With the rod, he beats the drum while he reads a text telling the drum to listen to the words of the Buddha when it enters the temple. The monk explains to the drum that inside the monastery it shall not make noises nor do things that are inappropriate.

This ritual of taming the temple drum is a kind of symbolic transformation of a ritual shamanic drum, making it civilized and Buddhist. This brings to mind the wooden, shamanic drums from the Lua, Wa, and Eng, but also the ancient bronze drums, which we look at in chapter 7. There are common roots between the temple drum and drums from the culture of Monsoon Asia. The temple drums are considered to be alive and have to be consecrated, ceremonially tamed, and transformed into a Buddhist sacred drum before they are brought into the monastery and used. For the Wa people, hollowing a new drum was a major event in religious life: "Before felling the tree, shots were fired in the air to chase away the spirit inhabiting it. Then, a hole was made in the trunk to drill through it, to 'kill' it" (Formoso 2013, 130–31). It is also noteworthy that temple drums have one male and one female side, similar to the Wa spirit house, with two drums, one male and one female, positioned close together.

Once all these preparations and rituals are completed and the temple drum hangs in its place in the assembly hall, it has been transformed into a Buddhist sacred drum. In every religious festival, the drumbeat is used to mark the transition from worldly life to a sacred time of contemplation and listening to the Buddha's words. It is a time to make merit (*puñña*) by abiding by extra ethical rules that lead to the virtue of good karma. Elderly laypeople often wear white clothes and stay overnight in the monastery. Beating on the temple drum finishes the religious feast as it was started.

Temple drums are present in the whole of the Tai Yuan- Khuen-Lue cultural area, though they are probably more prevalent in Chiang Tung. The sacred rituals of the Khuen temple drum when it is manufactured, consecrated, and installed in the assembly hall are probably unique. In Luang Prabang and northern Laos, drums often hang in a drum tower in the monastery area instead of inside the assembly hall. Mani Samouth Doré has studied drums in the Lan Na culture of Northern Thailand and Laos. She believes, as I do, that these drums have a very ancient origin, with roots in rituals from pre-Buddhist shamanistic times in southern China. According to her, they can be traced back to the mythical Xia (Hsia) dynasty. Although the temple drums in Lan Na have basically the same design and function as those in Doré's study, they also have local characteristics. They vary in the mythical stories of the drums and how they are used in Buddhist rituals, but also in the rhythms that are played. Doré also emphasizes that the drums have been associated with power and politics, and they play an important role in the mythology of Luang Prabang's first ruler and his coronation (Doré 2008).

Drums were also connected to power in Chiang Tung. The old palace had a large drum in the same shape as a temple drum, but bigger. It was used to warn of dangers of different kinds, or, with different rhythms, the officers at the palace could gather people. J. George Scott describes the palace drum from his first visit to the ruler of Chiang Tung in 1890, noting that it resembled a beer or wine barrel. One hit on the drum marked that the ruler had ascended to the throne. Two hits meant he had left the palace. Three hits were used to gather the officials and the armed guards. Scott was told that the drum had been made by mountain people, but not exactly by whom (Mangrai 1965, 211). This particular drum was destroyed and removed when the palace was demolished by the Burmese military in 1991. Burmese soldiers punched holes in its skins, seeking precious metals, gems, or other valuable objects inside it. They had probably heard about the sacredness of the drum. Today, this palace drum sits broken in Wat Phra Sao Loang, the temple that inherited the Mahāmuni Buddha image. It was made from one hollowed teak trunk, one of a set of three made from the same trunk. One of the other two is currently in the royal temple of Wat Ho Khong.

Rituals and Literature

Ceremonies with recitations of Buddhist texts take place in the sacred space of Buddhist assembly halls. People gather in the *vihan* on sacred Buddhist days, listening to and visualizing Buddhist stories such as that of Prince Vessantara. The most popular Buddhist ritual in Chiang Tung is probably the *Dham Vessantara Jātaka* recitation, held at different times at different monasteries, mostly from February to May. To conduct Buddhist ceremonies requires literature. Like elsewhere in Buddhist Southeast Asia, monasteries in Chiang Tung have played a key role in the creation, production, and conservation of these religious texts. Justin McDaniel investigated the existence of literature in monastic libraries in Thailand and Laos and concluded that Pāli canonical texts are in the minority in these collections. Instead, the most popular texts are blessings, incantations, instructions for religious ceremonies, apocryphal *Jātakas*, and chronicles (McDaniel 2008, 191–94). This is also consistent with what appears to be the case in the monasteries of Chiang Tung (Peltier 1987).[5]

One important difference between Buddhism in Chiang Tung and in the rest of Myanmar centers on language, script, and literature. The *saṅgha* of Chiang Tung has a Buddhist Pāli canon (*Tripitaka*) written in the local *tham* script.[6] This *tham* script is almost the same as that which was used in Lan Na until this northern region was incorporated in the national state of Thailand and the old *tham* script was replaced by the modern Thai script. Since the *tham* script of Lan Na is not in use any longer in Northern Thailand, only some of the older monks can read the old manuscripts. However, in Chiang Tung it is still in use. Neither Burmese nor Shan people from the other Shan states can read Pāli written in *tham* script, making it next to impossible for monks from elsewhere in Myanmar or in Thailand to cooperate with Chiang Tung monks in their rituals. There are also great differences between Burmese and Tai languages, which has made the pronunciation of Pāli texts by Burmese monks and Tai Khuen monks quite distinct. Today many young monks from Chiang Tung study in Chiang Mai and have to learn to speak Thai and read Thai script. Therefore they don't have a problem participating with Thai monks in chanting Pāli together. But most Thai monks coming to Chiang Tung don't read *tham* script, and their pronunciation of known Pāli *suttas* has a slightly different rhythm.

Khuen literature reflects the great creativity of the Khuen people. In the words of McDaniel (2008, 216), "great stories are always stolen, always adapted, and always shared." The great stories of Khuen literature have their origin in the Tai Yuan-Khuen-Lue culture and the Buddhist tradition from the island of Lanka, written, rewritten, and shared from generation to generation, connecting tradition with change and transformation. The rich treasure of Khuen literature in the form of palm-leaf manuscripts and folder books teaches Buddhist morals and preserves the fundamental concepts of popular Buddhism. During the tradition of copying these texts, a sponsor gains merit for himself and the living and deceased members of his family. After a learned layperson or monk has recited it, the text in the shape of palm-leaf manuscripts and folder books is donated to the monastery to be kept in its library, manuscript cabinets, chests, or boxes. Figure 16 shows three manuscript cabinets high up under the ceiling in the assembly hall at Wat Baan Saen.

In addition to religious texts, there are other, more secular tales and legends belonging to an old oral tradition. Khuen literature is usually read before an audience. For example, a *māt* is a poem that can be read by one or more persons

FIGURE 16. Manuscript cabinets high up under the ceiling, Wat Baan Saen, in a Tai Loi (Lua) village in the mountains northeast of Chiang Tung. Photo by author.

at a time. The *māt* is recited in a tone between chanting and singing, creating a particular monotony. A learned reader inserts other forms of versification, which temporarily change the rhythm of the song. When it is read by many people at the same time, the several readers sit around an open, accordion-shaped book (*leporello*) with the text on both sides in opposite directions. More about *māt* recitation can be found in chapters 6 and 7.

There are many local Buddhist texts in the Khuen language written in *tham* script, such as *Jātakas*, also called Apocryphal *Jātakas*, which contain stories about previous lives of the Buddha that are believed to have been told by the Buddha himself to illustrate his teachings. These noncanonical *Jātakas* follow the structure of the canonical *Jātakas* about previous lives of the Bodhisatta, or Buddha-to-be. Some of these local *Jātakas* were composed early on in Southeast Asia, which is evident from references to individual stories in inscriptions and other early literary works that date back as far as the thirteenth century (Baker and Pasuk 2019, xiii). Local stories were given a Buddhist framing.

Some of these locally produced *Jātakas* were later gathered into collections called Paññāsa Jātaka, meaning fifty *Jātakas*. There are several such collections, some with fifty stories, but some with more or fewer stories, all named Paññāsa Jātaka. The process by which these stories were composed, circulated, and eventually assembled into collections probably extended over a long period of time and involved many different people in several different places. They were likely produced collectively within communities that shared similar sermon and storytelling practices (Baker and Pasuk 2019, xiv; Skilling 2017, 165).

Chiang Tung literature has much in common with literature from Lan Na and the rest of the Theravāda Buddhist world, and these bodies of literature resemble one another in the content of their texts as well as their stylistic form. Some examples of Khuen literature are *Sujavaṇṇa*, *Kalae Ok Hno*, *Maghavā*, *Chao Bun Hlong*, and *Candasobhā*, all of which have been transcribed to modern Thai script and translated to French and English by Anatole Peltier (1993, 1999, 2006a, 2006b, 2011). These are all written in the style of canonical *Jātakas*, beginning with the Buddha relating a story that took place during one of his previous lives. The story itself is derived from local tales and legends and ends with a Buddhist moral lesson. Many of the locally written *Jātakas* can be found in different versions among the Tai Yuan-Khuen-Lue cultural area.[7]

One of these locally written *Jātakas*, *Sujavaṇṇa Wua Luang*, has been the subject of analysis by McDaniel (2021). It is written in the local Khuen language, with parts in Pāli and in a style of canonical *Jātakas*, as its main character is a Bodhisatta and it involves self-sacrifice, renunciation, and the lives of royalty and the gods as well as some sort of journey (31). McDaniel discuss the use of

Pāli and points out that the text is not a local translation from Pāli. Instead, he writes, the Pāli framed the story and gave it a sense of religious authority and temporal authenticity; it could have been used to comment on contemporary events (29). The Khuen writers actively appropriated a classical literary structure and used it as a vehicle to carry their own religious beliefs and cultural practices. The *Sujavaṇṇa Wua Luang* reflects local innovations and creative engagement with canonical stories (45).

Khuen literature can be seen as a way the Khuen express their sense of belonging and cultural identity. All the hardships that afflicted Chiang Tung as a borderland between more powerful neighbors left deep traces in the culture and religion of Chiang Tung. Khuen literature has its roots in Lan Na culture, but the separation of Chiang Tung from the rest of Lan Na prevented further cultural exchange for a long time. That this literature of Chiang Tung uses the style of classical Buddhist literature to tell local stories is a way to give the stories a sense of religious authority, and connects the local with the global. This can be compared to the way Chiang Tung was established as a Buddhist sacred landscape connecting the local with the global through an asserted visit by the Buddha himself. Khuen literature, as well as other parts of the culture, reflects the everyday life of the people, their dreams, their hopes, and their religious beliefs and practices.

The collected literature forms the basis of Buddhist ceremonies that are held in the assembly halls. The most popular Buddhist ritual in Chiang Tung is probably the *Dham Vessantara Jātaka* recitation. *Vessantara Jātaka* is one of the 547 *Jātakas* included in the collection of canonical *Jātakas* in the Khuddaka Nikāya of the Buddhist Pāli canon. The text was probably first written on the island of Lanka and came to Lan Na during the fifteenth century, but the story was known earlier in Buddhist India and was depicted around the middle of the second century BCE on the northern gate of Sāñcī stupa 1 (Marshall and Foucher [1940] 1982, 122, 126, 225–26, plates 23, 25, 29, 31, 33). Therefore, this *Jātaka* belongs to the earliest part of the Buddhist tradition and has been very popular and presented in many different ways in Southeast Asia in texts, paintings, and rituals. Prince Vessantara (Vessandorn), the last life of the Bodhisatta before he was born as Gotama Buddha, focused on generosity (one of the ten perfections of *pāramī*), as it shows the prince prepared to give away everything important in his life, including his white elephant, his horse, a golden chariot, and even his wife and children. The Vessantara ceremony, in Thailand also called *Mahachat*, is very popular in Chiang Mai and elsewhere in northern Thailand, as well as in Laos and the rest of Thailand.

The ceremony of *Dham Vessantara Jātaka* takes three whole days and nights, and the text used in Chiang Tung is composed of twenty-six chapters, not just the thirteen main chapters narrating the story of Prince Vessantara. The first six and last two chapters are not found in any other Vessantara compilation.[8] They are considered to have been developed in Chiang Tung. Included in the *Dham Vessantara Jātaka* recitation are also two texts about Phra Malai. Section 7 is about Phra Malai's visit to hells and his report back to the people. Section 8 is about Phra Malai's visit to heavenly abodes, which he then narrates to people back in the human realm. In Lan Na, northeast Thailand, and Laos, the Phra Malai story has traditionally been part of the Vessantara recitation (Brereton 1995, 61). The widespread popularity of the story of Phra Malai in Thailand has been analyzed by Bonnie Pacala Brereton (1995).

It is impossible to date the origin of this ceremony, but according to the *Wat Pa Daeng Chronicle* (*WPD* §106) the great ceremony reciting the last life of the Bodhisatta was held at Wat Pa Daeng in Chiang Tung in the middle of the fifteenth century. In the *WPD*, the ceremony was named *Mahāpāng Dhamma*. Today the ceremony is called the *Dham Vessantara Jātaka* in Chiang Tung and *Tang Tham Luang* in Northern Thailand (Sommai and Doré 1992, 77).

There are two kinds of ceremonies and recitations about Prince Vessantara in Chiang Tung. One is annual and made by a group of local people from a village for the merit of the whole village. It can also be made to raise funds for monasteries, especially when new construction work in a monastery is planned (Sengpan 2016, 14). This kind of communal merit-making for a monastery in their own village is popular, since everyone in a village has a chance to participate, and each section of the ceremony can have one or several donors. Various kinds of offerings to the monks who conduct the *Dham Vessantara Jātaka* ceremony are placed in the assembly hall. Before the recitation and after the offerings, the main sponsors make offerings to the guardian spirits of the place.

Apart from this annual ceremony for the whole village, there is a great *Dham Vessantara Jātaka* recitation sponsored solely by a single family. This can be held at any time of the year, but it is often held between February and May when people are free from work in the fields. It takes three days and three nights and costs a lot of money. The recitation of the *Dham Vessantara Jātaka* is highly honored by the people of Chiang Tung. Any family that can sponsor this kind of performance is praised and honored for their generosity. It is believed that this kind of merit-making brings good luck to oneself as well as one's family and relatives, in this life and the next (Sengpan 2009, 125; 2016, 15–16). Because of the great expense required, there is a tradition of step-by-step merit-making to prevent extravagant spending.

Novice ordination (*paui sang long*) can be held at different times of the year, but it most often occurs from the fourth month in January/February to the seventh month of April/May. But there are also many annual ceremonies in Chiang Tung, which are held according to the Lan Na twelve-month tradition during the year:

TABLE 1. Important ceremonies in Chiang Tung

THE LAN NA TWELVE-MONTH CALENDAR	INTERNATIONAL (GREGORIAN) CALENDAR	IMPORTANT CEREMONIES
1st month	Oct./Nov.	Feast of Lights, finish of Buddhist lent, *Dham Vessantara* recitation, Kathina
2nd month	Nov./Dec.	Alm-giving ceremony, Zom Loi festival, Shan New Year
3rd month	Dec./Jan.	Parivaskam (*Parivasakamma*) ritual
4th to 7th months	Jan./Feb. to Apr./May	Novice ordination (*paui sang long*)
6th month	Mar./Apr.	Old Royal Market Day
7th month	Apr./May	Songkran
9th month	Jun./July	Venerating territory spirits (*sao baan* and *sao muean*)
11th month	Aug./Sept.	Start of Buddhist lent, *Dham Vessantara* recitation
12th month	Sept./Oct.	*Sujavaṇṇa Wua Luang* recitation

Another example of a Buddhist ritual with its origin in Lan Na culture is the *Parivaskam* (*Parivasakamma*) ritual (figure 17) for monks who violate any of the thirteen disciplinary rules and need to purify themselves. They do this by living in a quiet, isolated place in contemplation. In Chiang Tung, this ritual is performed annually in the third traditional month, December/January, and most of the time it is held in small huts outside in the monastery compound. The lay supporters of each village monastery are supposed to build a straw hut in the compound of one specific monastery. Each year, a monastery is selected to act as host to all the straw huts where the monks will dwell for ten days. The villagers make the huts according to a specific design, which takes both time and great skill. In January 2006, Wat Pa Daeng was the host, and at that time the huts were all made of straw. In December 2019 / January 2020, Wat Nong Kham hosted the ritual, with some huts replaced by tents decorated with straw.

One monk from each monastery in Chiang Tung spends ten days in contemplation in the huts. By his side is a young novice who attends to him. Every day, villagers come to make merit with food and other gifts for the village monk in the hut. In the countryside, village monasteries gather together for the *Parivaskam* ritual, but fewer monasteries participate. Besides the central ritual at Wat Nong Kham, at least two *Parivaskam* rituals were held in Khuen countryside villages in 2019/2020. Approximately ten monasteries participated in each ritual.

Parivaskam is an old Lan Na ritual. It was still being performed in Northern Thailand in the early 1990s, according to Sommai and Doré (1992, 99, 134–40). They claimed that, at that time, it was only performed at a few

FIGURE 17. *Parivaskam* ritual 2006, Wat Pa Daeng, Chiang Tung. Photo by author.

monasteries. Previously it was performed in the third month, just as in Chiang Tung. However, in later times, it was changed to be performed in the fifth month. One reason for abandoning this ritual in Chiang Mai was the difficulty of organizing it, according to an abbot interviewed by Sommai and Doré. Still, in Chiang Tung it continues to be very popular and is performed every year, though with a kind of modification to its meaning. The original purpose of the ritual as a kind of redemption for monks who violate any of the disciplinary rules has today lost its importance. Instead, the ritual is now more focused on the practice of meditation. Some monks connected to a Chiang Tung monastery who participated in the rituals of 2019/2020 were since living elsewhere, in Chiang Mai or other places. They have years of experience in meditation practice and come to Chiang Tung for this important ritual. Today the ritual is done more as a reward than for redemption. Though *Parivaskam* has lost its importance in Northern Thailand and changed meaning in Chiang Tung, it has found a new meaning because of the importance of meditation in present-day Myanmar.

People are born into a world of buildings and objects; some of these buildings and objects belong to everyday life, some belong to a sacred space. The Buddhist monastery is the sacred center of every village or block in Chiang Tung. From early childhood, memory takes root in the sacred space of the monastery, in objects, in stories, and in traditions of how to behave in the sacred room.

Throughout history, generations transmit sacred culture to succeeding generations, creating an emotional connection about the sacred place and the sacred past. Buddhist buildings and sacred objects allow people to connect with the sacred and to be part of a religious environment, but they also establish a common identity and a feeling of belonging to an imagined community. The sacred may be a place of belonging and reflecting in a feeling of affinity with Chiang Tung. The sacred visual and material culture of Chiang Tung reflects the close historical connection between Chiang Tung and Northern Thailand, which is based on a common origin. The Buddhist culture of Lan Na is clearly seen in the structure of monasteries, though most Chiang Tung monasteries have been rebuilt during the twentieth century.

Khuen literature and rituals are part of the sacred spaces of Khuen monasteries. People gather in the assembly hall on sacred Buddhist days, listening to and visualizing Buddhist stories at Buddhist ceremonies. Monasteries in Chiang Tung have played a key role in the creation, production, and conservation of Khuen literature. The rich treasure of Khuen literature in the form of palm-leaf manuscripts and folder books teaches Buddhist morals and preserves the fundamental concepts of popular Buddhism. During the tradition of copying these texts, sponsors gain merit for themselves and the living and deceased members of their family. There are many local Buddhist texts in the Khuen language written in *tham* script, such as local *Jātakas*, which contain stories about previous lives of the Buddha, written as if it were told by the Buddha himself to illustrate his teachings. They consist of many local tales and legends, end with a Buddhist moral lesson, and are part of Buddhist ceremonies.

The most popular Buddhist ceremony in Chiang Tung is from a canonical *Jātaka* about the story of Prince Vessantara and focuses on generosity. Buddhist ceremonies and Khuen literature are connected to the gold stenciling on the walls and the sacred objects in the assembly hall. The Khuen temple drums also reflect the influence of the indigenous people and the traditions from the ancient culture of Monsoon Asia.

6
RELIGIOUS CULTURE

> Each culture transformed Buddhist teachings and iconography into forms closer to its own heart, which led to the creation of beliefs, ideas and art forms that were neither purely Indian, nor indigenous and not even a fusion of the two, but were governed by a completely new aesthetic and world view.
>
> —Rajeshwari Ghose, *In the Footsteps of the Buddha*, 1998

The religious culture, particularly the Buddhist buildings and spirit shrines, can easily be seen in the sacred landscape of Chiang Tung. The first thing that one notices when coming to present-day Chiang Tung is the large number of Buddhist monastic buildings. This is not surprising, as the town is composed of many villages, and each of them houses a Buddhist monastery. The villagers have to bring food and other provisions to their monastery to provide for the monks. In return, religious ceremonies are performed for the families in the village. Monks from Khuen monasteries do not walk through town in the early morning for food donations. It is the villagers who come to take care of the monastery and its inhabitants.[1] Some more important monasteries have more than one village that takes care of them. Wat Pa Daeng, for example, is a large monastery and is provided for by three villages.

Walking around Chiang Tung, one frequently encounters altar-like shrines in front of big trees (figure 18). These shrines are dedicated to the territory spirits of each village (*sao baan*) and of the town itself (*sao mueang*). *Sao mueang* is the spirit of the whole town of Chiang Tung and is therefore regarded hierarchically as above the village spirits. The cult of territory spirits is a cult of the earth, of the place and the village itself, and of the people who have lived at that place. People in most cultures remember their past relatives and ancestors at specific graves or tombs. These are infused with memories of individual relatives and memories of the past. These memories form the bond of a common ancestry, connecting the present with the past. The same is true with shrines dedicated to territory spirits. They are infused with shared memories of local belonging of a long-gone past.

FIGURE 18. Village spirit (*sao baan*) shrine, Chiang Tung. Photo by author.

The cult of spirits is an ancient cult with close connections to agriculture and the monsoon climate, but it is still a living part of the religious life and worldview of the Khuen people. In the introduction I describe *mueang* as a principality or city-state with the surrounding countryside that includes many villages (*baan*). In the past, these city-states were semi-independent and loosely connected with one another, and a small *mueang* paid tribute to bigger ones. There is a hierarchical parallel between the social structure of city-states, villages, and the spirit world. The ancient background of spirit cults and the hierarchical parallel between the worldly and the otherworldly will be discussed later in this chapter.

The spirit shrine is often placed at a strategic location in the village.[2] Caring for and making offerings to the village spirit are symbolic performances for the village and all villagers. The shrine is almost always an altar-like construction in front of a big tree. Close by and connected to the altar is often a roofed space that seats ten to thirty people, made for offering ceremonies to the spirit. The village spirit is considered to be living in the shrine or in the ground, or it can be seen as the earth itself, but the spirit is not the tree or living in the tree. The shrine has no iconic, anthropomorphic figure; it is only an altar-like construction. Only in exceptional cases is there some human figure, which testifies to the Burmese influence.

Apart from the book's general goal to consider aspects of local belonging and a sense of place and belonging as identity for the people, in this chapter there are two areas of particular interest. First, I aim to understand the complex connection between tradition and change in religious culture. What happened when the Khuen traditional religious culture became divided by national borders in this historic borderland between more powerful nations? Second, I explore the relationship between Buddhism and the cult of territory spirits. These areas of inquiry are, of course, of interest for understanding Chiang Tung, but they are also of broader interest. To understand the cult of territory spirits in contemporary Chiang Tung and its relationship to Buddhist practice, we have to go back in time and ascertain the geopolitical and cultural-religious background of Monsoon Asia, which formed the spiritual culture of the Tai people.

Forested Mountains, Fertile River Valleys, and Agriculture

The ancient cult of spirits is still an important part of the sacred space of Chiang Tung. Every village has not only a Buddhist monastery but also a spirit shrine to take care of. This cult of the spirits has a long tradition in northern Southeast Asia, present far before the Buddhist tradition entered the scene. Important roots to religion and culture in Chiang Tung hide in the ancient culture of what has been called the Dong World by James A. Anderson and John K. Whitmore (2015, 2017), Southeast Asian Massif by Jean Michaud (2000), Zomia by James C. Scott (2009), and Monsoon Asia by Paul Mus ([1933] 2011). This geographical area of southern China and northern Southeast Asia, from the Yangtze Valley to the Southeast Asian lowlands and from the hills of southeast coastal China to the eastern edges of the Tibetan Plateau, comprises the highland river valleys.

Within this mountain world, the stream valleys (*dong*) form only a small percentage of the landmass, perhaps a tenth. The rest of this area is made up of the mountain slopes themselves. Many different ethnic peoples live and have lived on these forested upland slopes, predominantly above the stream valleys (Anderson and Whitmore 2017, 10–14). Catrine Churchman (2016) emphasizes the similarities and contrasts between the societies on the river plains of the Pearl River (South China) and the Red River (North Vietnam) and those societies on the mountains that lie between them. The borders of nation-states are less important. In this mountain world, the focus is not on whether people live in southern China or in another country of what is today Southeast Asia. Of greater importance is whether they are living in the lowland or in the highland. Chiang Tung is located in the lowlands of this large mountain territory of southern China and northern Southeast Asia, a geographical region that I will refer to as Monsoon Asia.

We can start this chapter's inspection of the religious culture of Chiang Tung by looking at the geopolitical environment and the cultural-religious background that formed the culture of the Tai people. At the center is the geographical landscape with high-forested mountains, fertile river valleys, and a monsoon climate, which has provided an opportunity for people to form a culture for a sustainable survival. The three distinct seasons of tropical monsoon climate—a cool, dry season; a hot, dry season; and a season with heavy rain from May until September—make wet rice cultivation the most significant agro-cultural phenomenon that has shaped the lowland culture of ancient Monsoon Asia. The climate formed the basis for the monsoon culture. Differences in geography create different agricultural and social systems. In the mountains, the land lent itself to slash-and-burn cultivation, and in the lowland plains and valleys the rivers carrying rich and fertile waters allow for wet rice cultivation. Wet rice production accumulated surpluses, and as a consequence, these cultures grew into city-states.

Rice was first domesticated in the Yangtze River Valley, probably around 4000 or 5000 BCE. Early rice farmers began to move south into Southeast Asia in the late third or early second millennium BCE. It was not a great migration; small groups of people moved south along the Mekong and Salween Rivers, each group bringing its own traditions and interacting with the local hunter-gatherers. They cultivated rice and millet and raised pigs, cattle, dogs, and chickens (Baker 2002, 9–12; Higham and Rachanie 2012, 82–85, 262–64; Higham 2014, 99–106, 127–29).

It has commonly been assumed that the Tai people originated from the region of the present-day Chinese provinces of Guizhou and Guangxi. However, this theory of the Tai people as having developed out of a single point of origin is not entirely correct. The migration process of Tai people into Southeast Asia is more complex and may not have been created solely by a succession of splits but also by different groups joining and participating in exchange (Baker 2002, 3–4). The Tai people immigrated into the region from approximately the eighth century, but it was not until the twelfth or thirteenth centuries that different Tai groups established more sustainable states. There are many foundational Tai legends in Southeast Asia with motifs of migration in search of good land suitable for rice production. The migrating Tai groups on their way south searched for a plain between mountains and a river ideal for growing rice, with a water supply coming from the hill streams (19).

When Tai-speaking groups migrated from southern China, they mostly came in contact with different societies of Mon-Khmer-speaking groups. One such group is called Lawa by the Siamese and Lua by the Tai Yuan in Northern Thailand (Grabowsky and Renoo 2008, 99n104). The history of Chiang Tung begins with these Lua people, who were defeated in the late thirteenth century by the

Tai people from Chiang Rai. According to legends, the Lua were the earthborn (autochthonous) people, believed to be born from the soil of northern Southeast Asia. These Mon-Khmer people also have their origin in South China but migrated from there at a much earlier date. In the chronicles of Chiang Mai, Lamphun, and Chiang Tung, the Lua are mentioned as a people living in the mountains; however, when Tai people migrated from the north, they had to defeat and drive away these people from the lowlands, as can been seen in Chiang Mai and Chiang Tung.

Tai people probably left their homeland in southern China for a combination of reasons, but most likely the pressure of the Mongols caused the migration southward. In the thirteenth century, the great dynasties of Bagan and Angkor had declined. In the absence of the major dynasties, the political landscape was fractured into many smaller states. Though there were several reasons behind the successful expansion of the Tai people in the region, the most important was probably that the Tai people were wet rice cultivators with sophisticated irrigation techniques.[3]

Research on the mainland Southeast Asian climate has advanced substantially in recent years. Lieberman and Buckley (2012) and Buckley et al. (2014) have pointed to the variability of the monsoon climate from circa 950 CE until the beginning of the nineteenth century. They suggest a relationship between climate and politics and particularly point out that the climate during the period 1250–1300 until 1450 affected the economic, political, and cultural collapse of Bagan, Angkor, and Dai Viet. At this time, the Tai people from the north could establish small city-states in the vacuum after the breakdown of Bagan and Angkor.[4] This period of cyclic fluctuations in monsoon rains caused droughts and floods, which are also described in the chronicles of Chiang Tung and Chiang Mai. The *Chiang Tung Chronicle* describes extreme droughts in 1410 (*CTC* §112) and 1674 (§161), and the *Chiang Mai Chronicle* tells of a heavy flood in 1524/25 (*CMC*, 156) where many inhabitants drowned.

The oldest rice cultivation system relied on annual rains and the flooding that followed. This was later replaced by more efficient irrigated systems. O'Connor (1995, 968) distinguishes between house gardening (horticulture) and irrigation, describing the Mon, Khmer, and Cham as horticulturists who took up rice. He also divides wet rice culture between rain-fed systems and irrigated systems, arguing that the wet rice irrigation system replaced the house gardening and rain-fed system. When Tai people moved south from the mountains and forests of southern China, they already had a developed wet-rice-cultivating irrigation system and a territory cult to the spirits of the earth.

Agriculture, the village community, and the cult of territory spirits were closely connected to one another in early Tai settlements in Southeast Asia. When groups of people settle in valleys and begin wet rice cultivation, they invest great amounts of human work on irrigation systems, water-management techniques, and other systems relating to lowland rice cultivation. The work of digging canals and damming streams to divert moving water through their fields requires a collective social arrangement. This in turn requires a need for irrigation associations, labor exchange groups, and village solidarity, favoring locally accountable leaders who make decisions based on customs and build consensus. This is, of course, the same for farmers all around the world, but wet rice farmers have to cooperate to a greater extent than other farmers. Important for wet rice farmers is recognizing communal rights to land and cooperating to build irrigation systems. O'Connor (1995, 976–78) argues that irrigation constructs a society as a roughly egalitarian and interdependent set of households, namely tightly integrated villages, in contrast to rice-growing garden farmers, whose villages were more like loose conglomerations of households.

These tightly integrated villages needed to be run by a respected leader who could promote cooperation and who acquired knowledge from previous generations when using water-management techniques. Old irrigation systems must be maintained, and new ones must be built. This is a matter of technology but also of old customs and experience. A respected leader has to be the link between the old irrigation constructions and the villagers as a group. He also needs to be just and promote cooperation. When immigrants found a good valley suitable for wet rice cultivation, it seemed natural for them to identify themselves with that specific place. The valley became their home, and the fertile soil became the basis for their survival. Nothing would be more natural than to worship the earth that gave them work, food, and a home.

Territory Spirits

Paul Mus emphasizes that throughout Monsoon Asia, there was an ancient indigenous cult of earth gods, guardian spirits, or tutelary spirits of a community (Mus [1933] 2011). All human societies throughout history, including wet rice–growing societies, are based on some kind of social construction of fictitious order, shared meaning, and myths. The cult of earth gods, or territory spirits, as I have called them, served as this kind of social construction for those people who settled in the valleys of Monsoon Asia in organized societies for wet rice agriculture. The territory cults, with offerings to the spirit of the soil, must have developed earlier in southern China, simultaneously with the development of agriculture and sedentism during the Neolithic period, or, at least with the development of societies with wet rice irrigation agriculture. The territory cult is an ancient interaction between a local group of people and a geographical place. Its origin is difficult to establish with certainty, but its ancient practice cannot be denied. John Clifford Holt has described its archaism: "If the spirit cults at the root of Southeast Asian religious cultures are not 'timeless' or 'primordial' in nature, to use now controversial and frequently discredited terms, then surely, at least, they must be recognised as archaic and ruggedly persistent" (Holt 2009, 15). It is undisputable that the territory cult had been established for a long time when the Hindu-Buddhist worldview entered Southeast Asia.

The territory cults of Monsoon Asia connect a group of people with a place. The annual rituals for the territory spirits establish a connection between a place on earth and a group of people, the "viable communication" between an imagined god and the human group (Mus [1933] 2011, 26). The village, with its territory cult, is a social unit for protection, representing a social contract between all villagers and between the village and a place on the earth. The territory cult also establishes a connection between the village and the history of that village, back through the ancestors, to the original headman of the village. Between the gods and the human group are priests, village headmen, and rulers. They have the magic power to conjure up the spirits and ward them off. The ancestors of the group, who are buried in the soil and thus restored to the soil, are also important intermediaries between the earth god and the group. In Chiang Tung, the original ancient village's headman and his followers are associated with the village spirit. The spirit of Chiang Tung (*sao mueang*) is likewise associated with a list of forty-three ancient rulers, and the oldest come from the earthborn Lua people. The spirit cult of Chiang Tung must be seen against this backdrop.

The *mueang* of Chiang Tung comprises independent villages, both inside the old town and outside in the countryside. They are called villages (*baan*), but inside old Chiang Tung they are more like city blocks or quarters. The village is not an administrative unit constructed by the state; it is a social community with ancient roots based on locality. Today, there are over fifty villages inside the town, with a headman as the elected chief of each village. Consequently, there are probably fifty shrines to honor all the village spirits in the town of Chiang Tung. The village headman has a close and intimate relationship with the spirit. He is regarded as a living human who, in the words of Mus, will act as one of the "intermediaries between the earth-god and the group" (Mus [1933] 2011, 30). Mus describes here a hierarchical parallelism between the worldly social structure of the city-states and villages and the otherworldly spirit world, with village headmen or rulers as intermediaries.

The village spirit is the spirit of the first leader of the village and all his descendants as headmen who have organized, taken care of, and built the village from ancient times until now. The present village headman is a natural intermediary between the ancient village spirit and the villagers. The Burmese authorities have tried to interfere in the choice of headmen in some villages, with little success. This is probably because the village headman has no real status in the official bureaucracy.

The traditional Khuen name for territory spirit is *sao*, sometimes transliterated in the literature as *chao* or *jao*. This contains the same element as in the name of a ruler, *saopha*, *chao fa*, or *jaopha*. The word *sao* means prince, ruler, or holy being, and *saopha* means a prince of the highest rank, the child of the king and his queen. *Saopha* is often translated as "lord of the sky" and was the royal title of Shan rulers in all the main Shan states. The spirits are therefore considered as lords of the earth in the same way as the local rulers, *saopha*, were lords of the sky. Occasionally, the words *phi*, *devata*, and *nat* are also used by some for these spirits, with the last one borrowed from the Burmese.[5]

Khuen people in Chiang Tung believe that natural objects are populated by several different spirits. Spirits can be dangerous if they are not respected properly. These spirits are located in many places in nature, such as trees, stones, mountains, rice fields, and rivers. *Phi* is the common word for spirits in the Thai language, but in Chiang Tung the word *phi* is mostly used for bad and malevolent spirits, such as spirits in the forest. The world of spirits is considered hierarchical, and territory spirits are above all others. Consequently, the most important spirits in Chiang Tung are territory spirits who protect the village (*sao baan*) and the city-state (*sao mueang*). Although the word *phi* is the common word for spirits in the Thai language, in the north Thai dialect, the word *sao* is also still used (Davis 1984).[6]

I have used the term "territory spirits" for the spirits of the earth. This can be questioned. O'Connor (2003) and Lehman (2003) have instead chosen to use the term "founders' cults" when writing about the cult of these spirits, which have sometimes been called guardian spirits, too. However, they both believe, as I do, that the initial and essential function of the cults of these spirits was agricultural. Farming households had to cooperate as a community, and the cult ties people to the land. The cult of the local territory spirit requires each household to contribute to a rite for the welfare of all. The spirits are also believed to punish misbehavior that upsets the local moral order (O'Connor 2003, 271–78). When the first human settlers cleared tracts of land, they had to make a contract with these spirit lords (Lehman 2003, 16).

This cult of the territory differs from the ancestor cult. A person must be born into the cults of ancestral spirits and remain a part of it throughout life. Ancestor cults are hereditary, and those who move to another place still belong to their original ancestral spirit (Rhum 1994, 52–54). The territory cult is, on the contrary, for all residents in a village, and if a family moves from one village to another, they have to become members of the cult of the new village. Newcomers have to accept the village spirit and, in theory, be accepted by the spirit. The beliefs and practices of spirit cults also undergo changes. In a village in Lampang district in Northern Thailand, according to Michael R. Rhum (1994), the territory spirit of the village has almost totally disappeared in favor of ancestor cults.

The Spirit of Chiang Tung

There are three annual celebrations for the spirit of Chiang Tung (*sao mueang*). The main annual offering to the spirit occurs in the ninth month (June/July) of the Lan Na twelve-month tradition. Another is held in March during the Old Royal Market Day, when four centrally located villages in Chiang Tung organize the offering. The last one is in April during the Songkran festival and will be described further in chapter 7. All the celebrations include offerings of food and rice liquor, a *māt* recitation, and a social gathering where the food and liquor from the offering are consumed.

The first time I visited a ceremony for the spirit of Chiang Tung was at the Songkran festival in 2013. At a central place in town, close to the mausoleums of the seven last rulers and where the old market once was located, there is a shrine for the spirit of Chiang Tung with a roofed space where people can gather. I visited the roofed portion of the spirit shrine and can testify to the veneration and offerings made in front of the *sao mueang* shrine. The ceremony was held before noon on the second day of the festival. I was sitting close to the shrine, watching and listening to the offering and recitations, as the drumming outside by the Tai Loi (Lua) people created a rhythmic background. The rites started with food and liquids offered on plates in front of the altar (figure 19). Sixteen plates with eggs, fish, rice crackers, and vegetables were presented together with small cups of liquor. The liquor was slowly spilled on the plate while a man read from a sacred text.

After the offering of food and liquor, a group of about ten elderly men sat in a circle around an accordion-shaped folded book (*leporello*). The book had the same text on two sides, facing both directions, so that all men could follow along, read, and chant (figure 20). The recitation technique is special, with an exceptional rhythm and intonation, sounding rather odd and melodious, very different from a monk's recitations. Two of the men, sitting opposite each other, had sticks in their hands and led the recitation, pointing to each syllable in the text to be read and, on occasion, making peculiar movements with the stick, so everyone could follow the text and take part in the recitation. The text in *tham* script is a mix of Khuen and Pāli words, with symbolism and metaphors expressing the admiration for the spirit who takes care of the *mueang* Chiang Tung. The result is a song of many voices, thus adding to the harmony of the poem. Sometimes

FIGURE 19. Offering to the spirit of Chiang Tung, at the 2019 Songkran festival. Photo by author.

FIGURE 20. *Māt* recitation, Songkran festival, 2013, Chiang Tung. Photo by author.

the *māt* recitation is repeated a second time, and occasionally two groups of men read the *māt* recitation at the same time. Afterward, people sit and talk and share the food and liquor that have been offered to the spirit. This special *māt* recitation to the spirits is also made on other occasions where the spirits are venerated, such as at the annual offering to the village spirit, when a new house has been built, and at the beginning of the growing season.

The main annual offering to the spirit of the town is made in late June or early July and is more or less the same as described above. The exact date depends on the local calendar and the people involved; it cannot be set before every village has completed its own individual annual offering to the village spirit. This annual offering, corresponding to the ninth month in the Lan Na twelve-month tradition (Sommai and Doré 1992, 223–56), has its counterpart in Chiang Mai at the same time of the year. There the celebration occurs in the eighth and ninth months of the Lan Na twelve-month tradition, focusing on the worship of guardian territory spirits, including the city pillar Inthakhin and the ancestors of Chiang Mai, Pu Sae Ya Sae (see Sommai and Doré 1992, 40, 204–22, 242–56; Tanabe 2000; Fukuura 2022; Johnson 2014).[7] Though this book does not go into detail about the ceremony in the city-state of Chiang Mai, it is important to note its connection with the indigenous Lua people, called Lawa, in the Thai context.

The annual offering to the spirit of Chiang Tung is made at the spirit shrine in the center of town, close to the place where the royal palace once stood, and not far from Wat Phra Sao Luang containing the Mahāmuni image (figure 21). The shrine was moved and installed in this location by the last Khuen ruler, Sao Sai Long, who planted the tree from a Sri Lankan sapling.

The cult of *sao mueang* is complex because there is more than one shrine and three different annual ceremonies, indicating a confusion in the beliefs about the territory spirit of Chiang Tung. The spirit shrines are located in strategic places around the town, but they are not considered as shrines to spirits of

FIGURE 21. The central shrine to the spirit of Chiang Tung. Photo by author.

a delimited part of the town but conceived as spirits of the whole town. The differences between them are not geographical but stem from history, as they are all connected to a specific ancient ruler. Each ruler has a name, but, to my knowledge, there are no biographies connected to these rulers. This is in line with the connection between the village spirit and the first village headman. These spirits are all venerated annually in June or early July, depending on the calendar. The names of these rulers connected to spirit shrines are all mentioned in a list of forty-three Chiang Tung rulers. It is worth noting that the first two of these rulers were from the earthborn Lua ethnic group. The last six Khuen rulers, from 1881 to 1962, are not considered as spirits to worship. These six last rulers are all buried in a mausoleum located very close to the shrine where the Old Royal Market Day and the Songkran festival are held. They are so closely situated that, if it were possible, the former rulers could witness the celebrations.

The Village Spirits

There is a hierarchy among spirits, with the *mueang* Chiang Tung (*sao mueang*) considered higher and more important than all the village spirits (*sao baan*). Before the annual offering to the spirit of Chiang Tung can be performed, all the village spirits must have already been celebrated. In Thailand and Laos there are small spirit houses on almost every family's property, resembling miniature Buddhist temples. In Chiang Tung, aside from the shrines to the village spirits, there are no such spirit houses around town. Holt (2009, 18) is of the opinion that these spirit houses seem to indicate the domestication of the spirit cult. The absence of these miniature spirit houses in the streets of Chiang Tung may indicate the lack of domestication, or rather the lack of Buddhisization, of the spirits of Chiang Tung.

All villagers have one spirit in their community, the spirit of the village. In theory, the village spirit belongs to and serves all residents in the village, independent of religious or ethnic belonging. The spirit cult promotes cohesion and solidarity in the village. It is believed that the spirit takes care of Buddhists and Christians alike, but not everyone cares about the spirit nowadays. For example, a newcomer Christian Akha family must relate to the spirit cult, but they do not need to participate. The village headman considers them as belonging to the village and to the spirit, regardless. Family members who temporarily move to another city or abroad to study or work can, if they want, still consider themselves as belonging to their family village spirit. As far as I understand, this is a matter of individual choice for the family.

There are two kinds of ceremonies for the village spirit, one annual and one made to protect the village after some misfortune. The annual ceremony is called the village offering and is held in June/July. Every village chooses for itself a perfect day for the ceremony to be held, depending on the local calendar and time for the people involved. The ceremony takes two days but has to be prepared in advance by the village headman. He visits every family in the village to collect money for the ceremony. The money is used for all expenses during the ceremony, including food, liquor, decorations, and the cost of inviting monks. In the evening on the first day, the village spirit is offered food and liquor, and a *māt* recitation is made by the village headman and a couple of respected men in the village. When the offering and recitation are finished, all people participating in the ceremony start eating and drinking the offerings. This can continue until late at night and sometimes includes card playing and similar amusements. The *māt* recitation requires knowledge and experience that is not found in all villages any longer. Therefore not all villages can arrange a *māt* recitation but instead perform an abbreviated version of the ceremony.

No monks take part during the first day's ceremony, but they are invited to come the next morning. When they arrive, they carry sacred water to the village shrine. After they have been offered food, they sanctify the village. Not all villagers are present at the ceremony, neither this day nor the day before. Instead, they are represented on the second day by a piece of cloth. Every family in the village can bring a piece of cloth to the shrine for every family member. The cloths are placed under a pyramidlike structure made of bamboo poles. Holy water is sprinkled on the clothes, and sacred texts are recited by the monks to give protection to the owner when he or she wears the cloth. There is a belief that power may be transferred from one object to another. A string connects one object with another or to a sacred Buddha image so that protection power is transferred to all the clothes before they are taken home to the family members. They are protected both by the power of the Buddha and the village spirit. This annual ritual establishes what Mus calls "a viable communication" between a god and the human group (Mus [1933] 2011, 26), even if not all villagers take part in person.

The other ceremony is called village cleaning or village preparing. It is done to cleanse the village of bad and evil fortune, such as when someone living in the village dies outside the village or when an unmarried woman is having a baby. Events like these are believed to disturb the order of the village and therefore upset the village spirit and bring bad luck. Therefore offerings must be made to the spirit quickly. Later in this chapter, I will explore the relationship between Buddhism and the cult of territory spirits.

The History of Buddhism in Lan Na

To address the question that began this chapter about what happens when a traditional religious culture becomes divided by national borders, we first must look at the early history of Buddhism in Lan Na, including the controversy between the two Sinhalese monastic orders and the relationship between rulers and the Buddhist community. In chapter 3 I mentioned that when King Mangrai in the thirteenth century united the region and expanded his territory, he adopted Buddhism as a legitimation of universal power. The local cult of territory spirits was not enough to hold together a socially complex and expanding society. In contrast to the locally grounded territory cult, the Indic Hindu-Buddhist worldview was universal and created a model by which Southeast Asia rulers could aspire to a status that reached beyond their specific locality. The Indic Hindu-Buddhist worldview had already been in place in Southeast Asia for several centuries before Mangrai gathered some small city-states under his leadership. Mangrai and the new Lan Na kingdom needed the universal Buddhist culture for an expanding society, so Mangrai turned his eyes toward the Buddhist Mon tradition of Haripuñjaya. That the spirit cult is local, and that Buddhism is universal, are, of course, rough generalizations.

The origin and early history of Buddhism in Lan Na and Chiang Tung can be divided into three different traditions: first, a Mon tradition of Haripuñjaya established in the thirteenth century, and, later, two traditions from the island of Lanka. The first Buddhist monks who came to Chiang Tung must have belonged to the old Mon (Haripuñjaya) Buddhist tradition, since Buddhism from Sri Lanka came later, though this is not specifically expressed in texts or in oral tradition. Legends about the founding of Haripuñjaya include the indigenous Lua/Lawa people, as do the legends of Chiang Tung and Chiang Mai. Haripuñjaya is usually associated with a late settlement of the Mon Buddhist tradition of Dvāravatī, centered in central Thailand at sites like U Thong, Nakhon Pathom, Sri Thep, and Lopburi. Buddhism has been practiced in Dvāravatī at least from the sixth or seventh century, evidenced by the many Buddha images from that time. In this early period, Buddhist art shows strong influence from Gupta art, specifically the Sārnāth style (Brown 2014, 190).

Mon inscriptions have been found in Haripuñjaya, and the art there has typical Mon features. However, the connection of Haripuñjaya with the Dvāravatī kingdom is problematic. One very typical architectural style in Haripuñjaya is the pyramid-shaped *chedi* of Ku Kut, with niches on five upper stories. Altogether, there are sixty niches, each holding a standing Buddha. The influences must have come from South India or Lanka but may also have to do with the

Mahābodhi temple at Bodh Gayā (Woodward 2005, 174). Betty Gosling is of the opinion that in Haripuñjaya they practiced a distinctive and now poorly understood *Sarvāstivāda* Buddhism, sometimes referred to as Ariya Buddhism, with roots in Burma (Gosling 2004, 160–61). If this was the case, the first Buddhist monks who arrived in Chiang Tung would have practiced some kind of tantric cult.

This Mon (Haripuñjaya) Buddhist tradition had an important symbolic role in the establishment of Buddhism in early Lan Na. When King Mangrai moved his capital south from Chiang Rai, he first built it in Wiang Kum Kam, just outside modern-day Chiang Mai. The building there of the pyramidic *chedi* Ku Kham, with sixty standing Buddhas like the famous Ku Kut in Haripuñjaya, gives witness to the importance of Haripuñjaya Buddhism as a way for Mangrai to establish his authority and power. The importance of Mon traditions can be attributed to a legend about the Buddhist mission by the South Asian king Aśoka in the third century BCE. It is told there that Aśoka sent two learned monks, Sona and Uttara, to Suvaṇṇabhūmi (Sanskrit: Suvarṇabhūmi). Legends have identified this with Southeast Asia. The legends from the Lankan chronicles Dīpavaṃsa and Mahāvaṃsa were repeated in the Kalayani Mon inscription at Pegu in 1476 CE. References to the region are to be found in Indian sources describing sea journeys to the lands of gold, naming the region as the Suvaṇṇabhūmi.

The Mon city-state of Haripuñjaya had a powerful impact on early Tai state formation and culture. The ruler of Chiang Mai, Phaya Khuena (Ku Na), had heard of the reputation of the Sinhalese order and invited a monk named Sumana to stay at Wat Phra Yun in Haripuñjaya. Establishing Sumana initially at Wat Phra Yun provides continuity to the pre-Thai mythical, legendary, and historical traditions of Haripuñjaya. Moving him later to Wat Suan Dok, a new monastery built by the ruler Kuena on the royal property in Chiang Mai, symbolizes the transition to a new cultural and religious center (Swearer and Sommai 1978, 24–25). This indicates the importance of Haripuñjaya Buddhism for Lan Na and the symbiotic relationship between the religion and the state.

According to one chronicle (*CTC* §79), Mangrai's son Namthum brought Buddhism to Chiang Tung and embodied the prophecy made by the Buddha. Mangrai also commanded Namthum to build the palace and rule the state from the same site where the Lua ruler had his palace. He sent two monks to Chiang Tung, who brought four Buddha images with them. But on their way, one of the images fell into the water, and only three arrived. Therefore, we can state that the monks who arrived in Chiang Tung must have belonged to the old Mon (Haripuñjaya) Buddhist tradition because the Sinhalese Buddhist movements arrived in Chiang Mai and Chiang Tung later.

Wat Suan Dok

Most important for Buddhist history in Chiang Mai, as well as Chiang Tung, was the arrival of two different monastic orders from the island of Lanka, the Flower Garden (Suan Dok or Pupphārām) and the Red Forest (Pa Daeng). These Sinhalese Buddhist movements of the Mahāvihara interpretation of Theravāda Buddhism had important impacts on the whole of Lan Na.

Buddhist chronicles have often been used by scholars for historical reconstructions. However, this should be seen as risky. These chronicles were not composed for purely historiographical purposes. They are subjective texts with other aims. Anne M. Blackburn (2015) warned that these works were sometimes written long after the events they purport to describe, then transmitted through unstable scribal practices that did not necessarily privilege verbatim copying. Further, they were often composed by a particular monastic group in the context of a competitive monastic conversation, or debate, about the purity and authenticity of various lineages and their practices (Blackburn 2015, 316). She implies that references to Lanka in texts written in Lan Na, or elsewhere outside Lanka, function to add value in some way (318). This is certainly true, and the goal here is not to reconstruct the factual history of Buddhism in Chiang Tung. On the contrary, events documented in the chronicles represent a living tradition transmitted throughout generations, revealing a definite self-awareness of the local Buddhist Chiang Tung people. The arrival of the two Sinhalese orders, the controversy between them, and the rich Buddhist culture during the Golden Age of Lan Na history have become a chosen point of glory for many generations of Chiang Tung Buddhists, regardless of whether there is any historical truth to these events. It is the Buddhist history in the minds of Chiang Tung's local Buddhist people I want to tell.

Monks traveled between different places in and out of Lan Na. An important goal was to visit the island of Lanka (Sri Lanka), which was considered the most important place for true Buddhism, at least according to the tradition of Theravāda. This was considered to be the place where Buddhist texts originated. Monks traveled from Lan Na to Lanka several times during the 250 years of the Lan Na Golden Age. They brought texts, Buddha sculptures, and relics back to Lan Na, but, more importantly, monks underwent the Buddhist ordination in Lanka. It was considered to be a more authentic ordination, compared to the one monks underwent in Lan Na. It was important to be properly ordained in direct succession from the hand of the Buddha. Theravāda ordination traditions are strictly concerned with lineal descent and genealogy, and consequently the two monasteries ended up fostering two similar but separate ordination lines (Veidlinger 2006, 65).

The Buddhist culture also spurred the production of important art, architecture, and literature. Artists, architects, and construction workers moved between different places and made contacts when working with Buddhist buildings in different city-states around Lan Na. Buddhist monks from Southeast Asia took the dangerous trip all the way to Lanka, stayed there for years studying, and became reordained. Finally, they went home, intending to reform the local *saṅgha*, but for this they needed the support of the local ruler. The reformation movement of the Buddhist *saṅgha* was thus part of local politics.

The first Sinhalese order established in Chiang Mai, and later in Chiang Tung, was the order of Wat Suan Dok (the flower garden monastery), also called the Pupphārām order. The monk Sumana, a native of Sukhothai, went to study in Martaban in Lower Burma as a disciple of the Sinhalese monk Udumbara Mahāsāmi. The Sinhalese monastery of Udumbaragiri was a branch of Mahāvihara, a forest-dwelling order outside the royal city of Polonnaruva in Lanka. Udumbaragiri was known for high standards of scholarship and followed strict monastic disciplines. Sumana went to Martaban, was reordained, and became a disciple of the Udumbara order. He spent ten years there and received the grade of Thera.

The ruler of Chiang Mai, Kuena, had heard of the reputation of the Sinhalese order for scholarship, discipline, and magical powers, and in 1369 he invited Sumana to stay at Wat Phra Yun in Haripuñjaya. The chronicles tell of daily miracles performed on the way from Sukhothai to Chiang Mai, using the relic that Sumana brought with him. He also brought a copy of the Buddhist scriptures given by the king of Sukhothai (Griswold 1975, 20–23). After two years, he moved to the newly built Wat Suan Dok, the flower garden monastery, just outside Chiang Mai. Wat Suan Dok was a forest-dwelling order (*araññavāsi*), in contrast to the old Mon order, which was city-dwelling (*nagaravāsi*). The Suan Dok order was brought to Chiang Tung and is today upheld by the Wat Yang Kuang (spelled Vat Yanggong by Saimong Mangrai [1981]). As already mentioned, to build a new monastery, Wat Suan Dok, on the royal property in Chiang Mai, for Sumana and his monks was an attempt to merge the old Buddhist tradition of Haripuñjaya with the new Buddhist tradition from Lanka and place it under royal protection.

Wat Pa Daeng

Wat Suan Dok was not the only and most important Sinhalese order. After approximately fifty years, a new Sinhalese order came and challenged the old one. According to *Tamnan Mūlasāsanā Wat Pa Daeng* (*TMWPD*) (Sommai and Swearer 1977, 87), a Chiang Mai monk named Siddhanta visited the island of Lanka. When the Sinhalese monks heard the recitation by Siddhanta, they decided that the monastic rules (*kammavācā* and *pātimokkha*) of Chiang Mai were incorrect. Therefore, no one in Chiang Mai could be considered being an authentic Buddhist monk in the eyes of the Sinhalese. Siddhanta had to return home with a message that the monastic traditions of Suan Dok were invalid. He reported to the *saṅgha*, "Your ordination is not valid, and none of you is a monk" (*TMWPD*, 87).

The *Wat Pa Daeng Chronicle* also states that the monks of the old Suan Dok order did not follow the strict recitation of the words of the Buddha: "They followed the dictates of their hearts; they invented when they could, never followed the sounds of the alphabet which Lord Buddha had laid down" (*WPDC* §114).

Therefore, a couple of years later, a group of twenty-five monks under the leadership of Nāṇagambhīra went to Lanka to become reordained. Traveling to the island took four months, and they stayed there for five years, were disrobed, and later were reordained. After they had studied the dharma for five years, they went back via a merchant junk in 1428, carrying with them a Buddha image, a branch from the bodhi tree, and a copy of Buddhist texts. Afterward, they went upcountry to Ayutthaya, Phitsanulok, Sukhothai, Haripuñjaya, and finally to Chiang Mai. It is told that at every place they stopped, they reordained monks to the new purified order, the Red Forest order (Wat Pa Daeng) of Sinhalese Mahāvihāra.

Back in Lan Na during the reign of Sam Fang Kaen, the new forest-dwelling order arrived around 1430, and a divisive controversy began between the two Sinhala schools. Although the text states it was Wat Pa Daeng who emerged victorious in the religious battle, we know from inscriptions that during the reign of Phaya Kaeo (Bilakapanattu) (1495–1526) all three Buddhist traditions, Mon-Haripuñjaya, the old Lanka order (Suan Dok), and the new Lanka order (Pa Daeng), still lived side by side in Chiang Mai (Swearer and Sommai 1978).

However, the king of Chiang Mai, Sam Fang Kaen, did not support the new Pa Daeng order, while his son Tiloka did. Sam Fang Kaen openly supported the old order, which prompted Tiloka to rebel against his father and subsequently kill him. We can question whether Tiloka initiated a palace revolution because he was a devout follower of Pa Daeng and their reformed Buddhism, or if he did this only to grab power. Nāṇagambhīra and his group of fellow monks reportedly spent some time in Chiang Saen after they came back from Lanka. Swearer and Sommai (1978, 20–33) therefore propose that the ruler Sam Fang Kaen backed the old Wat Suan Dok order and expelled Nāṇagambhīra and his followers from Chiang Mai, deporting them to Chiang Saen. Around 1441, after Tiloka seized power, he invited Nāṇagambhīra back to Chiang Mai.

It is even possible that the reordination of monks from the Suan Dok order was a way for the ruler to take land and money from the Buddhist order that had been given as merit donations. This we do not know for sure, but the text recounts that monks from the Suan Dok order handled money and property. This may suggest that the old order had become rich from merit donations and owned large properties.[8] In the inscription of Wat Pa Daeng in Chiang Tung, we can follow how rulers were involved in religious donations. Tiloka, the ruler of Chiang Mai, bore the cost of a *chedi* at Chiang Tung, and the inscription (*EHS* 19, IV/15–19) also states that land and slaves were presented to the monastery by the royal family of Chiang Tung (Griswold and Prasert Na Nagara 1978, 72, 86).

The new Sinhalese order (Pa Daeng) was also established in Chiang Tung. The establishment of both these orders, first in Chiang Mai and later in Chiang Tung, reflects the close connection between Chiang Mai and Chiang Tung during this formative period. According to the *Jinakālamālī* (*JKM* 136), it was the year 1448 when Nāṇagambhīra sent Somacitta with four companions to Chiang Tung. At Chiang Tung, a dispute between the old Sumana Sinhalese order and the new order began. The *WPDC/TMWPD* describe this dispute, but we cannot trust the details, especially as the chronicle was written by monks from one of the two contesting parties, the new Sinhalese order. The dispute is presented as a break between Nāṇagambhīra and his former teacher, Dhammakitti. When Nāṇagambhīra insisted that the ordination of the old order was invalid, monks argued that he had shown disrespect to his teacher, Dhammakitti. To resolve the dispute, the king called a meeting and used magic to put the two orders on trial. To find out who was properly ordained, he wrote the name of the head monks on two different palm leaves and threw them into a fire: "The name of the teacher of the Suan Dok tradition was destroyed, but the name of Nāṇagambhīra was not burned" (*TMWPD*, 108).

This new Sinhalese order was more strictly concerned with lineal descent, the way of dressing, and the prohibition of handling money and property. However, the main concern was probably a more proper pronunciation of the Pāli language during ordination. In the *Wat Pa Daeng Chronicle* (*WPDC* §44–53) there are several paragraphs that describe how to use correct Pāli words and grammar. The use of the Pāli language was certainly more difficult for the Tai people from Chiang Mai and Chiang Tung, in contrast to the Sinhalese. The text also corrects errors and incorrect use during recitations made by Lan Na monks of the Suan Dok school. The higher ordination to be a monk (*upasampadā*) has been immensely important throughout the entire Buddhist tradition. It is believed to go back to the time of the Buddha, with the idea that a proper ordination will make the aspirant a real disciple of the Buddha himself. A proper ordination must be conducted within the confines of a consecrated ordination boundary (*sīma*) with a minimum of ten, or five, fully ordained monks who have been ordained for at least five, or sometimes ten, years. The incorrect ordination was the main reason the monks who went to Lanka had to first be disrobed. They were not considered proper Buddha disciples by the Sinhalese monks and therefore had to be properly reordained in the Mahāvihāra monastic discipline.

From the *WPDC/TMWPD* we can, so far, understand the importance of strictly following the Buddhist monastic discipline and the importance of a proper ordination. There is much in the chronicles about monastic rules (*vinaya*) as well as the history of kings, monks, Buddha images, bodhi trees, rituals, and relics. However, there is not much about the teachings and doctrines (*dharma*). The burning of the palm leaves with the written names to resolve the dispute may indicate the importance of magical power in written texts and the ordination and a strict following of monastic rules. It is also possible, as we have seen, to understand the religious controversy as involved in a political struggle. From the chronicle, but also in the inscription, we can conclude that donations were an important act of merit-making.

The tradition of writing Pāli manuscripts in the Lan Na script started in the fifteenth century, probably connected with the arrival of the Pa Daeng order from Lanka. Before that time, the Buddhist culture in Lan Na was largely an oral one, despite being a society where writing was known (Veidlinger 2006, 57–58). However, this changed from the time of Tiloka (1441–1487) until that of Phaya Kaeo (Bilakapanattu) (1495–1526), a time that saw the creation of many literary works in Pāli and local languages. The Buddhist literature during this time expanded and reached a peak, with monk scholars producing learned Pāli texts of various genres. Writing was probably considered less important among the older city-dwelling order but played a more important role within the new Sinhalese order, inspired during the visit to Lanka (Veidlinger 2006, 85, 101–2). As already mentioned in chapter 5, literary texts written on palm-leaf manuscripts were collected in boxes and kept in libraries, often in separate elevated buildings in the monastery compound. During the time of Tiloka, a Buddhist council was held in 1477 at the Mahābodhi monastery (Wat Chet Yot) outside the town of Chiang Mai. This is remembered in Thailand as the Eighth Buddhist Council. It was a large gathering of learned monks, some most likely from Chiang Tung.

Many written copies of Pāli texts were kept in libraries largely as symbols of royal power rather than as scholarly tools (Veidlinger 2006, 101). The Buddhist culture was, to a large extent, mostly an oral culture, but texts were also read aloud at rituals. As we have seen during the controversy between the two Sinhalese orders, the written word was thought to contain magical power. Although the rulers donated written copies of Buddhist texts and libraries, the sponsoring of Buddha images, *chedis*, and relics was considered to be at least as important.

The close connection between Buddhism in Chiang Tung and the rest of Lan Na lasted for approximately 250 years. In 1558, the whole of Lan Na was invaded and conquered by troops from the rising Burmese Toungoo dynasty. As a result,

Chiang Tung strengthened its bond with areas to the west of the Salween River and in the Shan states. The Golden Age of Lan Na was over, and the production of Buddhist literature was no longer as it had been. Nevertheless, we must assume that much of local religious life continued for a long time as before. Then, in the eighteenth century, after the fall of Burmese suzerainty over Lan Na, there was a considerable cultural and economic revival with the production of many new and old manuscripts (Lagirarde 2012, 92).

The *Saṅgha* and the State

When Mangrai united Tai city-states in the thirteenth centuries, he adopted Buddhism from Haripuñjaya as a legitimation of universal power, in contrast to the locally grounded cults of territory spirits. Later rulers, from the time of the Chiang Mai ruler Kuena, who in 1369 invited the monk Sumana from the Udumbara order, sought legitimation from the universal Sinhalese Buddhist movement. The Buddhist worldview created a model by which rulers could aspire to a universal status as a righteous ruler that reached beyond the specific locality.

This Buddhist worldview was not a means to political ends; it was the end itself. However, it serendipitously united several small city-states into a kingdom with a shared Buddhist worldview. There are ideas about the righteous world ruler (*cakkavattin*) in early Buddhist texts, and the legend of the great Mauryan King Aśoka has been used as guidance during the long Buddhist history, inspiring rulers of Southeast Asia to follow his example as a generous and righteous monarch, a *cakkavattin*, a universal monarch, or world conqueror.[9] The ruler and the court had to establish hereditary leadership using the ruler's charismatic personality, establishing a Buddhist sacred landscape and presenting the ruler as a protector and promoter of the Buddhist religion. However, Lan Na rulers did not generally cultivate pretentions toward the status of a *devarāja* or god-king, as was the practice among the kings of Ayutthaya. The rulers took more local names because this northern part was never under Khmer influence (Sarassawadee 2005, 83).

When a new ruler in Chiang Tung assumed his role and became installed as *saopha*, the Tai Loi (Lua) people symbolically handed over to him the ownership and the rights of land, and the Buddhist *saṅgha* handed over to him the power to rule. When an old ruler died, the practice was to hand the state over to the Buddhist *saṅgha* until a new ruler could be installed and crowned (Scott and Hardiman 1901, 1:400; Scott 1932, 320). The royal court, the Buddhist *saṅgha*, and the Tai Loi (Lua) people had the responsibility of establishing continuity in the Mangrai dynasty. The installation, performed with the coronation ritual we saw in chapter 2, instituted the new monarch as a legitimate Buddhist ruler.

The historical writings of Chiang Tung distinguish several rulers as charismatic leaders and promoters of the Buddhist religion: Mahā Dhammikarājā, who ruled over a long and peaceful period in the seventeenth century and built Wat Suvaṇṇarāma; Sao Mahakhanan, who repopulated Chiang Tung, rebuilt the defensive wall, withstood several invasion attempts during the Chiang Tung War in the middle of the nineteenth century, and also offered one hundred monk robes and one hundred palm-leaf manuscripts to the *saṅgha*; Sao Intaleng, who ruled during most of the colonial times, sent monks to Lanka, and oversaw the casting of a replica of the Mahāmuni image; and Sao Sai Long (1947–1963), who received the Tooth Relic from Lanka and restored the *chedi* at Wat Chom Kham.

The reason Buddhism became so deeply rooted in Lan Na and elsewhere in Southeast Asia was partly that it filled an important geopolitical role. The rulers needed a unified worldview to claim their role as rulers and adopted Buddhism as a legitimation of universal power. But the Buddhist order was also needed by the state as support. We can read in the old chronicles how the early rulers of Chiang Tung and other city-states in Lan Na used Buddhism to legitimize themselves. The rulers sponsored Buddhist monasteries and built many religious buildings for both religious and worldly prestige and legitimacy. They built *chedis*, redistributed relics, donated robes, sponsored the production of Buddha images and literature, and sent monks far away to Buddhist countries. Without the interdependence between the *saṅgha* and the state, we would not have such a rich Buddhist culture as we have in Chiang Tung. Donald K. Swearer has described this relationship as "mutually symbiotic" (Swearer 1999, 194).

There are also many oral stories about how the Buddha, during his lifetime, visited places and predicted that certain areas would flourish under a Buddhist ruler. These stories recount how Chiang Tung and other places in Southeast Asia would become Buddhist domains and therefore gain the interest of the rulers. Buddhist monks traveled between different cities and monasteries across Lan Na, creating a large network of contacts. Buddhism and Buddhist monks created a common culture and worldview. The presence of the Buddha in many city-states throughout Lan Na acted as a "cosmogonic event that creates an ordered, meaningful world" (Swearer 2004a, 157). The presence of the Buddha in legends about his visit to places, in relics, and in images, created a network of city-states as a Buddhist sacred landscape throughout Lan Na, in contrast to local territory spirits and the so-called uncivilized earthborn people. King Mangrai and later rulers needed a unified worldview to bring together all the different city-states in northern Southeast Asia.

Important in the reciprocal relationship between the Buddhist *saṅgha* and the political power of Chiang Tung was a Buddhist sacred landscape connecting places (*mueang*) in Lan Na with the Buddha and with the international Buddhism of Lanka, Bodhgaya, and elsewhere. Swearer (1987), McDaniel (2002), Prakong (2012), and others have demonstrated that local places in Lan Na nearly always are associated with Buddhist relics. According to Anne M. Blackburn, the Buddhist landscape "served the consolidation and projection of royal power within the context of local and regional competition" (Blackburn 2007). The role of place in Lan Na stories of images and relics may have been inspired by the sense of place found in stories about the Buddha arising from classical Pāli sources, such as the *Mahāparinibbāna Sutta* and the *Nidānakatā* of the *Jātkaṭṭhakathā* (Chiu 2015, 115; 2017, 85–87). John S. Strong (2004, 7) emphasizes that relics are extensions of the Buddha's biography. The Buddha's relics do not just recall events from his life but have adventures of their own.

Again, as seen in myths and memories, Chiang Tung was established as a Buddhist sacred landscape through an account of a visit by the Buddha himself, narrated in the *Chiang Tung Chronicle* (§12). The text states that the Buddha visited the lake where Chiang Tung later would be established. He stood on one of the hills, or islands, and made a prophecy that a sacred Buddhist city would be established at the site. He also left behind eight hairs from his head that were later enshrined in the golden *chedi* of Wat Chom Kham, which is still standing on a hill in Chiang Tung. The prophecy and the relic from the Buddha make the place a sacred landscape, with Buddhist sites as symbolic markers of authority for local rulers. This Buddhological geography, to use a term coined by Thongchai (1994, 22), with a sacred relic from the Buddha planted in the ground and enshrined in a sacred *chedi*, establishes an association between the Buddha, the place of Chiang Tung, and the ruler and the Khuen people. Or in the words of Angela S. Chiu, "the images in place are unifications of Buddha and place" (2017, 97). This sacralization of the place legitimizes Chiang Tung as a Buddhist sacred place—a Buddha-land.

At Wat Pa Daeng monastery, there is an inscription dated 1451 (*EHS* 19: IV/15–19) that gives us more information about Chiang Tung as a city-state in Lan Na and how the rulers legitimated themselves with relics of the Buddha. In the inscription, Wat Pa Daeng was still called Jayamantārāma, and it was less than three years after the new Pa Daeng order was established in Chiang Tung. The text tells that Saddhamma Rāja Cuḷāmaṇi ruled Chiang Tung starting in 1443 or 1444, but he left his duties as ruler to spend one year as a monk. He died in 1449 and was succeeded by his son. The ruler of Chiang Mai, King Tiloka, donated relics of the Buddha to Chiang Tung, which were preserved together with the remains of the ruler. Thus, Rāja Cuḷāmaṇi was buried together with the Buddha in a casket made by his widow Siridīghā (Griswold and Prasert Na Nagara 1978, 72, 82). This episode speaks to the close connection between Chiang Tung and Chiang Mai at the time of King Tiloka, who actively supported the Wat Pa Daeng order. It also tells of a powerful and pious woman at the court of Chiang Tung, Queen Siridīghā, who carried out religious acts, such as reconstructing a monastery and creating an ordination hall (*bot*). This inscription is one of the few instances where a woman's legacy is preserved in the early history of Southeast Asia.

At the same time that the Buddhist ruler King Mindon (reigned 1853–1878) of Mandalay was the main protector of Buddhism for the whole of the Koungbang dynasty, the ruler of Chiang Tung was the protector of Buddhism in the territory he ruled. Chiang Tung was a vassal state and had to send tributes to the king of Mandalay, but as long as the ruler was loyal to the greater king, he could govern his territory and strengthen his authority as a righteous Buddhist protector.

Rulers in Buddhist kingdoms were devoted Buddhists. The *Wat Pa Daeng Chronicle* describes that in the middle of the fifteenth century, the Chiang Tung ruler went to the monastery every year to donate robes to the monks at the *kaṭhina* celebration (*WPDC* §106). Wat Pa Daeng was a large monastery at that time, with two hundred monks and novices who needed new robes. The chronicle also describes in the same paragraph that the ruler spent every new and full moon at the monastery sleeping at night in the assembly hall and observing the eight *sīlas*. We do not know details, but he was probably only dressed in white, sleeping together with the ordinary lay devotees.

Still during British colonial rule, the local ruler protected Buddhism and as a consequence legitimized himself as the ruler. Sao Intaleng functioned in such a manner during the colonial period. First, Intaleng sponsored the casting of a replica of one of the most venerated and famous sculptures in Burma, the Mahāmuni Buddha. The original Mahāmuni Buddha image came from Arakan (Rakhine State), and the tradition places the construction as far back as the lifetime of the Buddha. Historical documents date the Mahāmuni image to the fifth century, when a statue was installed as a royal shrine of one of the early kings of Arakan. The image has been highly venerated throughout Burmese Buddhist history, and many kings have attacked Arakan to take the Mahāmuni Buddha. King Bodawpaya invaded Arakan in 1784 and brought the image to his new capital in Amarapura, on the outskirts of present-day Mandalay. This highly venerated Buddha image captivated Sao Intaleng so much that he commissioned a replica to be cast in 1920 and sent officials to Mandalay to oversee the casting. The image was thereafter brought in pieces to Chiang Tung by boat and a bullock cart. In Chiang Tung, the image was installed in a temporary building until 1926, when it was finally installed in Wat Phra Sao Luang, a temple built close to the palace solely to house the image. (There will be more about this Mahāmuni Buddha later in this chapter.)

In a second example of royal protection of Buddhism, Sao Intaleng sent monks on a pilgrimage to British Ceylon to pay homage to the so-called Tooth Relic and to study sacred Buddhist texts. As far back as the fourteenth and fifteenth centuries, religious travelers had gone to the island of Lanka, but at that time the trip went through Chiang Mai, Sukhothai, and Martaban. This time, the religious trip started in Chiang Tung in December 1929 with mules, heading over the mountains and across the Salween River. Cars were waiting on the other side of the Salween to take the travelers to Taunggyi. At Taunggyi, they got medical examinations and the documents for the journey. The final trip down to Yangon was by car and train. It was politically impossible during colonial times to take the easiest way down to the sea, from Chiang Tung through Chiang Mai, down to Martaban, as monks had done in the fifteenth century. In the *sanad*, it was strictly stated that the ruler "shall abstain from communication with states outside British India" (Mangrai 1965, xxxvi)—therefore they had to take the more difficult route. At the time the island of Lanka was a British Crown colony, Ceylon, so it was relatively easy to visit for the travel group from Chiang Tung.

Thirteen monks from Chiang Tung left Yangon in January 1930 on a ship, sailing for two weeks to the island. Together with the monks, Sao Intaleng had sent a guide and interpreter named Thiem Khek, who wrote a poem about his memories of the trip. Because of lack of resources, the travelers had to stay on the deck the whole journey, and according to the poem, they were uncomfortable: "On the ship, the atmosphere was very gloomy. Those who had means were happier than us" (Peltier 2012). On Lanka the governor welcomed them and allowed them to make a pilgrimage to the Tooth Relic, the Jetavana stupa, Abhaya Giri, Dambulla, and the Thuparama stupa before they returned to the capital, Colombo. They shared the merit they received through the pilgrimage with their families, teachers, and the ruler of Chiang Tung (Peltier 2012, 67). On their way home, they stayed in Yangon for seven days and visited Shwedagon and the Mahāmuni Buddha image.

Sao Intaleng was fifty-five years old when the monks made their trip, and we can speculate that he sponsored the trip for his own merit. He died five years later, in 1935. The poet Noi Bunyao rewrote the poem into a *māt* poem in 1938, the year after the assassination of Sao Kawng Tai, the successor of Sao Intaleng. To recite this *māt* poem at religious ceremonies during the troublesome days after the assassination of the ruler and protector of Buddhism was probably a way to remember the more glorious days of the leader's rule. The awareness of Buddhism in Chiang Tung as part of a universal Buddhism, with its connection to Lan Na and Sinhalese traditions, still is important for people in Chiang Tung today.

Buddhism between Borders

Buddhism from Lan Na has sometimes been called Yuan Buddhism, which comes from the ethnic term "Tai Yuan" for the majority of people living in Northern Thailand. The term "Yuan Buddhism" was first coined by the missionary William Dodd in his book *The Tai Race* ([1923] 1996). Later, it was used by anthropologists like Keyes (1971) and Cohen (2001). This term has been questioned by Akiko Iijima (2009) and Sean Ashley (2013), as it has never been used by the local people, and they believe it is an invention by Western missionaries and academics.[10] I believe that a geo-ethnic demarcation can be useful as a working term, but in that case, "Yuan-Khuen-Lue Buddhism" would be better.

Buddhist traditions constantly underwent transformation and, as in all other religions, became adopted in local traditions and practices. Chiang Tung is no exception; tradition and change, generation to generation, transformed the religious tradition of the Tai Khuen people. Religious traditions from the ancient monsoon culture as well as Buddhism adopted from the tradition of Lan Na and the island of Lanka are entwined into the religious worldview of contemporary Chiang Tung. As we have seen, a long and turbulent history, with wars, forced relocations, and hardships, separated Chiang Tung from the rest of Lan Na, even before the colonial times, which split Lan Na with national borders. Chiang Tung became part of Burma/Myanmar, Chiang Rung in the north was incorporated into China, and the rest of Lan Na became a part of the national state of Siam/Thailand. This section highlights the effect of these political shifts on Buddhism and looks at what happens when a traditional religious culture becomes divided by national borders.

The Buddhist culture of today's Chiang Tung is connected to the local history. It is a continuation of the historic Lan Na Buddhist tradition, with roots in the Sinhalese Buddhism established in the fourteenth century. Myths and memories about the Buddha predicting that there would come a king who would build a prosperous Buddhist city established a connection between the local place and Buddhist beliefs and practices. Chiang Tung, as a Buddhist sacred landscape, connects local identity with religious identity.

Chiang Tung has an exclusive, independent Buddhist *saṅgha*, in practice not reliant on the Burmese government or other governments. All monks in Chiang Tung belong to one of two of the nine officially recognized monastic orders (*nikāya*) of Myanmar: either Sudhamma (Thudhamma) Nikāya or Shwegiyn Nikāya. According to official documentation by the State Sangha Maha Nayaka Committee, in 2016 there were 10,384 monks belonging to Sudhamma Nikāya and 872 monks belonging to Shwegiyn Nikāya in the Eastern Shan State.[11] Altogether there were more than eleven thousand monks in the Eastern Shan State.

Most of them were Khuen monks, but an unknown number must have been Western Shan (Tai Yai) and Burmese monks. In practice the Buddhist monasteries in Chiang Tung are more or less independent and without official government control. It is quite possible to speak about an unofficial Chiang Tung monastic order because the monastic practice belongs to the tradition from Lan Na, not from Myanmar.

The particularity of Buddhism in Chiang Tung is characterized in brief by a decentralized and independent Buddhist *saṅgha*, a hierarchy built on seniority, an old Buddhist calendar, Buddhist rituals and literature written in the *tham* script and recited in Pāli and Khuen language, a tradition of charismatic holy monks, and a specific Buddhist visual and material culture. This traditional Buddhism is an important identity marker for the people living in Chiang Tung. It connects Buddhism with the local history of Chiang Tung by creating a Buddhist sacred landscape believed to be predicted by the Buddha himself. It is not only for the Khuen people but also for most of the Tai Buddhist people living in Chiang Tung, including the Tai Loi (Lua), Tai Lue, Western Shan (Tai Yai), and Tai Nuea, who are more or less assimilated in the traditional Buddhist culture of Chiang Tung.

If we look at developments on the other side of the border in Northern Thailand, we see a strong nationalization of the Buddhist culture. The changes in Northern Thailand were drastic at the beginning of the twentieth century. Bangkok used educational and religious reforms to expand north and incorporate Lan Na into the national state of Siam. West of Siam, the British occupied Burma, and to the east the French colonized what they called Indochine Française. The Siamese government managed to stay free from Western colonizers, but they embraced a colonial policy themselves against the north. With foreign powers on both sides of Siam, the rulers in Bangkok became afraid that the colonial powers would take the north. Ratanaporn Sethakul argues that "Western colonialism was a catalyst for the full colonisation of the North into Siam" (Ratanaporn 2018, 81). This process to incorporate the north into Siam took place over several decades, starting with the Chiang Mai Treaty of 1874, and it has been described by many scholars, such as Keyes (1971), Swearer (1999), Bowie (2017), and Ratanaporn (2018).

In Bangkok, authorities realized that political centralization was not enough to forge national unity. By imposing the Sangha Administration Act of 1902, they standardized the *saṅgha* and incorporated Lan Na into the national *saṅgha* under direct control of the state (Ratanaporn 2018, 84). Without controlling the *saṅgha*, King Chulalongkorn could not control the provinces. Cholalongkorn's half brother Prince Wichirayan was the main architect of the changes. The Sangha Administration Act brought the *saṅgha* from all parts of the kingdom under a single hierarchy, with the Council of Elders (Mahathera Samakhom) at the helm. Officially, the Council of Elders was to act as adviser to the king in all affairs concerning the religion, administration, and support of the *saṅgha*.

The purpose of the Sangha Administration Act of 1902 lay in the creation of the Council of Elders, which expanded the hierarchical structure of the *saṅgha* and included every village and monastery in the kingdom. Furthermore, it brought the *saṅgha* into a program of national integration, steered by Bangkok (Khammai Dhammasami 2018, 132, 143–44). The act also had a conscious educational policy to assimilate the people into Siamese culture and prevent children from being Christianized in the missionary schools (Ratanaporn 2018, 88). One circumstance that made the reforms difficult was the language differences. There were differences in pronunciation, vocabulary, and script between the Siamese Thai language and the Tai language spoken in the north. The Siamese Thai language had many more loan words from Pāli, Sanskrit, and Khmer than the northern Tai dialect of the Lan Na people. Therefore, northern monks were sent to Bangkok to study with the goal that they would bring new educational plans back to Lan Na (Ratanaporn 2018, 88). Recitation in regional dialects was discouraged, and reforms were made to normalize ritual chants in Pāli. In the 1940s, the government even authorized the burning of palm-leaf manuscripts written in the Lan Na (*tham*) script (Swearer 1999, 203). In summary, the Sangha Act of 1902 incorporated all monks in Siam into a national structure, established a hierarchical principle of authority with the Council of Elders at the top, and established a national system of clerical education. This colonization of the north brought every principality in the former Lan Na into the national state of Siam, except those that were considered outside Bangkok's control: Chiang Tung and Chiang Rung (Sipsong Panna), which at that time belonged to the British and the Chinese, respectively.

The unification and incorporation of Lan Na monasteries into a national *saṅgha* was not completely painless. Some charismatic monks from the north, such as Khruba Faihin (1832–1913) and Khruba Siwichai (1878–1939), resisted the new authorities. After Khruba Siwichai refused to obey them in 1935, he was sent to Bangkok and not allowed to return to the north until he signed a document affirming his willingness to abide by the regulations of the Central Thai *saṅgha*. Additionally, more than three hundred monks who were part of his lineage were disrobed (Bowie 2017, 29). Integrating Lan Na Buddhism into the national Thai *saṅgha*, starting with the Chiang Mai Treaty of 1874 and followed by the Sangha Act of 1902, can be seen as finished when Khruba Siwichai signed the document of affirmation in 1936. From that time, northern monks were under the control of the national ecclesiastic hierarchy of the Department of Religious Affairs, and the northern *sangha* became part of the Siamese *sangha* (Bowie 2017, 53).

At the same time that Lan Na Buddhism was integrated into the national Thai *sangha*, the British had conquered Burma, though the Shan States belonged to the Frontier Areas, still under British protection but ruled by the traditional *saopha* ruler. Unlike the authorities in Bangkok, the British did not interfere in religious affairs but let the local ruler continue as protector of the local Buddhist tradition. The Buddhist tradition in Chiang Tung was part of this same Lan Na Buddhist tradition that had more or less been destroyed, or at least transformed, by Bangkok authorities. However, in Chiang Tung the tradition survived, evolved, and preserved much of its traditional character. The separation of Chiang Tung from the rest of Lan Na had become a reality in the late eighteenth century when local leaders in Lan Na swore allegiance to the Siamese king and in the beginning of the nineteenth century when Sao Mahakhanan joined the Burmese in fighting against Kawila's forces from Chiang Mai. This separation was further strengthened during the colonial period with many restrictions on trade and cultural exchange. The exchange between Chiang Tung and the Shan states on the west side of the Salween River and with Burma was instead increasing, despite the distance between Mandalay and Taunggyi and Chiang Tung.

Sangha Organization

The rivalry between the two Sinhalese Buddhist orders is of no importance in the monasteries of today's Chiang Tung. The *sangha* was protected by the ruler before and during colonial times, but since the military coup of 1962, the *sangha* has had no protector. It tries to maintain independence from any outside power. Authority in the *sangha* comes from seniority in years since ordination, not from age or some standard monastic education system. According to Ratanaporn Sethakul, the traditional Lan Na *sangha* was an independent social institution "built on the basis of seniority, charismatic qualities, and lineage, i.e., the relations of teachers and ordained students" (Ratanaporn 2018, 84). This corresponds in many ways to the present state of the *sangha* in Chiang Tung.

At the head of Buddhism in Chiang Tung is a patriarch with the title *atyatham* (or *somdej atyatham*). He is the head of the Sangha Council and a guarantor of local traditions and customs for monasteries in Chiang Tung. All the monasteries in Chiang Tung are largely independent but have to follow decisions by the *atyatham* and the Sangha Council. The Sangha Council elects a new *atyatham* when the old one passes away. The present *atyatham* is old and resides in Wat Chiang Yuen since there is no head monastery in Chiang Tung. Therefore, when a new *atyatham* is elected, he will stay at the monastery where he presently lives.

Below the *atyatham*, seniority is also established according to the number of years since ordination. At the top is a category of monks called *khruba*, who are members of the Sangha Council. This is an official ecclesiastical title for monks who have been ordained for fifty years or more. The levels below are named *swamee* for those living as monk for forty years or more and *swati* after a monastic life of more than thirty years. Monks do not automatically enter a higher level. The proselyte has to be respected by the other members of that level, and between each level there is a rite of passage that every monk has to pass through. The ritual is performed in a temporary hut at the monastery, symbolizing that the monk leaves one level and enters a higher one. The monk enters the hut, and his parents or relatives pour sacred water over his body from two tubes connected to the hut, one decorated with silver and one with gold.

One important duty of the *atyatham* is to be the expert on the Chiang Tung Buddhist calendar. The monks of Chiang Tung are proud of their ancient calendar and believe it is much older than the calendars of neighboring peoples. It is the responsibility of the *atyatham* to make calculations for each new year and determine the dates of the full and new moon, along with all the Buddhist celebrations for the coming year. This calendar does not correspond to the Burmese Buddhist calendar but is believed to follow an old calendar from Lan Na times. Therefore, the full moon days do not always fall on the same days in Chiang Tung and the rest of Myanmar. In 2019, only full moon days in February, April, June, and August fell on the same day in Chiang Tung and the rest of Myanmar. The Chiang Tung calendar is unique and independent of outside authorities. Burmese local authorities in Chiang Tung have tried to persuade the *atyatham* to abandon the traditional calendar and follow the same Buddhist calendar as the rest of Myanmar, particularly to avoid different full moon days, but the present *atyatham* has completely deflected this effort.

Buddhist Charismatic Monks

The *ton bun* tradition of *khruba* monks is central in the religious tradition of Chiang Tung as well as in northern Thailand. The title *khruba* is also an official title in the hierarchal structure of the Chiang Tung *saṅgha*. In this context, *khruba* is a charismatic *ton bun* monk who has accumulated great merit (*bun*) and perfections (*barami*) in a past or present life.

As previously mentioned, the Chiang Mai monk Khruba Siwichai opposed the Bangkok hierarchy. Renowned for his asceticism and as a meditation master, Khruba Siwichai was very popular and gained much support. Even today, he is still worshipped by many at his shrine outside Chiang Mai, on the way up to Doi

Suthep. There are other present-day monks who are considered having similar reputations as Khruba Siwichai, with extraordinary powers as a *ton bun khruba*.

Ton bun can be translated as "person of merit" or "source of merit," and people make pilgrimages to such a person in hopes of being in his presence, to receive some of his merit. One of the most respected and adored monks who fit in this *ton bun* tradition is Khruba Bunchum. He was born a Thai citizen and ordained in the Thai monastic order but spent a long time in the Shan State and also served as an abbot in the Eastern Shan State (Amporn 2017, 191). His transnational characteristics make him popular among ethnic minorities, and he has a good reputation in Chiang Tung, which he regularly visits.

Khruba Bunchum has traveled extensively throughout the northern Mekong borderlands, building and renovating religious monuments and sharing merit with the laity. He is said to have gained his reputation as a *ton bun khruba* through moral living, ascetic practice, and meditation. Beginning in April 2010, he retreated for three years, three months, and three days of meditation in an isolated cave in Lampang Province in Northern Thailand, without seeing or talking to anyone (Amporn 2017, 202–8). Khruba Bunchum is probably considered one of the most venerable monks by the Tai Khuen as well as the Tai Loi (Lua). He has lived in the Eastern Shan State, very close to the borders of Laos and Thailand, though he spends most of his time in Northern Thailand. This doesn't prevent people from Chiang Tung from visiting him for merit donations. Border crossing is allowed for visitors to his place in Thailand, outside Chiang Saen. He receives more pilgrimage visitors than usual on his birthday in January. For a more detailed description of the *ton bun khruba* monks of the Lan Na Buddhist tradition see Cohen (2017).

Two of the prominent charismatic holy monks living in Chiang Tung do not entirely fit with the description of the *ton bun khruba* monks above. First, Sao Boon Tip is a Tai Loi (Lua) holy person living as a monk in the mountains about a one-hour drive from Chiang Tung. He is not regarded as a *khruba* and actually is not formally a monk. He has never been ordained, but he lives a life similar to that of a monk. He lives in his own temple compound close to Wat Zom Loi, a famous octagonal temple connected to the mythical history of the Tai Loi (Lua) people. As mentioned in the introduction, the indigenous Lua people are described as barbarous, uncivilized, and non-Buddhist, but also as the original landholders and therefore ritually superior to the Tai conquerors (Tanabe 2000, 298).

Sao Boon Tip was born in the mid-1950s, and at eighteen he decided to leave his worldly life and become a novice. He built a small hut beside a stream all by himself. Today, his temple still stands in the same place as his first hut. The temple is made out of merit donations from people, who regard him as a special holy person. Many people still come to make merit donations to him. No one calls him a *khruba*; we can call him a charismatic *ton bun* novice, but his life has some similarities to that of *khruba* monks. His reputation comes from his moral lifestyle and ascetic practice. He is vegetarian, and the answer he gives, when asked why he was never ordained as a monk, is that he only wanted to live a simple life, not be part of the Buddhist hierarchy. He considers the life he lives to be a missionary life.

He has not traveled transnationally to build or renovate temples, as most of the *khruba* monks do, but instead focuses on his own temple as well as educating the mountain people. He travels up in the mountains to remote villages and lets young boys follow him back to the temple and live there to study for two or three years. There are around fifty boys living in his monastery for education, taught by him and by visiting monks from the surrounding area. The young boys are from different ethnic groups, mainly Tai Loi (Lua), Enn, and Khuen, but also from non-Buddhist Wa and Akkha villages. Some come from faraway villages in the restricted area, away from the military's control. The travel by Sao Boon Tip to restricted areas has caused him trouble with military authorities, who are especially concerned about his contact with the non-Buddhist Wa people.

The second example of a charismatic holy monk, known as the "tiger monk," lives in Chiang Tung town at the Tiger Monastery, which has been renamed Wat Phra Singh. He is considered to possess supernatural powers, but his *khruba* title certainly belongs to the formal *saṅgha* hierarchy in Chiang Tung, indicating that he has been ordained for at least fifty years. He does not fit the description of a *ton bun khruba* monk, as he is not known for traveling and building *chedis* and other religious buildings. Instead, he is known for his supernatural powers. The tiger monk is said to bring good luck in business and to cure illnesses. To cure illnesses he uses several methods, such as astrology, smoke from pine trees, and the burning of sacred texts and diagrams inside hollow beeswax candles. In a case I observed, he put a woman in a trance on the floor. The woman had a balance disorder, and he located the root of the sickness in her head with the use of fire and embers. To cure her, he hit her several times with a knife on her neck, reading holy texts and massaging her head. He gave her some pine twigs to bring back home and instructed her daughter on how to blow pine smoke on her. Susan Conway (2014, 161–71) describes similar rituals performed by a Tai Yai monk living in Wat Tiyasathan north of Chiang Mai.

This tiger monk also is said to give protective power to people through a ritual that brings power through their clothes. There are two different magic beliefs in this ritual: the holy number nine, and the belief that power may be transferred from one object to another. I will briefly describe this ritual, which is carried out for fourteen or fifteen days between the new moon day and full moon day, for every morning until midday. The participants themselves are not present at the ritual. Instead, a couple of elderly women perform the actual service.

One part of this ritual involves transferring protective power from the Buddha and the monk to the non-present participants, using clothes as the link. Participant have to bring or send their clothes to the ritual, which is performed in a building next to the assembly hall. About twenty to thirty pyramidlike structures made of bamboo poles have been assembled in the building, and the women put all the clothes inside these pyramids early in the morning. A string combines the pyramids with a Buddha image. When the ritual starts, holy water is sprinkled on the clothes, and the monk recites sacred texts to infuse protective power in the clothes. Later, when people wear the clothes, they are thought to be protected. This ritual to infuse protective powers in clothes is similar to the one performed during the cult to the village spirit, and it also resembles the consecration rituals to install a new Buddha image. According to Donald K. Swearer (2004b, 96), "the chant becomes the medium through which the unseen reality of the Buddha (*dhammakāya*) is joined to the material reality of the image (*rūpakāya*)," which in this case is the clothes.[12]

One phase in the ritual includes placing fruits in nine magic squares. These squares are made on the floor with eight bamboo sticks, which are laid so that they form nine squares. Small baby fruits like pineapples and oranges are inserted into each of the different squares, depending on the day the participant was born. Terwiel described a similar ritual in Central Thailand, used when building a house. Various foods are placed in containers that have nine compartments. These containers are put in the most important foundation hole of the new house (Terwiel 2012, 175–76). The holy number nine relates to an ancient custom of the Indian subcontinent, exemplified by the nine planets, the nine plants, and the nine gems.

Buddhism and the Cult of Spirits

There has been a long-standing academic debate about the relationship between Buddhism and the cult of spirits, started in the 1970s between S. J. Tambiah (1970) and Melford E. Spiro (1978, 1982). Tambiah, from his anthropological research in northeast Thailand, treats religion as a living system, with Buddhist rituals and the cult of spirits linked in a single social structure (this is also my basic view). Spiro, on the other hand, discusses Buddhism in Burma as an ideological system. For him Buddhism and spirit cults are two poles representing two distinctive religions, where Buddhism takes priority over the spirit cults since the spirit cults have nothing to do with salvation, and Buddhism has nothing to do with mundane matters (Spiro 1978, 264–80).

Neither Buddhism nor the cult of spirits is in any way a pure and unchanged entity—that much is undeniable. Still, this study is about the cult of traditional territory spirits in Chiang Tung and its connection to Buddhist beliefs and practice. It does not include modern spirit-medium cults, nor does it involve detailed interviews with practitioners about how they view the difference between the Buddhist faith and the cult of various spirits. Instead, this section is a critical discussion mainly based on what I have experienced during my time in Chiang Tung, with a focus on some observations and discussions with monks and laypeople.

As previously discussed, the political geography of city-states has its origin in the monsoon climate and agricultural traditions of wet rice cultivation in the highland river valleys of Monsoon Asia. There is a mutual relationship in early Tai settlements between agriculture, the village community, and the cult of territory spirits. Nothing can be more local than the cult of the spirit of the place where people belong. When King Mangrai united Tai city-states in the thirteenth century, he adopted Buddhism as a legitimation of universal power, in contrast to the locally grounded cults of territory spirits. The Buddhist worldview created a model by which Mangrai could aspire to universal status as a righteous ruler who reached beyond a specific locality. But Buddhism was not adopted to political ends; it was the end itself. This Buddhist worldview was not intended as a means to political power, but it turned out to serve this role. It united several small city-states to a loosely connected kind of kingdom with a shared worldview, with *mueang* Chiang Mai as the most important city-state.

Instead of regarding the spirit cult as subordinated in the relation to Buddhist beliefs and practice, Holt (2009, 45) assumes that the spirit cult provided the categories and concept of power that were used on the popular level to interpret Buddhist higher truths in a manner understandable to the many. This is certainly true, although the exact way Buddhism became integrated with local people and the local cult of spirits is difficult to establish. The sacred landscape, with stories and a visual culture connecting local places with the power of the Buddha, most certainly had a significant role for establishing Buddhism among local people. The cult of local spirits had already made a kind of religious map, a patchwork of places connected to groups of peoples identified by village headmen related to the spirit of the earth. This patchwork was easily absorbed by a coming Buddhist community, and still today every village and block in Chiang Tung and its countryside has both a spirit shrine and a monastery. Angela S. Chui (2015, 109–13) shows how motifs, themes, and structures of Buddhist chronicles reflect the relationship of Buddha and place, which includes the process in which Buddhist forms and values were integrated by Lan Na people with their own interests and sense of the landscape.

Today, the cult of spirits is a living tradition, mainly maintained by elderly males, but Buddhism is the main religious belief for monks and laypeople alike. Aside from young adults, I have never met a Tai Khuen person who has questioned his or her Buddhist faith. People today participate in the cult of spirits at the same time that they are seriously practicing Buddhists. The spirit cults are not considered as a competing religious belief. Instead, it is a tradition engraved in the geopolitical organization of early Tai *mueang* settlements and a traditional way of relating to the natural environment.

In myths and memories from the *CTC*, there are indications that the spirits are the place and the soil themselves, because the spirit of the place would not allow the Chinese to settle down at the site that would become Chiang Tung. This does not match what local people have told me, but the beliefs might differ from village to village and person to person. As previously discussed, there is a much more common belief that the spirit of the village is identical to the first leader of the village and, all his descendants as headmen and ancestors of the village headman.

The nature and existence of territory spirits in relation to the Buddhist worldview of impermanence and the principle of karma may be a starting point in understanding the relationship between the spirit cult and Buddhism. The doctrine of impermanence (*anicca*) teaches that all things that arise from a cause are subject to dissolution, and the principle of cause and effect, karma (*kamma*), affects one's future in the current life as well as future lives. Included in the Buddhist worldview are devas, ghosts, and many other creatures that are, like all beings, trapped in *saṃsāra* and subject to the law of karma. Good moral actions lead to happiness in rebirth, and bad moral actions lead to suffering in rebirth. If the territory spirit is identical to the first headman of the village as well as all his descendants as headmen and ancestors of the village headman, it makes no sense that territory spirits can perform actions that affect their future and cause them to be reborn as another being. It is hard to imagine that territory spirits who are stuck in place are included in the doctrine of impermanence and the principle of karma, but they nevertheless appear to be. When I asked persistently, it was explained to me that territory spirits like *sao baan* and *sao mueang* are part of the Buddhist worldview, including *anicca* and *kamma*. But exactly which actions the spirits perform that affect their future was difficult to discern. This example illustrates that the ancient territory spirits have been involved in a kind of domestication in the Buddhist worldview. The presence of Buddhist monks on the second day of the annual offerings to the village spirit can also be seen as a kind of Buddhist legitimization of the spirit cult. During Songkran, Buddhism is likewise interacting to a lesser degree in connection with spirits at the festival, mainly when people collect sand at the river and build sand *chedis*. Also, when inviting the spirit frog, Buddhist suttas are recited.

The cult of the spirit of Chiang Tung (*sao mueang*) is performed three times a year: There is the annual offering during the ninth month, the offering at the Old Royal Market Day, and the offering at the Songkran festival. This reveals that the cult of the spirit of Chiang Tung is still a living tradition, especially if we compare these practices with those in Chiang Rung, Sipsong Panna, and Luang Prabang, Laos. The spirit cult of Chiang Rung totally disappeared during the socialist transformation of Chinese society, although household and village spirits survived. When the *mueang* was replaced by the commune, protection from the spirits was no longer needed (Tanabe 1988, 16–18; Casas 2023, 280). In Luang Prabang, the cult of the *sao mueang* also disappeared, or, according to Holt (2009), was replaced by Buddhist practice.

John Clifford Holt (2009, 2017) has made an interesting observation about the connection between the cult of spirits and Buddha images in Luang Prabang. He argues that the state and the *saṅgha* in Lan Xang, the ancient Lao kingdom, were related in a dynamic of mutual legitimation, excluding the spirit cult. He describes how the Phra Bang Buddha image replaced the spirit of Luang Prabang as the power of the state and as a palladium, or protector, of Lan Xang mandala, expressed during the New Year Songkran festival.[13] According to Holt (2017, 37–41), this happened in the sixteenth century when King Photisarat ordered the old shrine of the ancestral guardian deities of Luang Prabang to be destroyed and replaced with a monastery. This Wat Aham was built to honor the king's deceased royal parents and was where he enshrined the cremated remains of his father.[14]

This makes Holt assume that the cult of the Phra Bang Buddha image replaced the cult of the spirit. His main argument is that the significance of the Phra Bang image of the Buddha has been affected by the spirit cult. The relative lack of institutionalization of the spirit cult indicates its nebulous nature. Following Mus, Holt argues that the territorial sacred power of the spirit cult derives from the identification between the place and the group of people living there, "as a result of the group's experience of the place, of the events that had occurred for the group in relation to it" (Holt 2017, 19). The Lao people attached this territorial sacred power to the Phra Bang Buddha image, which then became the palladium of the Lan Xang kingdom. For the ruler and the people in sixteenth-century Luang Prabang, the active Buddha presence embodied within the Phra Bang image may therefore derive power from the place itself. In the word of Mus, he is the god of the soil.

The Songkran New Year festival in Luang Prabang is, according to Holt, a renewal of social and cosmic order. He argues that the king and his ritual duties have, in today's celebration, been replaced by the beauty queen, Miss Lao New Year. Her ritual duties are to perform the veneration of the Phra Bang image, formerly undertaken by the king. "She embodies the 'welfare of the community' for the following year, just as former kings were emblems of the welfare of their kingdoms" (Holt 2009, 222).

Is, or was, there a corresponding Buddha image in Chiang Tung with a similar role as the Phra Bang image? The simple answer is no. There is no similar Buddha image with an active presence of the Buddha's power embodied within the image. There is nothing that is considered a palladium of the Chiang Tung nation, with the possible exception of one Buddha image, the Mahāmuni image at Wat Phra Sao Luang (figure 5), which will be discussed below.

The intimate relationship the people of Chiang Tung have with the place and territory where they are living is very strong. There is a close relationship between the village, the spirit of the village, and all the villagers, but there is also a close relationship between the village, the village monastery, and all the villagers. Therefore, both the village monastery and the village spirit shrine stand as symbolic centers of the village. In a similar way, there is also a close relationship between the *mueang* Chiang Tung, the spirit of Chiang Tung (*sao mueang*), and all the citizens of Chiang Tung. But as the symbolic center of *mueang* Chiang Tung, the spirit *sao mueang* stands alone. There is no monastery, temple, or Buddha image that can be viewed as a symbolic center of Chiang Tung. There is no specific monastery for the Buddhist patriarch, *atyatham*. After he is elected, he will stay at the same monastery where he previously lived. Neither is there any monastery holding a Buddha image as a palladium of Chiang Tung, as we have seen in Luang Prabang. The *sao mueang* stands alone as the symbolic center of Chiang Tung.

There is one Buddhist building and an image that have some qualities that suggest they could be a symbolic center and a palladium of *mueang* Chiang Tung. As already mentioned, the Khuen ruler Sao Intaleng ordered Mandalay craft workers to cast a replica of the famous Mahāmuni image. The original Mahāmuni image is special because it is believed to have been cast by the god Indra at Dhanyawaddy in Arakan during the lifetime of the Buddha, and it was brought to Amarapura in present-day Mandalay by the Konbaung king Bodawpaya after his invasion of Arakan in 1784. It is believed that the image is a true and exact likeness of the Buddha and that the Buddha breathed life into it. Therefore, the image has been highly venerated throughout Burmese Buddhist history, and many kings wanted it to claim legitimacy. Today the original Mahāmuni image in Mandalay gets a daily face washing at 4 a.m. while many devotees watch. For these reasons, the Mahāmuni image seems to have qualities similar to those of the Phra Bang image.

Sao Intaleng's initiative to make and install this replica may have been an attempt to make a Buddhist symbolic center for the *mueang*, with himself as the ruler. This is suggested in that he installed the replica not in one of the many monasteries of Chiang Tung but in a newly built temple close to the royal palace. Today, this is generally not considered a place for the Khuen people because the Burmese military controls the image. The possible royal connection of the Mahāmuni replica was, of course, ended by the military coup of 1962, if not earlier. But from 1996, when the Triangle Region Command was established in Chiang Tung, with its first commander Thein Sein, the military took control of the image, seizing symbolic power over it with a baldachin on top of the head with the names of the military commander and his wife. Everyone who enters and bows to the Buddha image also bows in front of the military power. Therefore, this image could never be considered as having a similar ritualistic role for the Khuen people as the Phra Bang image has for the Lao people. Today, in daily life, it is mostly Burmese people who venerate the Chiang Tung replica of the Mahāmuni image. Therefore, in the religious culture of Chiang Tung, we must turn away from Buddha images and instead focus on the role the spirit of Chiang Tung, *sao mueang*, has in the Songkran festival, which we will do in the next chapter.

Before turning to the Songkran festival, however, we must distinguish between the view of a Buddha image as a reminder of the Buddha and a Buddha image as the active presence of the Buddha's power embodied within the image. This distinction is at the heart of the Buddha as a palladium of a kingdom. According to Strong (2004, 20) and Collins (1998, 246–48), statues of the Buddha are thought to mediate the presence of the Buddha only if they contain a relic. This doctrinal interpretation does not match with practices found from early Indian traditions nor with contemporary practices in Southeast Asia. See Gregory Schopen (1997), who uses architectural and epigraphic materials to demonstrate the importance of what monks, nuns, and laypeople actually did and demonstrates the difference between early practice and precept. Cults of relics, stupas, and images of the Buddha by practiced laypersons and monks alike are well established, and the interpretations of these practices are dependent on historical situations and contexts.

What the presence of the Buddha means has different interpretations from many scholars of Buddhism. From the Theravāda world, there are special rituals to consecrate a new Buddha image when it is to be installed in a monastery. It was believed that if the rituals were performed correctly, the new image would take on the qualities of earlier statues, which together formed an unbroken chain back to the Buddha himself (Stratton 2004, xx). These consecration ceremonies (*buddhābhiseka*) seem to imply that the image is brought to life with an imagined divine presence of the Buddha.[15] Besides the Phra Bang image, there is in

Buddhist history several Buddha images that are considered to have a divine presence and have been used to claim political legitimacy. Most well-known are the Emerald Buddha (Phra Keo) of Bangkok and the Sihing Buddha of Chiang Mai, but there are also some lesser-known images linked to the Champassak Royal House in Laos (Baird 2017).

Today in the Theravāda world, it is normal to take active part in ritual practice without accepting a traditional, conservative belief system. Catherine Bell sees "ritual as a particularly effective means of mediating tradition and change, that is, as a medium for appropriating some changes while maintaining a sense of cultural continuity" (Bell 1997, 251). Holt expresses a similar viewpoint: "It is important to understand that ritual can house the participation of a great array of people who ascribe to varying sets of convictions and a multiplicity of perspectives" (Holt 2017, 4). Rituals are not something to think about but a continuity and tradition to follow, decreed by the ancestors. The performance of ritual action is often unrelated to the ancient original significance. This applies to the consecration ritual to open the eyes of the Buddha as well as the Songkran performance explored in the next chapter. The monks and laypersons in Chiang Tung who participate in these rituals may or may not believe that a divine presence of the Buddha is in the image. I have been told by monks that images of the Buddha are only reminders, although these consecration rituals are still important. For Jonathan Z. Smith a ritual is "a process of marking interest" and "an assertion of difference" between the way things are and the way things ought to be (Smith 1987, 103, 109). Opening the Buddha's eyes marks something out of ordinary life.

People in Chiang Tung, as elsewhere, are individuals and have different opinions. Religious traditions are constantly evolving and responding to social, economic, and political change, but at the same time, rituals preserve traditions. They are important for identity and a sense of belonging, or they can be performed just for fun. The Buddhist consecration rituals to bring to life the divine presence of the Buddha have established continuity within the Buddhist tradition, similar to the ordination tradition. Today, this cultural continuity has survived modern reinterpretations of Buddhism, and it is not seen as contradictory to perform these rituals seriously yet only see the Buddha images as reminders.

For more than seven hundred years, the traditions of Buddhism in Chiang Tung have been in a continuous process of transformation. Buddhism is in the heart of Khuen culture, blended with indigenous traditions from the ancient culture of Monsoon Asia. The reciprocity between the villagers and the village monastery, with food given to the monastery and knowledge and merits given back to the villagers, occurs in the sacred space of monasteries, the centers of every village.

At the center of every village is also a spirit shrine, devoted to the spirit of the village. It witnesses the ancient pre-Buddhist tradition cult of the spirit of the earth and a place of belonging, a tradition closely connected to agriculture and wet rice irrigation. The cults of spirits are hierarchical in structure and correspond to a political hierarchy, with the spirit of Chiang Tung considered higher and more important than all the village spirits, just as the ruler is considered above all the village headmen.

The reason Buddhism became so deeply rooted in Lan Na and elsewhere in Southeast Asia was partly that it filled an important geopolitical role. The local cult of territory spirits was not enough to hold together a socially complex and expanding society. The Indic Hindu-Buddhist worldview was universal, in contrast to the locally grounded territory cult. The Buddhist worldview created a model by which Lan Na rulers could aspire to a universal status as a righteous ruler, a *cakkavattin*, a status that reached beyond their specific locality. It was not means to political ends; it was the end itself. However, this model did, in fact, unite several small city-states, forming a kingdom with a shared Buddhist worldview. The ruler had to establish a hereditary leadership with his charismatic personality to create a Buddhist sacred landscape and be a protector and promoter of the Buddhist religion. Sao Intaleng was successful with this model; he ruled during most of the colonial times, sent monks to Lanka, and directed the casting of a replica of the Mahāmuni image.

The Buddhist sacred landscape, with stories and visual culture connecting local places with the power of the Buddha, has had a significant role in establishing Buddhism among local people. Even before Buddhism entered the scene, a kind of religious map, a patchwork of places connected to groups of peoples and local spirits, was already in place. This patchwork was easily absorbed by the incoming Buddhist community, and still today, in the center of every village in Chiang Tung and its countryside stand both a spirit shrine and a monastery.

It is surprising that Lan Na Buddhism with its *tham* script has been maintained to such a degree during the long and troublesome history of Chiang Tung. Communication with Chiang Mai was difficult to maintain for many years. At the turn of the nineteenth century, large parts of the population, together with the ruler and his court, were relocated to Chiang Mai, and Sao Mahakhanan had to repopulate Chiang Tung. During the Chiang Tung Wars in the middle of the nineteenth century, troops from Siam and Lan Na tried to conquer Chiang Tung but failed. Later at the colonial times, the British did not allow cross-border communication or trade, and the border to Siam was almost completely closed. Exchange increased instead with the Shan states west of the Salween River. In chapter 4 we saw how the military used Burmese visual culture to attempt to include Chiang Tung more centrally in the history of the Burmese dynasties, for example with the standing Buddha image with an index finger pointing at the town. Also noted was the resistance to the military's effort: it is considered downright dangerous to gaze in this Buddha's face. The replica of the Mahāmuni image sponsored by the ruler Sao Intaleng and installed close to his palace has today very little significance for the Khuen people because it is under the symbolic dominance of the Burmese military. This replica of the Mahāmuni image is not regarded as a palladium for *mueang* Chiang Tung, nor are any other images, leaving the whole nation of Chiang Tung without a main monastery and image.

This traditional Buddhist culture of Chiang Tung has an unofficial, independent Buddhist *saṅgha*, in practice not reliant on the Burmese government, although all monks belong to one of the officially recognized monastic orders of Myanmar. In practice, the Buddhist monasteries in Chiang Tung are more or less independent, with an elected Buddhist patriarch, *atyatham*, a Sangha Council, and independent monasteries. This Buddhism for the Khuen people also includes the Tai Loi (Lua), Tai Lue, Western Shan (Tai Yai), and Tai Nuea peoples who live in Chiang Tung and its countryside. Chiang Tung Buddhist culture has its roots in Lan Na and the tradition of Sinhalese Buddhism and is characterized by decentralized village monasteries, a hierarchy built on seniority, an old Buddhist calendar, Buddhist rituals and literature written in the *tham* script and recited in the Pāli and Khuen languages, a tradition of charismatic holy monks, and a specific Buddhist visual culture. This culture connects Buddhism with the local history of Chiang Tung by creating a Buddhist sacred landscape believed to be predicted by the Buddha himself. All the hardships that afflicted Chiang Tung as a borderland between more powerful neighbors left deep traces in the culture and religion of Chiang Tung. It is remarkable how well the religious culture has been preserved throughout the continuous process of both transformation and maintaining tradition. At the same time the culture of Chiang Tung has developed its own individuality and distinctiveness.

7
SONGKRAN FESTIVAL

> What we call our data are really our own constructions of other people's constructions of what they and their compatriots are up to.
> —Clifford Geertz, *Thick Description*, 1973

By looking at the history, the culture, and the religious background of Chiang Tung and the surrounding regions in the previous chapters, we have explored the larger context in which the Songkran festival takes place. This chapter brings the previous information together with a detailed description and analysis of the festival itself. The cult of spirits and the indigenous Tai Loi (Lua) people have a prominent place in the festival, along with the Songkran drum of luck and prosperity, a frog made with mud and clay down at the river, and a statue of the god Indra.

As mentioned in the introduction, I attended the Songkran festival in Chiang Tung for the first time in 2011. It was an amazing event that sparked my interest in uncovering its secrets and mysteries. Even on my first visit, I sensed that the festival somehow was connected with the origin and history of Chiang Tung. Since that visit, I have attended Songkran several times, and each time I discover something new. To understand the rituals of the festival, it is important to examine its connection to the ancient monsoon culture, the myths and memories from Chiang Tung, and the relationship between Tai Khuen and Tai Loi (Lua).

April 13 and 14 are the two main days of the Songkran festival, which finishes with a huge procession. These days are followed by one or two days devoted to Buddhist veneration. Songkran is a ceremony, but it is difficult to categorize it with any certainty. Is it a religious ceremony, a holiday festival, or a theater performance? The closest is what Milton Singer (1972, 71) called a cultural performance because it is somewhere between a staged play, community theater, a festival, and a religious ritual or ceremony. Singer writes, "I shall call these things 'cultural performances,' because they include what we in the West usually call by that name—for example, plays, concerts, and lectures. But they include also prayers, ritual readings and recitations, rites and ceremonies, festivals, and all those things we usually classify under religion and ritual rather than with the cultural and artistic" (71). Many different things happen at the Songkran, and I felt as Singer did when he says, "I do not mean that I could, even with the help of interpreters, always understand everything that went on at one of these performances or appreciate their functions in the total life of the community" (71). My own account is an interpretation, involving layer after layer of information, and as Clifford Geertz put it in his famous essay, *Thick Description*, "What we call our data are really our own constructions of other people's constructions of what they and their compatriots are up to" (Geertz 1973, 9).

Songkran in Southeast Asia

The Songkran festival is celebrated in April all over Southeast Asia, and splashing water is at the center of it. Songkran marks the traditional New Year, with water as a symbol of washing away all that is bad. The month of April is in the middle of the hot season, when fields and small streams dry up. People await the rain to come. During the festival, a common ritual in Thailand and Laos is to take out Buddha images from the temples for ritual bathing. Sometimes, people carry them around the towns in order to allow everyone else to take part in the ritual bathing to receive merit. Richard Davis states, "In all these situations, water is used to *transmit* something: it carries away dirt, pollution and evil influences; it conveys the power of magic spells and Buddhist chants; it communicates aggressive and sexual impulses in the water throwing; and it conveys the good intentions of the host in welcoming a guest" (Davis 1984, 118).

The Holi festival, held in the spring in India, has many similarities with Songkran. Normally prohibited behavior is allowed. During this festival, people also drench each other with water as well as with colored powder. Holi, like Songkran, is a New Year festival at which the old year is destroyed and a new year is welcomed. With these similarities, it may appear that Songkran has its roots in the Holi festival of India, but it is more likely that similar climates and environments are behind the similar New Year festivals in South and Southeast Asia.

Songkran is also called Paveni Pi Mai (tradition of New Year), and according to Sommai Premchit and Amphay Doré, "it is the oldest and probably most primitive of all" (Sommai and Doré 1992, 175). Sommai and Doré suggest that it might "date from proto- or even pre-historic period" (39), and they state that "the Pi Mai festival intended to reenact the early high female status and to help the renewal of the nature through ritual sexual intercourse" (175). Sommai and Doré regard Songkran as a *cycle of nature* that aims at celebrating and participating in nature's renewal.[1] Thus it is likely just as old as or, most likely, much older than Indian influences in Southeast Asia.

Phya Anuman Rajadhorn (1953) describes the traditional celebration of Songkran in Thailand as a four-day period when the sun enters the sign of Aries, past midnight on April 13. On the eve of Songkran, April 12, people clean their houses and burn all the refuse. He continues, saying that anything bad belonging to the old year will be unlucky for the owner if left and carried into the coming New Year. On the afternoon of April 13 there is a bathing ceremony for Buddha images, and the abbot of the village monastery is also bathed. Anuman Rajadhorn describes the traditional water-throwing as quite different compared to today's celebrations. He states that younger people paid respect to elders by pouring scented water into the palms of their hands. In earlier days, he says, young people helped the elderly take an actual bath, change their old clothing, and put on new clothes that the young people presented to them. Today, the Songkran festival in many parts of Thailand is like a party for young people, with drinking, dancing, and intensive water splashing.

Anuman Rajadhorn also says that in some parts of the country, the guardian spirits of the village and town receive offerings on Songkran days, which he believes are reminiscences or traces of ancestor and animistic worship (Anuman 1953, 20-21). In connection to the Songkran festival, people build sand pagodas for making merit. Inside, they put a coin or a leaf from a bodhi tree. The pagoda is decorated with flags and banners and sprinkled with scented water. These sand pagodas are often built at the monastery area, but people who live near riverbanks build sand pagodas near the water with the belief that their sins will be transferred to the sand and washed away by the running stream.

The New Year festival in Burma/Myanmar is called Thingyan. As in Thailand and Laos, it is celebrated in April and includes water splashing. In the late nineteenth century, J. George Scott described how royal astrologers in Mandalay had to calculate at what time the *nat* king Thagyamin would descend upon the earth and the New Year's festival would begin. This always occurred sometime between the ninth and twelfth of April (Scott [1910] 1989, 347–55). Thagyamin is the highest-ranking *nat* (spirit) in traditional Burmese beliefs and is derived from the Hindu god Indra, called Sakka (Sanskrit: Śakra) in Buddhism. In Buddhist mythology Sakka is believed to be the king of the gods who resides in Tāvatiṃsa heaven. Today, Thingyan is a big party filled with young people drinking, dancing, and splashing water on one another.

The celebration of Songkran is much the same in Laos as in Thailand, with the exception of a very special ritual festival in the former royal city of Luang

Prabang. It has many similarities with the Songkran festival in Chiang Tung, but, as mentioned in chapter 6, the main focus is on the Phra Bang Buddha image, the palladium of Luang Prabang. Water throwing and its importance as a symbol of fertility is clear, but the cult also focuses on the Thevada Luang, the spirits and semihuman mythical ancestors who are believed to have once prepared the ground for the ancient kingdom. These mythical ancestors are represented during Songkran festivities with a ritual dance by three characters, the mythical grandparents (grandfather and grandmother Nyeu) and a long-nosed lion. The political contract between the Tai Khuen people and the earthborn Tai Loi (Lua) in Chiang Tung also has its counterpart in Luang Prabang. The opposition between the Tai-Lao and the Mon-Khmer people, the Khamu/Kasak, is played out in an annual ritual game similar to hockey, which the Lao always win (Aijmer 1979, 739; Stuart-Fox 1998, 51). According to Ing-Britt Trankell (1999, 193–94, 206), "the New Year ceremonies were dedicated to the ritual confirmation of the political dominance by the Lao royalty over the aboriginal inhabitants of the surrounding areas, and issues of ethnicity were, and are still, therefore dramatically displayed during the ritual." She adds that in Laos today, the role of ethnic minorities has changed from one of serfs for the royals to a position of national citizens.

There is one very central ritual in Luang Prabang that is absent in Chiang Tung: the lustration of the Phra Bang Buddha image by Miss Lao New Year. As mentioned in chapter 6, Holt (2009, 222) demonstrated that Miss Lao New Year now has the role that the king formerly held in the Songkran rituals, representing the welfare of the community for the following year. Holt (222) states that the Phra Bang Buddha image functioned as an emblem, or a palladium, for Luang Prabang and the Lan Xang kingdom, and today Miss Lao New Year also represents the Lao national state. However, as we have seen, there is no Buddha image that serves as legitimacy and power to the ruler of Chiang Tung. In Chiang Mai, however, the Phra Sihing Buddha image is taken out on the streets for veneration by the local people during the Songkran festival.

To my knowledge, we have records of only three early witnesses from the Songkran celebration in Chiang Tung. They are all from colonial times and give some important insight into the Songkran. The first is from J. George Scott, who witnessed a Songkran procession during his visit in the late nineteenth century, shortly after the British incorporated Chiang Tung in their empire. We do not know exactly what year he was there, but it was somewhere between 1890, when the British took control, and 1900, when Scott published his work *Gazetteer of Upper Burma and the Shan States*. The other two accounts are from the early twentieth century, during the colonial period when Sao Intaleng was the local ruler. One is from the Presbyterian missionary William Clifton Dodd and his wife, who visited Chiang Tung around 1913. The other is from Captain C. M. Enriquez, who visited Chiang Tung in 1915. They were all invited to the palace to celebrate Songkran together with the ruler.

Scott describes the procession down to the river, where an "indecent figure is paraded and obscene antics indulged in all along the route" (Scott and Hardiman 1901, 1:440). He also mentions that the spirit in the shape of a frog is thrown in the river and that the feast is held every year because it is essential for public welfare.

The festival activities are most vividly described by the Dodds, who recount the intense water splashing they encountered in the streets of Chiang Tung: "The custom seems to be universal among all the Tai, of throwing water at that time. But never have we seen it carried to such an extent as among the Kün" (Dodd [1923] 1996, 203). They state that people came out of doorways and corners with cups of cold water and squirt guns. Most of the descriptions from the Dodds, however, were of what they saw inside the palace, not out on the streets. They were invited to the palace by Sao Intaleng, together with representatives from all the eighty-six districts of the Chiang Tung state. Twice a year, these eighty-six representatives were invited to visit the ruler, and Songkran was one of these two days. Therefore there must have been more than one hundred people in the big assembly hall, when, after one hour of obeisance and offerings made by the officials, the ruler went out and changed from his state robes. He returned dressed in his everyday clothes as the great wooden doors were closed, with a Sikh guardian stationed at each one. Big jars of water with silver bowls were placed inside the hall at each of the tall pillars. For the two foreigners, there was nothing to do but join the water splashing: "High carnival followed, shrieks and screams of laughter and running to and fro, pursued by the dignitaries of the palace, the court, and the eighty-six districts all anxious to pour water over us. They did not think they had treated us with proper respect if they had failed to assist in performing this rite in our behalf" (Dodd [1923] 1996, 203).

Enriquez was also invited by Sao Intaleng to celebrate Songkran in the palace when he visited Chiang Tung in 1915. His description of what happened during the celebration does not include the same level of detail as that of the Dodds, but we have no reason to question that he had a similar experience to theirs. He states that "some people say that water is thrown about to cool the World, because the Thagya Min descends from his Heaven at this parched season, to succor the Earth" (Enriquez 1918, 27). Of special interest is his description of a procession that goes through the town, which he had the opportunity to witness from the palace garden. This procession, which he calls *Thin-chyan*, "passes through the town, and is squirted at from the houses on both sides of the street as it goes" (26–27). He also mentions the procession as a phallic cult (27).

Drums and Frogs in the Monsoon Culture

Drums and frogs have important symbolic roles in the ancient culture of Monsoon Asia, and as we will see, they have a prominent part in the Songkran festival of Chiang Tung. But before detailing what happens during the annual Songkran days of April, we should look at the symbolic role drums and frogs have had, and still have, in the ancient culture of Monsoon Asia.

The drum is one of the most essential and widespread musical instruments in the history of human cultures. Beating sounds have been with us since the beginning of human existence. In the womb, we are woven into a sensual soundscape, which persists deep within matured bodies. Across religious traditions, drums invoke the gods, protect people, create rain, unite communities, and bring us to the point of ecstasy. The drum and the drumming have religious and ritual significance in many cultures, sometimes to achieve a state of trance, to invoke the gods, or to identify holy time by starting and ending a ritual. Drums can be seen as living beings themselves, with or without their sound (Plate 2014, 99–101).

The manufacture and use of bronze drums, commonly called Dong Son drums, rain drums, or frog drums, are probably among the oldest continuous art traditions of South China and Southeast Asia, and date back as early as the first millennium BCE. Commonly called the Dong Son Culture after an important archaeological site in North Vietnam, the production, distribution, and cult of the bronze drums are intimately connected to fertility, but the drums were also traded and distributed as valuable and prestigious materials expressing power. This cultural-religious worldview emerged from the monsoon climate and is an intimate part of irrigation agriculture and the production of rice. At the Chiang Tung Songkran in 2013, one of these bronze drums was placed in front of the main drum (figure 22).

The bronze drums found in Dong Son in northern Vietnam (a style classified as Heger I) are famous for their decorative beauty. The bronze drums found in South China in Guangdong and Guangxi south of the Pearl River (Heger II) are much larger but decorated in a much plainer style. The sheer number and size of the Heger II drums indicate the existence of large and complex societies beyond the reach of the Chinese administrative system (Churchman 2015, 62). Early bronze drum styles in both South China and North Vietnam are decorated with frogs and radiating sun motifs, closely connected to fertility. Bronze drums have been made and used by many different peoples, but, according to Catherine Churchman (2016, 6–7), the earliest bronze drum casting tradition was probably in present-day central Yunnan.

FIGURE 22. Bronze drum, Songkran festival, Chiang Tung. Photo by author.

Made by the lost-wax casting process, the bronze drums are very impressive artifacts and testify to the rise of powerful chiefdoms in the cultural area of South China and North Vietnam, at least from the fifth century BCE. The use of bronze drums spread over most of Southeast Asia and China, from Burma in the West to Indonesia in the South. Decorations on the drums include realistic images, geometric patterns, and scenes of rituals featuring musical instruments and elaborate costumes. The technology required to produce these bronze castings with such refined and intricate decoration suggests highly skilled artisans with wealthy patrons. Ceremonial performances that included bronze instruments were clearly an integral element of elite society in ancient Southeast Asia.

The symbols on these drums are mostly derived from animals and plants, and some of the most prominent symbols are frogs or toads and egret birds. Frogs seem to have had particular significance, because on a large number of the drums, frogs were depicted in high relief near the edge. The frogs are sometimes depicted in groups of three, on each other's back (figure 23). Frogs are such a common motif that the drums are sometimes called frog drums (*kloong kop*). When the drum is to be played, it hangs horizontally by a rope and is allowed to swing freely a few inches from the ground. One of the most ancient uses of the bronze drums was in rainmaking ceremonies. The sound of the drums has been likened to both thunder and to the croaking of frogs. Both sounds are predictive of rainfall.

Firsthand descriptions of the use of these bronze drums are not easy to find. However, there is an early fifth century Chinese text (*Guangzhou Ji*) describing a ceremony to celebrate the casting of a new bronze drum among the Li and Lao.

FIGURE 23.   Frogs on bronze drum, Chiang Tung. Photo by author.

When first completed they are hung up in the courtyards and on an appointed morning they set out wines and invite those of the same tribe. The guests crowd the gates, and the sons and daughters of the rich and prestigious people among the guests take gold and silver made into large forks and after beating on the drums with it they then leave it for the owner of the drum.... Those in possession of these drums are extremely powerful. (Churchman 2015, 63)

The Karen ethnic group has been associated with the ritual use of bronze drums. Cooler (1995, 30) discusses the origin of the Karen bronze drums and believes that they were brought from Yunnan. The Karen are not metalworkers and do not make the drums themselves (Fraser-Lu 1983) but buy them from Shan craft workers and craftspeople from other ethnic groups. The Karen use drums during funerals, both to make appropriate sounds and as grave goods, and they almost certainly associated the drums with frogs and rainfall (Cooler 1995, 38).

During the second day of Songkran in Chiang Tung, a great procession with many hundreds of people leads the drum and the Indra statue down to the river. At the river, a frog made of mud and clay is waiting. This meeting is supposed to bring rain and fertility. The central place of the frog in the Songkran festival shows the strong connection of the culture in Chiang Tung with the ancient monsoon culture. Frog worship can be found all over the region of Monsoon Asia, and the animal is considered auspicious. The modes of life drastically change for these creatures with the monsoon rain. Frogs estivate during the dry, hot summer and emerge at the beginning of the mating season. The croaking of the frogs indicates the end of the dry summer and the beginning of rain, accompanied by thunder and lightning. Plants sprout new leaves and flowers, and the mating season starts for many creatures. It is not difficult to imagine that the cult of frogs is highly connected to rain, fertility, and food production.

The Zhuang people of Guangxi in southern China still uphold a tradition of frog worship, which includes beating a bronze drum for ritual purposes.[2] The Zhuang own many bronze drums, which are considered a sacred inheritance. The people worship frogs during the Maguai festival, which is held for a good harvest. Locals believe that when winter comes, frogs hibernate underneath the earth, but once spring arrives, they are refilled with life and start to reproduce. The earth not only has its mysterious reproductive capability but also represents the origin of reproduction itself (Li Song 2015). In the Zhuang frog songs and myths, frogs are the children of the thunder spirit, and the people who slaughtered the frogs incurred the wrath of the thunder spirit. Only after the people undertook a solemn funeral ceremony for the frogs did the thunder spirit allow rain to fall. Yu Shi-jie retells a story from Tian-er of a drought in ancient times where the Zhuang placed frogs on top of the bronze drums as offerings. The frogs were touched by the sincerity and suffering of the people and called for their father to let rain fall. Although these stories differ in detail, the common core is that the thunder spirit controls rainfall, the frogs are his children, and they have been sent to earth as messengers. Humans who want a bountiful harvest should worship the frogs or risk devastation by drought (Yu Shi-jie 2001).

In the Songkran festival in Chiang Tung, the frog has a central role. The frog is called Rāhu, and in Indian mythology Rāhu is a demon who seizes and swallows the moon and the sun and thus causes eclipses. He also causes lack of rain, as he gathers up rainwater in order to cool his body (Malalasekera 1974, 735–36). In Chiang Tung, Rāhu is deeply embedded in the symbolism of water and fertility. The morning of the second day of Songkran, people gather at the river to make a frog to bring about rain, as it is told in the myths.

According to the *Chiang Tung Chronicle* there was an extreme drought in Chiang Tung six hundred years ago. Both the *Wat Pa Daeng Chronicle* (*WPDC* §192–97) and the *Chiang Tung Chronicle* (*CTC* §112) describe this drought and how to bring about the rain again, which is the rationale behind the very special celebration of Songkran we witness still today. The ruler asked for advice from an astrologer on how to summon the rain. The astrologer said that the people had to create a sand *cetiya* (stupa) and a frog, holding a moon in its mouth, at the bank of the Khuen River. The frog should be worshipped by soldiers, elephants, horses, and sword-and-shield dancers for the years to come. And four monks should recite the *Buddhavaṃsa sutta* in front of the frog and the *cetiya*. "At that moment the sky roared and so much rain fell that the lords had to run away from the rain" (*WPDC* §195).

This event is the basis for how the Songkran festival has been celebrated and is still celebrated today. The *WPDC* indicates that the drought happened in the year Tausi Sakkaraja 754 (1392 CE), but in the *CTC* the year is specified as Kodyi Sakkaraja 772 (1410 CE). The people of Chiang Tung trust the dates from the *CTC* and therefore believed that the year 2011 marked the six hundredth anniversary of the drought. The Songkran was an extraordinary celebration that year.

The wooden ritual drums from the indigenous Palaungic Mon-Khmer-speaking people have similarities with the ancient bronze drums, the Khuen temple drums, and the Songkran drum. For one, they are all used horizontally. Wooden ritual drums are important among the Wa, Lua, Eng (Enn), and other Palaungic Mon-Khmer-speaking people. I visited an Eng village in the mountain around Chiang Tung, where the people are not Buddhists or Christians but still practice their traditional religious way of life. Inside the house of the village shaman there was a wooden drum (figure 24) very similar to the temple drum, but it was in a stand, not far off the floor. I was told about the complicated rituals during the manufacturing and consecration of the drum and was strictly forbidden from touching it.

In the late nineteenth century, J. George Scott visited the so-called Wild-Wa who lived across the Myanmar-China border and were, at that time, regarded as

FIGURE 24. Ritual drum, Eng (Enn) people. Photo by author.

headhunters. He described a wooden drum in the spirit house, made of a huge log, the interior of which had been laboriously hollowed out.

> These drums are sometimes ten or twelve feet long and three or three and a half feet thick. They are beaten with wooden mallets and give out deep vibrating notes which travel very long distances. This gong is sounded at all crises and moments of importance to the village, but chiefly when heads are brought home, or when sacrifices are being made, or when a village council is to be held. Outside this spirit-house the sacrifices to the spirit are made, the buffaloes, pigs, dogs, fowls, are killed and their blood smeared on the posts, and rafters, and thatching, and their bones hang in clusters round the eaves. (Scott and Hardiman 1900, 1:502–3)

The Wa people believe that they originate from frogs, as Scott tells in a legend of the origin of the Wa.[3] The Wa people also believe, according to Scott, that the primeval Wa couple, Ya Htawm and Ya Htai, spent their youth as tadpoles in a legendary lake at the Nawnghkkeo mountain. When they became frogs, they moved to a place called Nam Tao and grew to be ogresses living in a cave. Scott describes them as father and mother spirits, the parents of all the Wa. Offerings to them were to be fowls, pigs, bulls, and buffaloes, but for special occasions, such as marriages, the beginning of war, death, and the founding of a village, the putting out of a human skull was advisable (Scott 1932, 291–94).

Bernard Formoso visited the Wa people in 1997 and described their rituals and the process of making the hollowed-out drums. The log is treated as if it were alive and has to be killed before making the drum. He states that the drum could be the true village guardian spirit and was "considered to be the main [tool] for communicating with the creator and supreme god of heaven, Muhidjae" (Formoso 2013, 130). Magnus Fiskesjö also mentions the production of a Wa drum: "Its creation and installation was a lengthy process, from the selection and felling of the right giant tree ... to the moment it was dragged home in the company of throngs of villagers. It was then made to 'wait' for three days before being brought in through one of the village fortress gates" (Fiskesjö 2021, 56).

Chapter 5 describes the temple drum and the rituals observed during its manufacture, consecration, and installation (figures 14 and 15). The connection between the wooden ritual drums of the indigenous Wa, Lua, and Eng people and the Khuen Buddhist temple drum is clear. The Khuen temple drum is considered to be a dangerous living being before it is installed in the monastery. The drum is transformed into a Buddhist sacred object during the consecration and installation rituals. The ancient bronze drums, the cult of frogs, the ritual drum of the Palaungic Mon-Khmer-speaking people, the Khuen temple drum, and the Songkran drum all show evidence of a common monsoon culture.

Songkran Cultural Performance

The Songkran festival in Chiang Tung is a holiday with drinking and constant water splashing, like Songkran elsewhere in Southeast Asia. But at the same time, it is a different and a much more remarkable event. The Songkran festival in Chiang Tung is a cultural performance, celebrated as a special local tradition, deeply embedded in myths and memories of the Tai Khuen people and the community of Chiang Tung. The festival in Chiang Tung can be seen as a kind of performed history of Chiang Tung and of the imagined Khuen nation. It is performed every year for the survival and continued existence of the nation, a kind of cultural staging of ancient Khuen history with elements of fertility, prosperity, and the symbolic ownership of land. The main theme, the ancient relationship between the Tai people and the earthborn mountain people, is symbolically repeated in the Songkran festival with the Tai Loi (Lua) people drumming for wealth and prosperity to Chiang Tung and the Khuen people.

What I will describe in this chapter is somewhat similar to what Clifford Geertz (1980) calls an organized spectacle of a "theatre state," designed to dramatize the ruling obsessions of (in his case) Balinese culture. Here, this organized spectacle is the annual Songkran performance, which dramatizes a kind of symbolic agreement, or an informal political contract, about the ownership of land, established between the Tai Khuen and the indigenous Tai Loi (Lua) several hundred years ago through a coronation ceremony. It is consequently also a drama about the meeting of the Indic Hindu-Buddhist culture and the indigenous culture of Monsoon Asia. Thus the Songkran festivities may be seen as a social drama and a symbolic cultural performance representing Chiang Tung as a place of belonging for the Khuen people.

The following is a detailed description and analysis of the most central parts of the Songkran festival, witnessed during the years 2011, 2013, 2016, and 2019. The festival site is the Old Royal Market, a sacred, fenced area in the middle of the town, which includes the shrine of *sao mueang*, the spirit of Chiang Tung. Inside the fence and close to the shrine are two big trees and a roofed place for worship. Opposite the sacred festival site is a mausoleum, which holds the funeral monuments (tombs) of the last seven rulers of Chiang Tung, making it a sacred area for traditional Khuen culture.

A group of Tai Loi (Lua) young men play an important role in the festival. They are invited to Chiang Tung before the Songkran festivities begin, to prepare themselves for their role in the celebration. Much of the preparations and organizing of the Songkran is done by a special organizing committee, which has its office just behind Wat Phra Sao Luang, in the center of the town. At the back of the office there is a place for the Tai Loi (Lua) men to stay, sleep, and make their own food during the festival. In the days before the celebrations begin, some of the younger Tai Loi (Lua) men spend time at the market or walk around the town, collecting money for their expenses during the celebration, probably to cover the costs of food and alcoholic beverages.

On the first day of the celebration, April 13, people gather around 11 a.m. at the festival site, where the statue of Indra and the Songkran drum, the drum of luck and prosperity, are already in place. The drum is stored in a nearby temple and is used only once a year at the Songkran festivities. All throughout the festival, water is constantly splashed on the Indra statue and the drum. At the end, the drum skin is so soaked from all the water that it sometimes must be replaced the next year. One year a bronze drum, the so-called Dong Son drum or frog or rain drum, was placed close to the main drum, probably just for its cultural symbolism of ancient fertility rites or rain ceremonies.

The Songkran festival, and especially the procession down to the river, is a male-dominated space. Women mainly perform dances in traditional dresses, run market stands, and provide different services. The organizing committee is made up of elderly men, and *māt* recitations and the accompanying food offerings (but not their preparation) are for male participants only. The procession down to the river is male dominated, with young adult men in a collective gathering.

The statue of Indra is prepared days or weeks ahead of time by a local artist and is brought to the place early in the morning (figure 25). Opinions differ about just what the statue represents; sometimes it is called Avatar or Bramar, although this is probably a reference to Indra appearing on the earth as a Brahman in Buddhist stories. In any case, the artist who created the statues was certain that it represented the god Indra. As mentioned early in this chapter, the tradition of Thagyamin in Burma/Myanmar is a manifestation of Indra, who descends upon earth during the Thingyan New Year festival in April. It is likely the Indra statue has its background in the Burmese celebration of the New Year, and it would not be surprising if it was the Indra statue that replaced the phallic object during British colonial times.

The god Indra is associated with war, lightning, thunder, storms, rains, and fertility. The Rigveda defines his chief characteristics as power and strength. Though a warrior god, he is also associated with fertility and rain and appears as a creator of the cosmos. When the demons attacked the gods and threatened their very existence, the young Indra fortified himself by drinking three beakers

FIGURE 25. Statue of Indra, Songkran festival 2013, Chiang Tung. Photo by author.

of the sacred soma, then went out alone to do battle with the demons. As a result of Indra's victory, the waters, which had been pent up in mountain caves, were set free and flowed downward for the welfare of humans (Basham 1990, 12–13). This myth of bringing the monsoon rain to the people clearly explains the role Indra has as Thagyamin in the Thingyan in Burma/Myanmar and as Indra in Songkran in Chiang Tung. He is here also a representation of the Indic Hindu-Buddhist culture, rather than the indigenous monsoon culture. Initially a Vedic god, he is also associated with Buddhism as Sakka (Pāli) and Śakra (Sanskrit). The Buddhist Sakka often descends to earth disguised as a Brahman in order to test the virtue of the Buddha's disciples. Many stories are told about how Sakka interacted with the Buddha in his last or previous life. Sakka is connected with the birth of the Buddha and also accompanies the Buddha to the heaven of the thirty-three gods to preach to his mother.

The statue is made with straw, papier-mâché, and colorful paint, and Indra is always depicted riding on a creature or animal. What kind of creature or animal differs, depending on which weekday Songkran falls. The Khuen calendar states that when the second day of Songkran falls on Sunday, Indra shall ride a *naak* (water dragon), on Monday a snake, on Tuesday a *khut* (Garuda bird), on Wednesday a buffalo, on Thursday a horse, on Friday a cow, and on Saturday an ogre. Astrological calculations are made to regulate which direction Indra should go and what paraphernalia he will bring. In 2013, he had a sword and an arrow in his hands and rode from north to west. The statue is made according to these stipulations. Once at the river, the statue is immediately destroyed by young men, who want part of the statue as a trophy.

Places for people to sit at the sacred fenced area are already prepared, and a special grandstand is built for prominent people representing the local government, the Burmese military, and the Tai Khuen civil society. The first day of Songkran begins with dance performances and donations. The donations consist of baskets with precious foods, which are submitted by prominent military and civil servants, mostly of Burmese descent, to representatives of the local organizing committee. In 2011 and 2013, the Burmese military had a prominent role in making donations and taking part in the Songkran activities, but this changed in 2016, when Myanmar switched to a nominally civil government. The high-ranking military were replaced by Burmese civilian authorities.

Beating the Rhythm of Belonging

A highlight of the festival is the twenty-four-hour drumming performance by the Tai Loi (Lua) people. Every year, some thirty-five to forty Tai Loi (Lua) young men dressed in red are invited to Chiang Tung to beat the Songkran drum, the drum of luck and prosperity. The drumming is performed under constantly splashing water for wealth and prosperity for Chiang Tung and the Khuen people (figure 26). It begins at noon the first day and continues throughout the night until noon the next day. The second day these men bring the drum and the statue

FIGURE 26. At the 2013 Songkran festival in Chiang Tung a Tai Loi (Lua) beats the Songkran drum while a Khuen man (*at left*) pours water on a bronze drum. Photo by author.

of Indra down to the frog at the river. The procession is a grand culmination of Songkran and has elements of fertility symbolism.

The custom of Songkran drumming most likely began during the reign of Sao Intaleng at the beginning of the twentieth century. Sao Intaleng chose a Khuen family (the Zar family) to organize the festival. The procession throughout the town and down to the river is mentioned by both Scott and Enriquez, but Scott, Dodd, and Enriquez do not mention the drumming. However, I have been told from several local people that Sao Intaleng chose a group of Tai Loi (Lua) from a village north of Chiang Tung called Eleven Hills to come down to Chiang Tung every year to perform the drumming.

It is highly credible that Sao Intaleng reformed the festival at the advice of the British. The drumming must have started as a replacement for the coronation ceremony, which was forced to cease sometime after 1897 when Sao Intaleng was installed as the new ruler. As mentioned in chapter 2, the Tai Loi (Lua) are the descendants of the Lua people who were defeated when the Tai conquered what became Chiang Tung. After they were defeated, their leaders came down from the mountains to be part of the coronation ceremony every time a new Tai Khuen ruler was installed. During this coronation ritual, the indigenous Tai Loi (Lua) symbolically gave away the ownership of land. This symbolic change of ownership has today been replaced by the Tai Loi (Lua) drumming ceremony during the Songkran festival.

Today the young Tai Loi (Lua) men who take part in the drumming ceremony mainly come from villages not far from Chiang Tung. One of the older members of the group reported that he had long ago been forced to leave his traditional longhouse village in the mountains and settle outside Chiang Tung because of fighting between the Burmese army and guerrillas.

One may wonder why these young Tai Loi (Lua) men agree to this ritual drumming. Is it voluntary? Do they get any prestige or profit for their participation? They do get some food and necessities from the organizing committee, and local people also donate money when the young men walk around in the market and elsewhere the days before the festival. It seems that most of the young Tai Loi (Lua) men want to show their strength, endurance, and at the same time have some fun. They probably do not think about the symbolic meaning of drumming prosperity to Chiang Tung and the Khuen people, nor of the symbolic change of ownership.

As previously mentioned, on the first day of the festival, places for people to sit are already prepared, and just before the celebration begins, prominent people take their places on the special grandstand. The ceremonies open with dance performances by girls in traditional dress and symbolic donations made to the Khuen organizing committee from prominent Burmese military members and civilians.

At noon, the main performance starts with a blessing of the drum by a Khuen ceremony master, who sits in front of the drum reciting a text in the Khuen language. Thereafter, two local old men read a dialogue aloud about the reason and purpose behind the drumming. They sit face to face at a table, reading questions and answers in Khuen. The dialogue is also translated to Burmese and read by two young girls for the Burmese-speaking visitors. Briefly, the dialogue expresses, in seven points, that the drumming is performed to make the bad luck of the old year disappear and to welcome the New Year in order to bring wealth and prosperity to the ruler and the community. Below is an informal translation of the answers, point by point, mentioning seven motives for drumming the Songkran drum of luck and prosperity. The text is written in poetic form with many old words.

> Beat the drum for the prosperous ruler of the nation.
> Beat the drum for the people to have good fortune and peaceful lives.
> Beat the drum for the ruler to fight enemies and prevent an invasion of the nation.
> Beat the drum for the people to have wealth and good business.
> Beat the drum for the ruler and the villagers not to be angry at each other so that the city will be filled with peace, prosperity, and good fortune.
> Beat the drum for the villagers so that they will be healthy, wealthy, and wise.
> Beat the drum so the thundering sound of the drum will be witnessed by the whole universe.

It is worth remembering that the Tai Loi (Lua) people who do the drumming are descendants of the earthborn Lua people, who were defeated in the thirteenth century by the Tai people. Therefore the dialogue expressing a sense of place and belonging is also a symbolic agreement, and an informal political contract, between the Khuen and the Tai Loi (Lua) about the ownership of land. These indigenous people within Tai traditional political systems have been described as "ambivalently and contra-distinctively represented as barbarous, cannibal, uncivilized, and non-Buddhist on the one hand, and on the other hand as original land-holders, and therefore ritually superior to the Tai conquerors, particularly in relation to the tutelary spirits of domains" (Tanabe 2000, 298).

After the initial recitation and before the Tai Loi (Lua) people get access to the drumsticks, the drum and the Indra statue have to be blessed. This blessing was previously done by the ruler or other senior officers at the court. However, today the role to start the blessing has been taken over by the Burmese government officials, who consider themselves the rulers of Chiang Tung. When I attended Songkran in 2011 and 2013, the highest-ranking Burmese commander of the Triangle Region Military Command in Chiang Tung started the drum blessing (figure 27). He walked up to the drum and slowly beat it seven times with a golden stick. Afterward, he got a small twig, which he dropped in water and then used to sprinkle the drum and the Indra statue, while slowly walking around them. This was repeated by some elderly Khuen men and others using a silver stick. In 2016 a prominent Burmese civil servant took the place of the Burmese commander because Myanmar changed over to a nominally civil government. The Burmese military commander and the prominent civil servant who started the blessing clearly represented power and authority, taking the role of the deposed Khuen ruler.

The Songkran ceremony is closely connected to traditional powers and the traditional *saopha* Khuen ruler. During the coup on March 2, 1962, the ruler Sao Sai Long was arrested, and the Songkran festival was not held in the years that followed, as the ceremony is so closely connected to the ruler and the court. A few years later, however, some of the remaining officials from the old court secretly restarted Songkran, and slowly it became more and more organized. Later, probably not before the 1990s, the Burmese military became interested in joining the celebration and showing authority.

FIGURE 27. The Burmese military commander of the Triangle Region Command in Chiang Tung prepares for the blessing of the drum at the 2011 Songkran festival. Photo by author.

The real drumming starts when the leader of the organizing committee hands over the working drumsticks to the group of Tai Loi (Lua) men. First, a short, stylistic martial arts performance with the drumsticks by one of the older Tai Loi (Lua) men starts the drumming. Then the young men join with the rhythmic drumming, beating the rhythm of life under constant water splashing. The temple drum discussed in chapter 5 uses only slow, gentle beats. The Songkran beat, in contrast, is like the heart rhythm after running, an ecstatic drumming of life into the festival. This drumming continues under intensive water splashing, hour after hour, all afternoon, the whole night, and through to the morning of the next day (figure 26).

In the evening of the first day, as the drumming continues, the festival site is filled with families and groups of teens, bringing small plastic buckets of water. They walk around slowly, splashing water on the drum, the statue, and the drummers with small twigs or with cups of water. Many of the festivalgoers, especially the elderly or families with small children, bless the drum and the statue on this evening because it is difficult to come close to the drum during the huge procession the next day. The Tai Loi (Lua) young men alternate at the drum all night long and continue until noon the next day when the drum is taken down to the river in a big procession.

Morning of the Second Day

On the morning of the second day of Songkran the drumming continues, with the skin of the drum now thoroughly soaked by water. Before the procession down to the river takes place, an offering must be made to the spirit of Chiang Tung, and a frog has to be made by the river.

Several Khuen men have already set to work on the frog down by the river, just as it is told in the chronicles (figure 28). The frog is made out of clay and mud, and an image of the moon is placed in its mouth. The men work on the frog with both seriousness and laughter. They decorate it with small sacred flags (*tung*), and in front of the frog they make a small pond containing the image of a fish. Then a female spirit from the mountains has to be invited to take up residence in the frog. The invitation is made by a ceremony master. He quickly transports himself to the river from the main festival space to facilitate the invitation of the female mountain spirit into the frog, reading from the text of the *Buddhavaṃsa sutta* as it is told in the chronicles. In 2011, four monks were actually present and read the text, though usually it is a lay ceremony master who recites it. The ceremony master kneels when reciting legends of the twenty-four Buddhas in the *Buddhavaṃsa sutta*. The making of the frog and the invitation of the spirit must be finished before the procession down to the river can begin.

FIGURE 28. Making a frog down by the river at the 2011 Songkran festival in Chiang Tung. Photo by author.

Meanwhile, at the festival site, people prepare for the offering to the *sao mueang* at the spirit shrine. Food is carried to the site and set on tables in front of the shrine.[4] The offerings actually start the day before the Songkran festival, as several spirits have to be invited to the sacred fenced festival site. In 2013 I was invited to follow the ceremony master as he visited seven different spirit shrines all around Chiang Tung. We went by motorbikes to shrines at a gate, at the lake, at a cemetery, and at the spirit shrine close to the place where the old palace once stood (figure 21). Today there are three different spirits at the *sao mueang* spirit shrine in the center of town. Two of the spirits from the old, demolished palace had to be removed and enshrined here when the palace was destroyed. The ceremony master invites the spirits, one by one, with a ritual. After all the spirits have been invited, they are believed to enter the sacred festival site and hang around there until the morning of the second day when they are worshipped together with the main territory spirit.

On the sacred site the second day of Songkran, visitors make offerings and merits in front of the spirits shrine. Plates with eggs, fish, rice crackers, and vegetables are presented together with small cups of liquor (figure 19). After the offering, a *māt* recitation is performed (figure 20), as described in more details in chapter 6. A group of about ten, mostly elderly, Khuen men sit on the floor in a ring around the accordion-shaped manuscript and read aloud a text to *sao mueang* in *tham* script, which consist of a mix of Khuen and Pāli words, abundant with symbolism and metaphors. The rhythmic drumming heard from outside the spirit shrine, together with the rhythmic *māt* recitation coming from inside, becomes a melting pot of disparate rhythms and cultures, a symbolic imagination of the meeting of the so-called civilized lowland and so-called uncivilized highland cultures, as well as of Indic and indigenous monsoon cultures.

The Procession

At noon on the second day, the Indra statue and the drum are carried down to the river in a great procession called Sending the Drum. The account by Enriquez mentions how this procession "passes through the town, and is squirted at from the houses on both sides of the street as it goes" (Enriquez 1918, 26–27). Scott describes the procession that he witnessed during his visit to Chiang Tung in the late nineteenth century, mentioning that an "indecent figure is paraded and obscene antics indulged in all along the route. On arrival at the river a small image of the Lahu nat is thrown in. This is in the shape of a frog—the spirit which the Shans say swallows the moon when an eclipse occurs. After leaving offerings at the river, the people return to the town. It is considered essential to the public welfare that this ceremony should be performed every year" (Scott and Hardiman 1901, 1:440).

Scott does not mention any drum or drumming. His account makes it clear that there actually was a phallic object carried down to the river, which later was replaced, presumably because of its perceived obscenity. It may have been the Indra figure, the drum, or both that replaced the phallic object in the procession. Enriquez also mentions that the procession he witnessed in 1915 was performed as a phallic cult: "Incidents in this procession suggest phallic cult, though possibly of Tai Loi and not of Shan origin" (Enriquez 1918, 27). This supports the idea that, at that time, the Tai Loi (Lua) people had an active role in carrying the phallic object down to the river.

I have been told that the procession down to the river earlier was called Sending the Phallus instead of Sending the Drum. It is generally believed that before Sao Intaleng reformed the ritual, it was a crafted phallus that was brought to the female frog spirit by the river. During the time when Sao Intaleng ruled, British administrators and Christian missionaries lived and worked in Chiang Tung. One can speculate that it was the prudish foreigners who wanted to remove the phallus and transform the phallic cult. I have been told by local people that no more than a generation ago, there still was a phallic object brought to the river, but at that time it was sent in secrecy, together with the drum and statue. Even today, a hidden object can follow the procession, but I have not witnessed this. Chapter 2 recounts a legend about Japanese samurais who visited and settled in Chiang Tung. The crafted phallus may be of Japanese origin, possibly referring to the Honen fertility festival at the Tagata Shrine in Nagoya.

The procession at noon on the second day is the culmination of the festivities. Before it begins, a large number of mostly Khuen young adult men gather around the Indra and the drum, waiting for the procession to start. The constant rhythmic drumming of the last twenty-four hours by Tai Loi (Lua) young men continues to beat. The offering to the spirit with a *māt* recitation has ended, but some of the men are still sitting under the roof, chatting. Some of the Khuen young men party wildly and make noises, as if they were going to watch their favorite football team.

Leading the whole procession is a male member of the Zar family riding a horse, a custom established by Sao Intaleng. A group of Tai Loi (Lua) men lift the Indra statue, and another group of Tai Loi (Lua) men do the same with the drum, ready to carry them to the river. Slowly, the long, unruly procession starts to move. The large crowd moves slowly but fitfully gains speed, sometimes slowing almost to a stop and sometimes advancing rapidly.[5] The crowd of young adult men moves forward with incredible noise, a mix of rhythmic drumming and collective walking and shouting, all the way to the river, with the Indra statue in front and the constantly beaten drum close behind. Many of the young men hang around the statue and the drum, walking and running close together in a kind of union with the Tai Loi (Lua). The rhythmic sound of the drum and the yelling of the crowd of young adult men can be heard all along the way, with thousands of people on both sides of the streets watching and splashing water and colored powder on the procession (figure 29).

I witnessed the crowd of young men, walking and running together to the sensual drum rhythm, and sensed an intense emotional state of communal shared experience. It can be described as *collective effervescence*, a concept coined by Émile Durkheim, which refers to when a group of individuals embodies a collective emotional experience: "Once the individuals are assembled, their proximity generates a kind of electricity that quickly transports them to an extraordinary degree of exaltation" (Durkheim [1912] 2001, 162). Victor Turner also discusses the concept of *communitas*, which addresses collective experiences beyond social structures and categories. The bonds of *communitas* are antistructural, implying egalitarian relationships between people outside the normal structure of society (Turner 1974, 274). All the young men gather in a mass of familiar and unfamiliar fellows in ecstatic collective behavior, as a *communitas* beyond social and ethnic limitations. I don't want to overemphasize the symbolic significance of the procession, but there clearly is an absence of both the social and the ethnic structures. The Tai Loi (Lua) men drum alone from the start of the Songkran, but during the procession it seems that they have entered into a community with the Khuen men, which ends when they reach the river. One year I was part of the intense shared emotional experience, walking and running in the crowd behind

FIGURE 29. Procession to the river during the 2011 Songkran festival in Chiang Tung. That year, the Indra and the drum were carried by trucks. Photo by author.

the Indra and the drum. I became part of a collective energy, sharing a common purpose, with water splashing from everywhere. The rhythm of drumming and the rhythm of walking, screaming, and yelling together form an ecstatic collective experience of belonging. This ecstatic collective behavior corresponds with a wide range of such experiences, from the ecstatic devotional *bhakti* (*bjajanas*) movements, to the European football supporters on their way to a local match, and even to the crowd of ecstatic bodies participating in a unified state of flow on the electronic dance music floor.

When the crowd finally arrives at the river, a chaotic tumult ensues. They rip and tear the Indra statue, competing with one another in breaking the statue into pieces. The young men who have managed to stay close to the front of the procession rush around Indra and the frog, trying to catch some of the remnants. After about fifteen minutes, nothing is left of the statue. Aggressive behavior toward the frog implies symbolic intercourse, and what is left of the frog is just a pile of mud and straw. The fragments the young men catch are believed to bring them wealth and good luck in love affairs throughout the new year to come. This tumultuous fertility finale of the procession is believed to call the rain and bring water from the mountain down to the valley of Chiang Tung, a necessity for a wet rice agriculture society.[6]

After this final part of the procession, the drum is taken back to town and returned to the Khuen organizers. The Tai Loi (Lua) men have then completed their obligations and can go back to their villages. In former days, the Tai Loi

(Lua) young men were not allowed to enter the town on their way home, as they had symbolically given it away, but today there is no such rule.

The Songkran festival in Chiang Tung is not much of a Buddhist festival, except for the last two days. As a grand finale of the festival, on the third day people collect sand from the river and use it on the fourth and final day to make Buddhist sand pagodas (*chedi*) at the village monastery. People use plastic buckets to collect the sand, and as compensation they make offerings to the spirit of the river with cakes made of sticky rice, peanuts, and sesame seeds, wrapped in banana leaves. These cakes are hidden inside small pagodas, made in the shallow river. Young Tai Loi (Lua) boys and girls try their best to grab these cakes. The circle is complete: the Tai Loi (Lua) have drummed away their land, and the Tai Khuen exchange sand for rice cakes so that the young generation of Tai Loi (Lua) get rice cakes for the future. It is on the morning of the fourth and last day of the celebration when large, decorated sand pagodas are built at the monastery compound (figure 30). This is a collective task for the village, with people coming to donate sand and jointly make *chedis* for merit. The Songkran ends as a Buddhist ceremony, with laypeople staying at the temple most of the day and some elderly staying overnight, dressed in white, taking the eight precepts (*sīla*).

The Songkran festival is an ancient tradition deeply embedded in the fertility culture of Monsoon Asia. This festival in Chiang Tung is performed as a symbolic legitimation of power and a communal veneration of the place of belonging for the Tai Khuen people. The Songkran performance has its roots far back in the myths and memories of the Khuen people. After the defeat of the earthborn Lua

FIGURE 30. Sand *chedi*, Songkran festival, Chiang Tung. Photo by author.

people in the thirteenth century, the Tai Khuen built their palace at the same place as the Lua palace and continued to venerate the same spirits as did the Lua people.

An informal political contract between Tai Khuen and Tai Loi (Lua) can be seen either as one of domination and subordination or as a mutual dependence between the newly arrived lowland people and the indigenous highland people. This political contract was established historically through symbolic actions connected with the Chiang Tung royal court and relating to a symbolic ownership of land. The displaced Tai Loi (Lua) came down to the Khuen royal court and were part of a symbolic banishing during the coronation ceremony to install a new Khuen ruler. This symbolic banishing has today been replaced by the Tai Loi (Lua) drumming ceremony during the Songkran festival.

Songkran was a symbolic legitimation of power for the Tai Khuen traditional ruler until the military coup in 1962 when the last ruler, Sao Sai Long, was arrested and the Songkran ceremony was banned. Later, the festivities were resumed in secret, and the fertility symbolism of Songkran continued. Much later, the Burmese military joined the celebration, aware of the symbolic performance of the ownership of land. The military commander assumed the role of the former ruler, blessing the drum and the Indra statue. This is in line with the ethnic policy of the Burmese military in the 1990s to use culture and religion to rewrite the history of Chiang Tung and include it more closely in the history of the Burmese empires.

The Songkran festival serves as the focus of communal veneration and manifests an enduring sense of place and belonging for the Tai Khuen people. This is clearly expressed when two Khuen men sit face to face in front of the drum, reading aloud a dialogue in the Khuen language about the reason and purpose behind the drumming. Briefly, the dialogue expresses, in seven points, that the drumming is performed to make the bad luck of the old year disappear and to welcome a propitious New Year, bringing wealth and prosperity to the ruler and the community. During the second day, before the procession to the river, the rhythmic drumming heard from outside the spirit shrine, together with the rhythmic *māt* recitation coming from inside, becomes a melting pot of disparate rhythms and cultures. The mix of Tai Khuen text recitation and Tai Loi (Lua) drumming becomes a symbolic imagination of the meeting of the so-called civilized lowland and the so-called uncivilized highland cultures as well as the meeting of Indic and indigenous monsoon cultures.

The symbolism of fertility is highlighted when the procession with the drum and the Indra statue reaches the frog at the river, and the frog and the statue are torn apart in a chaotic tumult, where young men try to catch some of the remnants. Drums, frogs, splashing of water, and the Indian god Indra are all charged with the symbolic meaning of renewal of nature, fertility, and power. This symbolic fertility manifestation is believed to bring the young men wealth and good luck in love affairs and to call the rain and bring water from the mountain down to the valley of Chiang Tung, a necessity for a wet rice agriculture society. The performance of Songkran, with its rhythmic drumming by Tai Loi (Lua) people, together with offerings and a *māt* recitation to the spirit of the place, signifies an enduring sense of place and belonging for the Tai Khuen people. Deeply rooted in the wet rice irrigation monsoon culture, the Songkran festival is a manifestation of and homage to the place and the culture of the Khuen.

CONCLUSION
A Sense of Place and Belonging

In this book, a sense of place refers to the physical place and how people endow the place with significance and meaning. This is an interdisciplinary study about the meaning people project onto their home, which includes cultural, religious, and historical aspects of their place. It presents Tai Khuen culture, connecting the local with the global, the present with the past, and tradition with change and transformation.

Myths and memories of a chosen history, Buddhist rituals, visual and material culture, local literature written in the *tham* script, locally based cults to the spirit of the earth, and the Songkran performance of wealth, prosperity, and ownership of land, all testify to a sense of place and belonging for the people of Chiang Tung.

With this in mind, the conclusion of this book focuses on themes that shape Chiang Tung's and the Tai Khuen people's relationships to the place they call their home: a history of independence, localized ethnic identity, the spirit of the place, the Tai Yuan-Khuen-Lue Buddhist culture, and the merging of Indian and indigenous monsoon culture.

History of Independence

Chiang Tung, located in the Eastern Shan State of Myanmar, sits at the historic borderland between the large and powerful nations of the Chinese, the Burmese, and the Siamese. During the time of the Second (Toungoo) and Third (Konbaung) Burmese dynasties, Chiang Tung was politically dependent and had to pay tribute to the Burmese rulers but still enjoyed a large degree of independence. The religious culture from the 250 years of Lan Na times could continue because of Chiang Tung's isolated geographic location, although for most of the time Chiang Tung was dependent on the Burmese. The culture of the Tai Yuan-Khuen-Lue region during the Golden Age of Lan Na, from the late thirteenth century until the middle of the sixteenth century, is still a prominent part of the culture and religion of Chiang Tung. It is a remarkable testament to Chiang Tung's relative independence that the culture of Lan Na is still so vibrant in contemporary Chiang Tung, considering the drastic changes in the area's official government.

During colonial times, Chiang Tung, the rest of the Shan states, and all the territory outside Burma proper became known as the Frontier Areas and was administrated under indirect rule by the British. The ruler of Chiang Tung still had the practical and symbolic power as the main ruler and protector of Buddhism during the colonial period. The border to northern Thailand was virtually closed, and during that time, interchange between Chiang Tung and the Shan states west of the Salween River increased.

Chiang Tung (officially Kyaingtong) is today an integrated part of the Republic of the Union of Myanmar, with Burmese as the national language taught in school and a lingua franca for all the ethnic groups in the country. In many ways, Chiang Tung has been well integrated into the political and administrative systems of Myanmar since the end of colonial rule. However, Chiang Tung has always maintained a degree of independence and still does so in culture and religious matters today.

Localized Ethnic Identity

In the myths and memories of the origin and early history of Chiang Tung, there is a close connection between the origin of the Khuen ethnic group and the place Chiang Tung. During the existence of Chiang Tung as a frontier state against the Mongols of China in the thirteenth century, Chiang Tung was re-established in what seems to have been a political decision to unite a local Tai group with soldiers from Chiang Rai. The conquest by the Tai people and reestablishment of Chiang Tung as well as the integration of a new ethnic group of inhabitants highlight common ancestry and a sense of place and belonging for the Khuen people living in Chiang Tung.

Khuen identity, in short, is connected to Chiang Tung's long history, despite the realities of forced resettlement and displaced people. The control of human power, not the conquest of land, was the crucial factor for establishing, consolidating, and strengthening state power in precolonial Southeast Asia. In the early nineteenth century, large parts of the population in Chiang Tung were forced or persuaded to move south and relocate in Chiang Mai, which was in great need of a growing population. Chiang Tung was left deserted and defenseless until Sao Mahakhanan, who managed to escape the deportation to Chiang Mai, later move back to Chiang Tung, allying with the Burmese. This decision was momentous for the future of Chiang Tung. During his reign, Sao Mahakhanan prepared for future conflicts by repopulating the city and started a major restoration project of the defensive wall. Chiang Tung was repopulated in part with people from the surrounding areas, from Tai groups, but also from other ethnic groups. Through intermarriage and immigration in the nineteenth and twentieth centuries, different people, such as Western Shan (Tai Yai), Tai Lue, and Tai Neua, are today well integrated in Khuen culture and society.

The Spirit of the Place

A territory cult is an ancient interaction between a local group of people and a geographical place. In Chiang Tung, it has its origin in the geographical landscape of South China and northern Southeast Asia with high forested mountains, fertile river valleys, and a monsoon climate, which made it possible for the development of wet rice irrigation. Agriculture, the village community, and the cult of territory spirits were closely connected and still leave their mark upon the present Buddhist culture of Chiang Tung. The cult of territory spirits is a cult of the earth, the place, and the village itself as well as the people who have lived in that place. The cult expresses a sense of belonging to a place and is very locally grounded. The territory cults are, in the words of Richard A. O'Connor (2003, 271, 282-84), a "lingua franca of localism" because villagers need to mark boundaries, respect precedence, and recognize prior owners. The cults act as a diplomatic language of interestedness. The villagers, the village headman, and the founder of the village are the territory spirit as a collective.

There is a belief that the spirit of the village *is* the first leader of the village and, to a certain degree, all his descendants as headmen and ancestors of the village headman. The present village headman is therefore a natural intermediary between the village spirit and the villagers. Offerings to the village spirit are made to ensure good harvests and prosperity, but they have social meaning as well: to meet and socialize around the village spirit. The spirits have connections with ancestors, former headmen, and rulers, connecting the present with the past and establishing a link to a chosen history.

This local cult of the spirit of the earth was challenged by an Indic Hindu-Buddhist worldview. The gods of the new religion were universal rather than locally grounded and thus created a model by which Southeast Asian rulers could aspire to a status that reached beyond their specific locality. The cult of local spirits had already made a kind of religious map, a patchwork of places connected to groups of peoples identified by village headmen related to the spirit of the earth. This patchwork was easily adapted to themselves by a growing Buddhist community. The sacred landscape, with stories and a visual culture connecting local places with the power of the Buddha, most certainly had a significant role in establishing Buddhism among local people. When King Mangrai united Tai city-states in the thirteenth century, he adopted Buddhism as a legitimation of universal power, in contrast to the locally grounded cults of territory spirits. The Buddhist worldview created a model by which Mangrai, and later rulers, could aspire to a universal status as a righteous ruler who reached beyond a specific locality. But Buddhism was not adopted to political ends; it was the end itself. This Buddhist worldview was not intended as a means to political power, but it turned out to serve this role. It united several small city-states (*mueang*) to a loosely connected kind of kingdom, with Chiang Mai as the most important city-state. Today, the cult of the spirit of the earth and the Indic Hindu-Buddhist traditions are intertwined; every block and village in Chiang Tung, along with its countryside, has both a spirit shrine and a monastery.

The cults of spirits are hierarchical in structure and correspond to a political order, creating a parallelism between a this-worldly social structure and the otherworldly spirit world. In the hierarchy of spirits, the spirit of the *mueang* is the highest and is above all village spirits. Before the ritual of *sao mueang* can take place, all villages have to maintain their ritual offerings. Village spirits are below the spirit of the *mueang*, just as all the village headmen are below the ruler. The village monastery and the village spirit shrine stand together as a symbolic center of the village. But as the symbolic center of *mueang* Chiang Tung, the spirit *sao mueang* stands alone; there is no monastery, temple, or Buddha image that can be viewed as a symbolic center, or a palladium, of Chiang Tung.

The Tai Yuan-Khuen-Lue Buddhist Culture

Buddhist traditions constantly underwent transformation and became adopted into local traditions and practices. In the words of Rajeshwari Ghose, "Each culture transformed Buddhist teachings and iconography into forms closer to its own heart" (1998, 1). The heart of the Tai Khuen people of Chiang Tung is truly filled with Buddhist beliefs and practices; it is not just an echo of foreign

Buddhist texts and doctrines. Culture and religion are not timeless and unchanging but embedded in a thick context of traditions and changes.

It is remarkable how well the traditional Lan Na Buddhist culture (Tai Yuan-Khuen-Lue culture) has been maintained during the long and troublesome history of Chiang Tung. At the turn of the nineteenth century, large parts of the population, together with the ruler and his court, were relocated to Chiang Mai, and Sao Mahakhanan had to repopulate Chiang Tung. He could not have any contact with his relatives, who had been sent to Chiang Mai. During the Chiang Tung Wars in the middle of the nineteenth century, troops from Siam and Lan Na tried to conquer Chiang Tung but failed. Later, during colonial times, the border to Siam was almost completely closed. Altogether, communication between Chiang Tung and Chiang Mai has been restricted for a long time, but still a good deal of the traditional shared Buddhist culture has largely been maintained.

The Buddhist culture of Chiang Tung is characterized by a decentralized and independent Buddhist *saṅgha*, a hierarchy built on seniority, an old Buddhist calendar, Buddhist rituals and literature written in the *tham* script and recited in Pāli and Khuen languages, a tradition of charismatic holy monks, and a specific Buddhist visual and material culture. All monks in Chiang Tung belong to one of two of the nine officially recognized monastic orders of Myanmar, but in practice the Buddhist monasteries in Chiang Tung are more or less independent and without official government control. At the head of Buddhism in Chiang Tung is a patriarch with the title *atyatham*. He is the head of the Sangha Council and a guarantor of local traditions and customs for monasteries in Chiang Tung.

Chiang Tung's close connection to Lan Na Buddhist culture appears clearly in rituals and literature about Prince Vessantara and locally produced *Jātaka* stories. The visual and material culture of Buddhist monasteries, with assembly halls and sacred objects, also reflects a common origin in the Tai Yuan-Khuen-Lue region. The cultural traditions of Chiang Tung are constantly evolving and responding to social, economic, and political changes, but at the same time, Chiang Tung's core identity is preserved.

Rituals and artistic expressions such as literature and visual and material culture preserve old traditions and infuse in their users a sense of community and group identity. With this in mind, it is interesting to note the attempts by the Burmese military to use culture and religion to include minority regions like Chiang Tung in the history of Burma/Myanmar. The military wanted nothing less than to rewrite the history of Chiang Tung and include it more closely in the history of the Burmese empires. However, this has not fully worked. The large Buddha statue built by the military on one of the Chiang Tung hills is still very controversial within local Khuen culture. People know that it is not built in traditional

Khuen style and believe that it was not consecrated in a proper way. The strong connection between the Khuen people and their traditional culture and religion makes most of local people reject the Burmese military's attempts to reconstruct history. People know that Khuen Buddhism has its roots in Lan Na and the island of Lanka, not in Bagan.

The Burmese military ruined the old Chiang Tung ruler's palace and built statues that mediate traditional Burmese culture, religion, and power, and it also tried to take control of the Mahāmuni Buddha and the Songkran festival to manifest its own dominance and power. Still, the celebration of the Songkran festival has continued to maintain vibrant and unique local cultural traditions.

The Merging of Indian and Indigenous Monsoon Culture

The celebration of the Songkran New Year is an ancient tradition deeply embedded in the culture of Monsoon Asia. It marks the traditional New Year, with water as a symbol of washing away all that is bad. The symbolic importance of water, frogs, drums, the Indic god Indra, and the cult of territory spirits all together give witness that Chiang Tung culture stands with one foot in the indigenous ancient monsoon culture and the other foot in the Indic Hindu-Buddhist culture.

The Songkran is also a continuation of an informal political contract between the Tai Khuen and the Tai Loi (Lua) about the ownership of land. This symbolic agreement was established after the Tai people defeated the Lua people in the thirteenth century and was reenacted through a symbolic deporting during the coronation ceremony of a new ruler at the Chiang Tung royal court. A group of Tai Loi (Lua) chiefs were called down from the mountain, given a meal to eat, but before they could finish their meal they were carried away from the throne, and the new Khuen ruler ascended the throne; the symbolic succession to the throne was in place. This coronation ritual can be described either as a symbolic relationship of domination and subordination relating to ownership of land, or as a mutual dependence between the newly arrived lowland people and the indigenous highland people.

This coronation ceremony ended during the colonial period and was replaced with the drumming by the Tai Loi (Lua) at the Songkran festival. Every year at Songkran, Tai Loi (Lua) people are called down to Chiang Tung for a twenty-four-hour drumming ceremony to make the bad luck of the old year disappear and to welcome the New Year to bring wealth and prosperity to the ruler and the community. This is expressed in a ritual dialogue between two Khuen men, just before the drumming begins. The indigenous people in Chiang Tung and elsewhere in northern Southeast Asia have been conflictingly represented as barbarous and uncivilized, on the one hand, and on the other hand as the indigenous earthborn inhabitants of the land and therefore ritually superior to the Tai conquerors. For the Tai Khuen, the drumming by Tai Loi (Lua) of prosperity and symbolic change of ownership of the land confirms Chiang Tung as a sense of place and belonging for the Khuen people.

The Buddhist *saṅgha* was also part of this symbolic relationship. The royal court, the Buddhist *saṅgha*, and the Tai Loi (Lua) people had the responsibility of establishing continuity for the Mangrai dynasty. When the old ruler died, the power was handed over to the *saṅgha* for a short period until the new ruler was installed and crowned. Buddhism still has minor roles in the Songkran today, especially on the last day of building sand pagodas. In Chiang Mai and Luang Prabang, Buddhist statues have played the central role in the Songkran festival. In Chiang Mai, the Phra Sihing Buddha is taken out from the Lai Kham assembly hall in Wat Phra Singh, onto the streets for veneration by the local people. In Luang Prabang, the Phra Bang Buddha image is also taken from its temple to Wat Mai for veneration by Miss Lao New Year, the mythical grandparents Nyeu, and local people. These statues, the Phra Sihing and Phra Bang, are regarded as palladiums for Chiang Mai and Luang Prabang respectively. Instead, in Chiang Tung, the Songkran festival and the cult of the spirit of Chiang Tung (*sao mueang*) confer legitimacy and power to the rulers.

Until 1962, when the Burmese military took control over the country, the local ruler was the rightful leader of the Songkran. After the coup, the celebration of the Songkran festival ceased, but later it was revived in secret. The Burmese military, as it took over as the ruler of the nation, became interested in the power symbolism of the Songkran festival. During the Songkran festival in 2011 and 2013, the highest-ranking Burmese military official of the Triangle Region Command in Chiang Tung started the blessing of the drum with seven slow beats from a golden stick. In 2016, the highly ranked military figure was replaced by Burmese civilian authorities, as Myanmar nominally now had a civil government. During the COVID-19 pandemic, Myanmar closed much of the country, but authorities decided that the Songkran should be celebrated for the wealth and prosperity of the nation. Because of the pandemic, the festival was arranged with many fewer participants in 2020 and 2021, but it was not canceled. Songkran must be held every year to bring wealth and prosperity to the place and the people of Chiang Tung.

The Songkran festival and the local religious culture in Chiang Tung both reflect the meeting of the Indic Hindu-Buddhist culture and the indigenous culture of Monsoon Asia. Culture and religion are not timeless and unchanging but embedded in a thick context of traditions and changes. In the case of Songkran, it is clear that the ancient fertility symbols of the monsoon culture have a place in the hearts of Chiang Tung culture along with Buddhism.

Future Research

Very little has previously been written about the culture and religion of Chiang Tung. This is partly a result of the political situation in Myanmar along with Chiang Tung's relative geographical isolation on the borderland of northern Southeast Asia. Hopefully, my study will contribute to increased interest in this area, especially from local residents. Much remains to be studied and written about, and any of my mistakes will, I hope, be corrected in the future.

Finally, I would like to highlight two subjects that are in need of more specific analysis. First, the history, culture, and religion of the Tai Loi (Lua) people need more attention. Second, the rich tradition of Khuen literature is a field that should be explored more deeply. Anatole-Roger Peltier collected Khuen literature in the 1980s and translated some of it, but much remains to be done. The manuscript collection collected by Peltier will hopefully be digitized. But there is also still a rich cultural treasure of literature in the monasteries of Chiang Tung waiting to be preserved for future research (see figure 16).

Notes

INTRODUCTION

1. The eight northern provinces of Thailand usually included in the toponym Lan Na are Chiang Mai, Lamphun, Lampang, Chiang Rai, Phayao, Phrae, Nan, and Mae Hong Son.
2. Known to the Burmese as *main*.
3. Interestingly, Rāmaññadesa, the Mon kingdom in Lower Burma, was divided into thirty-two townships (*myo*) (Shorto 1963). Thus, to designate Chiang Tung as having exactly thirty-two towns seems to have some magical or sacred motive. There are several different lists of the thirty-two towns, and most, but not all, towns are the same on these lists.
4. The Salween is known as Nam Kong by the Shans, Nu in China, and Thanlwin in Burma. The river is powerful and rapid, and it passes through deep and narrow canyons, making it navigable only in its lower parts. For those traveling between Burma and Chiang Tung in earlier times, the Ta Kaw ferry was the only safe place to cross. J. George Scott states that until 1898, native boatmen still operated the ferry with their own boats, with subsidies from the British government. They had a landing ground on both sides and sufficient room for several hundred pack animals to load and unload (Scott and Hardiman 1901, 3:97–98).
5. The Shan are sometimes classified into four geographical entities: (1) the Northwestern Shan, living in northern Burma from the Indian border to Bhamo, (2) the Northeastern Shan, spread from western Yunnan down to the Irrawaddy, (3) the Eastern Shan, who are the Khuen and the Lue, and (4) the Southern Shan, who inhabit the central and southern Shan State (Sai Kam Mong 2004, 3).
6. Saimong Mangrai (1981) spells their name as Lva in his translation of the *CTC*. Other names for them used in different chronicles and inscriptions are Milakkha and Kha (slave).
7. The spoken language of the Tai Loi (Lua) needs further investigation. Some sources posit that it has transformed from a Mon-Khmer language to a Tai dialect closely related to Khuen, but with much substrate material from the Lua language. One of my informants reported that the languages of the Wa and the Tai Loi have almost 30 percent in common. Other information suggests that the Tai Loi (Lua) keep their native language but use the Khuen language when in contact with the Khuen.

1. LOCAL BELONGING

1. There are at least two more versions of the *CTC* that have been transcribed into the Thai script but not translated. These are published as *Tamnan Meuang Chiang Tung*, transcribed by Thawi Sawangpanyankun (Chiang Mai: Chiang Mai University, 1984), and *Tamnan Mangrai Chiang Mai Chiang Tung* (Chiang Mai: Social Research Institute, 1993). Only the English translation by Sai Saimong Mangrai has been used in this book. He translates the name of the document as *Jengtung State Chronicle*, but in line with recent literature I will instead use *Chiang Tung Chronicle*.

2. MYTHS AND MEMORIES

1. Comsak Hill is the hill in Chiang Tung where the Roman Catholic Church and the big Buddha statue stand today.

2. A similar story is told about a prince from Phayao, who chased a golden deer and came to the Chiang Dao Mountain north of Chiang Mai. That legend establishes the names of places where the Tai people would live in the future (Swearer, Sommai, and Phaithoon 2004, 63–67). To establish names for places with a legend like this is a common practice.

3. Kreangkrai Kirdsiri did an interview with the abbot of Wat Baan Ngaak in December 2004. The abbot told a story about Tai Loi (Lua) ancestors, Loi-mila, who lived at Wiang Chiang Lek for a very long time. The abbot told Kreangkrai that King Mangrai chased a golden deer and found that it was a good location to establish a city there. Therefore, he sent people to fight. The Loi-mila were defeated by Mangrai and then migrated to Baan Saen and Baan Ngaeg (Kriangkrai 2007). This is a story similar to that in the *Chiang Tung Chronicle*.

4. In ancient Luang Prabang the relationship between the Lao people and the indigenous Mon-Khmer-speaking group called the Khamu/Kasak was played out in an annual ritual game like hockey. Here, the Lao always won against the autochthonous people (Stuart-Fox 1998, 51). Further, the earthborn people had to undertake the task of cleansing the Luang Prabang royal palace of all negative influences when a new ruler was to be installed. They shot arrows against the palace façade in order to drive out evil spirits. Then the king rubbed a small ball of rice over his body and threw it in their direction, whereupon the indigenous people fled back to their village. Only then could the new king enter the palace (Lukas 2012, 109).

5. According to the *Chiang Mai Chronicle*, the king "led his retainers into the royal city by the White Elephant Gate on the north side, having the Lawa carrying their baskets going ahead. He entered and slept in the Chiang Khwang in front of Wat Chiang Man for one night" (*CMC*, 237). At royal processions in Chiang Mai during the reign of King Kawila (1781–1815) and Prince Kham Fan (1821–1824), the Lua/Lawa people, who were accepted as the original owners of the land, led dogs and carried baskets with chickens ahead of the king into the city. Dogs, chickens, and *chaek* baskets seem to be symbols of the Lua identity. The Lua use dogs and chickens in their rituals, and the *chaek* baskets were used by all Lua to carry things behind their backs (Aroonrut 2002; Sarassawadee 2005, 32; Grabowsky 2003, 113–14).

6. It is uncertain if this story is derived from the latest renovation of the defensive wall in the nineteenth century, made by Sao Mahakhanan, or if it dates back earlier, to the construction of the original wall in the late fourteenth or the fifteenth century.

7. There are indications that there were many folk stories in Lan Na about the Chinese in the past, but most of these stories were expunged from the official histories of Lan Na in later times (Grabowsky 2010, 201–2). One such story is preserved through the writings of Captain William C. McLeod. When he visited Chiang Mai in 1837, he was told by local people about another Chinese invasion and how the people of Chiang Mai had tricked the Chinese in a competition to build the highest pagoda. Local people had, he was told, built a high mound of earth with some brickwork on the top—a shortcut to make the Chinese believe that the people of Chiang Mai were very numerous (Grabowsky 2010, 201–2; Grabowsky and Turton 2003, 317–18).

3. PRECOLONIAL TIMES

1. Olivier Évrard and Chanthaphilith Chiemisouraj (2013, 65) have shown that Viang Phu Kha in northern Laos was conquered, abandoned, and rebuilt several times in the

course of its history. "Enslaved populations or refugees settled here, only to be later moved again by new invaders."

2. He started his journey from Moulmein to upper Southeast Asia together with his close friend David Richardson, who visited Karen, Red Karenni, and Kayan territories, as well as three Shan states inside Burma. McLeod described the fifty-five-year-old ruler as charismatic, with obvious authority. He mentions in his diaries that the prince had only one wife, and with her he had five or six children. This was unusual, as most other rulers had several wives or concubines. Marriages were intimately associated with politics, and having many sons was a guarantor of continuity to the throne, though sometimes the rivalry between sons led to bitter battles. Sao Mahakhanan's wife died in 1837, the same year that McLeod visited him, and after her death Sao Mahakhanan married a woman from the court in Chiang Khaeng and had two children. One of these children, Sao Kawng Tai, became the ruler of Chiang Tung in 1881.

3. Bryce Beemer (2009) highlights two interesting examples of cultural exchange by captured populations. One is the introduction of a sophisticated technique for lacquer decoration into Burmese society after the sacking of Ayutthaya in the sixteenth century. The other is the introduction of the *Ramayana* dance-drama to the Burmese court from Ayutthaya in the eighteenth century. It is also known that King Tilok of Chiang Mai deported famous potters from Chaliang to Chiang Mai and Chiang Rai (Grabowsky 2019, 32).

4. Volker Grabowsky approximates that fifty to seventy thousand war captives were deported to Lan Na during the late eighteenth and early nineteenth centuries (1782–1838). By the mid-nineteenth century, roughly 25–40 percent of the four hundred thousand inhabitants in the five Tai Yuan principalities of Chiang Mai, Lamphun, Lampang, Phrae, and Nan were war captives or their descendants. In particular, in Lamphun as much as 60–80 percent of the population were war captives or their descendants (Grabowsky 1999, 66; 2019, 51, 55n36).

4. FOREIGN RULERS

1. J. George Scott worked in Burma as a journalist and reported for several British newspapers, mostly as a correspondent for the *Evening Standard*. He also traveled all over the different Shan states, collecting information and documents. He wrote and published copious information from his time in Burma and the Shan states. His most important publication containing information regarding Chiang Tung is the *Gazetteer of Upper Burma and the Shan States*, published in 1900/1901 in five volumes.

2. Isabelle Massieu, who traveled between Taunggyi and Chiang Tung in 1897, wrote that "those who have spoken about the possibility of a railway line in this region have no idea about the chaos of mountains here, with steep crests that succeed each other like gigantic waves on a sea in full fury" (Massieu [1901] 2013, 119).

3. For the fascinating world of male and female clothing in Lan Na and the Shan states see Susan Conway (2002a, 2002b, 2003, 2006).

4. This palace would much later irritate the Burmese military rulers. They realized it could symbolize the time of independence for Chiang Tung and consequently destroyed it in 1991.

5. The long and bitter contest between Presbyterians and Baptists was, from the beginning, about sectarian differences, but it developed into a personal conflict (Swanson 1982). Now in Chiang Tung there are separate Baptist churches for Akha and Lahu, a remnant from the colonial times of ethnic separation.

6. For the history, myths, and significance of the Shwedagon Pagoda see Donald M. Stadtner (2011, 72–105).

7. For the myths of the Mahāmuni Buddha image and its place in the history of Burma see Stadtner (2011, 260–75) and Schober (1997).

5. SACRED SPACE

1. Shan people (Tai Yai) west of the Salween have immigrated into Chiang Tung, and a couple of Tai Yai temples are present in the city.

2. Aside from these Buddhist monasteries, there are also a few temples in Chiang Tung that do not belong to any monastery. One stands in the middle of the town (Wat Phra Sao Luang), built during the colonial time to hold a replica of the famous Mahāmuni Buddha image from Mandalay. Outside Chiang Tung there is a famous octagonal temple (Wat Zom Loi), where many people come for veneration. However, for the most part, Buddhist sacred places are monasteries (*wat*) with several buildings.

3. There are several old beautiful textile banners from Chiang Tung hanging in the Tai Khuen Museum at Wat San Kangpla, San Kamphaeng, Chiang Mai.

4. The number 1,000 seems to be a symbolic number in this ceremony.

5. A project to collect Khuen literature was organized by Anatole-Roger Peltier in the 1980s. Some 270 different texts were collected and copied in Chiang Tung and sent to Chiang Mai. The collection comprises "folk jatakas, Buddhist doctrines, life of the Buddha etc." and is presented in Peltier (1987) with abstracts in Thai, French, and English.

6. Numerous local variants of the *tham* script developed. The variants differ only slightly between *tham*-Khuen, *tham*-Yuan, *tham*-Lue, and *tham*-Lao.

7. Manuscripts of *Kale Ok Hno* exist in Khuen, Lue, Tai Loi (Lua), Tai Nua, and Tai Yai (Peltier 1999, 84–87).

8. The first six sections included in the recitation of *Dham Vessantara Jātaka* are (1) *Pāramī*, an explanation about the ten perfections; (2) *Uṇhassa*, explaining the results of past actions in various ways; (3) *Lokavuḍḍhi*, explaining how to be prosperous, wealthy, and healthy in this life and in the next; (4) *Suttanta*, demonstrating how to give gifts and the varied results gifts bring; (5) *Vinaya Piṭaka*, giving a brief history of the Vinaya and a summary of the four *pārajika* rules; and (6) *Abhidhamma Piṭaka*, the contents from the *Dhammasaṅgaṇi*.

6. RELIGIOUS CULTURE

1. Within the last fifty years or more, a handful of Burmese and western Shan monasteries have been established. These will be disregarded in this book. The monks and novices who are seen walking around for donations are from a Burmese or western Shan monastery.

2. Some villages have more than one spirit shrine. The village of Noi Naw, for example, in addition to the Sao Baan, also has a spirit shrine for Sao Woon Yone in the place where a famous warrior was killed some two to three hundred years ago. His life story is forgotten, but his spirit is venerated at his shrine.

3. See also Richard A. O'Connor (1995), Liew-Herres, Grabowsky, and Renoo (2012, 12), and Easum (2012, 43–45).

4. Lieberman and Buckley (2012) believe that the climate had a crucial role in the migration of the Tai people to Southeast Asia. From a seven-hundred-year reconstruction of hydroclimate, they suggest that "wide cyclic fluctuations in the reach and volume of monsoon rains contributed substantially to both the genesis and collapse of the charter civilisations of Angkor, Pagan, and Dai Viet" (2012, 1049) and consequently the opportunity for the Tai people to expand south.

5. Davis (1984, 260) discusses the word *sao* and believes it appears to be a convergence of two distinct words, *jao*, meaning lord, and *suea*, meaning shirt or jacket. Some types of spirits associated with particular localities or territories are known as *phii suea* (Davis 1984, 260). He proposes that the term *phii suea* denotes a spirit whose tutelage covers the territory like a shirt. Davis also suggests that the spirit of the *mueang* lies at the head of all other local spirits, and the cult of *phi mueang* is a relic of what may be the oldest form of religion in Southeast Asia (Davis 1984, 260, 273). For a more comprehensive discussion about the word *sao* and *phi* see Karlsson 2022.

6. The territory cults of Tai people are also described by Narujohn (1980, 101) and Davis (1984, 266–73) for Fang and Nan in Northern Thailand in the 1970s, by T'ien Ju-K'ang (1986, 58–60) and Pai-I people (Tai Lue) for Mangshih in the Chinese province of Yunnan during the 1940s, and by Pierre Petit (2020) at Houay Yong village in northeast Laos, close to the border of Vietnam. They all describe the cults of territory spirits, or guardian spirits as they sometimes are called, of both villages and towns as similar to those in Chiang Tung.

7. *Pu Sae*, the grandfather, and *Ya Sae*, the grandmother, are two of the guardian spirits of Chiang Mai who dwell at the foot of Doi Suthep. Two black uncastrated, undeformed water buffalo are sacrificed to them at this time of the year. The ritual also includes offerings to the last Lua/Lawa king, Khun Luang Vilanga, who is believed to have been defeated by Queen Cāmadevī in the eighth century (Sommai and Doré 1992, 247). In the ninth lunar month there is also a ceremony for the prosperity of the *mueang* Chiang Mai. According to Sommai and Doré, it is held right after the end of the celebration of Inthakhin. They also write that in the past there were two kinds of ceremonies performed to ensure that a city would be stable and prosperous, one when a city was peaceful and prosperous and one when a city met with troubles such as war, epidemics, floods, and droughts (Sommai and Doré 1992, 223–24; Notton 1926, 57–59, 64).

8. It is interesting to compare this with the relationship between merit sharing and sociopolitical status in Bagan, described by Michael Aung-Thwin (1985).

9. There are two myths in the Buddhist canonical literature about the origin of Buddhist kingship. One is about the Great Elect, King Mahāsammata, in the Aggañña Sutta of Dīgha Nikāya, and the other is about the Wheel-Turning King (*Cakkavatti*) Daḷhanemi in the Cakkavatti-Sīhanāda Sutta, also in Dīgha Nikāya.

10. Both Iijima and Ashley suggest that such a term implies a group of Buddhists who imagine themselves as part of the same religious community or lineal descent. This has never existed because Buddhists in Lan Na were decentralized, enjoying a high degree of autonomy. Ashley (2013) calls the term a meta-category because it comprises the geographical area that used texts written in the *tham* script. This is not a traditional Buddhist demarcation. Iijima (2009) views this geographical demarcation as a general outsider's viewpoint that fails to substantively clarify what is meant. He also questions whether there are any differences between this Yuan Buddhism and the Buddhist tradition in northeast Thailand, aside from script and literature.

11. According to 2016 statistics published by the State Sangha Maha Nayaka Committee, http://www.mahana.org.mm/en/religious-affairs/the-account-of-wazo-samgha-of-all-sect-m-e-1377-2016/.

12. For the magic belief systems in the context of textiles and clothes see Susan Conway (2014).

13. Palladia, or palladium, is a word named after Pallas Athena, the Greek goddess and protectress of various cities across the ancient world, including the city of Troy. The word has been used figuratively to mean anything believed to provide protection or safety. Stanley J. Tambiah was probably the first to use the term in a Buddhist context. He wrote,

"The possession of certain Buddha statues (and relics), rather than kinship, was interpreted as conferring legitimacy and power to kings and rulers, because these statues were treated as the palladia of their kingdoms and principalities" (Tambiah 1982, 5).

14. The spirits (the mythical grandparents Nyeu) are now regarded as living in two trees at the Wat Aham and are brought to life every New Year Songkran celebration.

15. For more about this subject see Strong (2004), Swearer (1995, 2004b), Terwiel (1st ed. 1975, 4th ed. 2012), and Crosby 2014, 48–53).

7. SONGKRAN FESTIVAL

1. This contrasts with the *agricultural ritual cycle*, which is to mobilize nature's force to cause rainfall for plowing paddy land and planting rice, and to stop rains when the rice stalks are tall enough. In order to cause rainfall, guardian territory spirits are worshipped and bamboo rockets are fired. For the cessation of rains, boats are raced, and illuminated vessels (*loi kratong*) are floated (Sommai and Doré 1992, 39–40).

2. The Zhuang people live in Guangxi, Yunnan, Guangdong, Guizhou, and especially the Kwangxi Autonomous Region of the Zhuang people of South China. They are connected with Tai people through the ancient Yue people.

3. When Scott speaks about the Wa people, he seems to mean all Palaungic Mon-Khmer-speaking people in northern Southeast Asia, including the Lua. He discusses the different names of the autochthonous people, mentioning the various names for the Wa, such as Lawa, Hkawa, Wa Hai, and Kha-La. He also divides Lawa into two closely related groups, the good La and the Wild (headhunting) Wa.

4. The main offering to the spirit of Chiang Tung take place in June/July, but it is performed at Songkran as well. Sommai and Doré (1992, 175) assume that the spirit cults of the Inthakhin and Pu Sae Ya Sae in Chiang Mai were previously performed at the same times as Songkran.

5. During the six hundredth celebration in 2011, the drum and the statue were transported on trucks.

6. This behavior resembles Magnus Fiskesjö's account of the Wa people at the end of the so-called headhunting or war ritual. The last stage of the ritual is the cutting of the calf's tail, which includes a violent slaughter of a single young bull. At the moment the tail is cut clear, all the men of the village throw themselves at the living beast with sharpened knives, competing with each other to cut it into pieces (Fiskesjö 2021, 158–61).

References

Aijmer, Göran. 1979. "Reconciling Power with Authority: An Aspect of Statecraft in Traditional Laos." *Man* 14 (4): 734–49.
Amporn Jirattikorn. 2011. "Shan Virtual Insurgency and the Spectatorship of the Nation." *Journal of Southeast Asian Studies* 42:17–38.
Amporn Jirattikorn. 2017. "Khruba Bunchum: The Holy Man of the Twenty-First Century and His Transnational and Diverse Community of Faith." In *Charismatic Monks of Lanna Buddhism*, edited by Paul T. Cohen, 191–216. Copenhagen: NIAS.
Andaya, Barbara Watson, and Leonard Y. Andaya. 2015. *A History of Early Modern Southeast Asia, 1400–1830*. Cambridge: Cambridge University Press.
Anderson, Benedict. 2006. *Imagined Communities: Reflections on the Origin and Spread of Nationalism*. London: Verso.
Anderson, James A., and John K. Whitmore. 2015. "Introduction: The Fiery Frontier and the *Dong* World." In *China's Encounters on the South and Southwest*, edited by James A. Anderson and John K. Whitmore, 1–55. Leiden: Brill.
Anderson, James A., and John K. Whitmore. 2017. "The Dong World: A Proposal for Analyzing the Highlands between the Yangzi Valley and the Southeast Asian Lowlands." *Asian Highlands Perspectives* 44:8–71.
Anuman Rajadhon, Phya. 1953. *Loy Krathong and Songkran Festival*. Bangkok: National Culture Institute, B.E. 2496.
Aroonrut Wichienkeeo. 2002. "Lua Leading Dogs, Toting Chaek, Carrying Chickens: Some Comments." In *Inter-ethnic Relations in the Making of Mainland Southeast Asia and Southwestern China*, edited by Hayashi Yukio and Aroonrut Wichienkeeo, 1–22. Bangkok: Amarin.
Ashley, Sean. 2013. "Narrating Identity and Belonging: Authenticity and Contested Ethnic Marginalization in the Mountains of Northern Thailand." *Jojourn: Journal of Southeast Asian Studies* 28 (1): 1–35.
Aung-Thwin, Michael. 1985. *Pagan: The Origins of Modern Burma*. Honolulu: University of Hawai'i Press.
Aung-Thwin, Michael, and Maitrii Aung-Thwin. 2012. *A History of Myanmar since Ancient Times: Traditions and Transformations*. London: Reaktion Books.
Aung Tun, Sai. 2009. *History of the Shan State: From Its Origins to 1962*. Chiang Mai: Silkworm Books.
Baird, Ian G. 2017. "Champassak Royal Sacred Buddha Images, Power and Political Geography." *South East Asia Research* 25 (4): 359–78.
Baker, Chris. 2002. "From Yue to Tai." *Journal of the Siam Society* 90:1–26.
Baker, Chris, and Pasuk Phongpaichit. 2014. *A History of Thailand*. 3rd ed. Cambridge: Cambridge University Press.
Baker, Chris, and Pasuk Phongpaichit, trans. 2019. *From the Fifty Jātaka: Selections from the Thai Paññāsa Jātaka*. Chiang Mai: Silkworm Books.
Basham, A. L. 1990. *The Sacred Cow: The Evolution of Classical Hinduism*. London: Rider.
Beemer, Bryce. 2009. "Southeast Asian Slavery and Slave-Gathering Warfare as a Vector for Cultural Transmission: The Case of Burma and Thailand." *Historian* 71 (3): 481–506.

Bell, Catherine. 1997. *Ritual: Perspective and Dimensions.* Oxford: Oxford University Press.
Bernatzik, Hugo Adolf. 1938. *Die Geister der gelben Blätter.* Munich: Bruckmann.
Blackburn, Anne. 2007. "Writing Buddhist Histories from Landscape and Architecture: Sukhothai and Chiang Mai." *Buddhist Studies Review* 24 (2): 192–225.
Blackburn, Anne M. 2015. "Sīhaḷa Saṅgha and Laṅkā in Later Premodern Southeast Asia." In *Buddhist Dynamics in Premodern and Early Modern Southeast Asia*, edited by D. Christian Lammerts, 307–32. Singapore: ISEAS.
Blundell Jones, Peter. 2016. *Architecture and Ritual: How Buildings Shape Society.* London: Bloomsbury Academic.
Bowie, Katherine A. 2017. "Khruba Siwichai: The Charismatic Saint and the Northern Sangha." In *Charismatic Monks of Lanna Buddhism*, edited by Paul T. Cohen, 27–57. Copenhagen: NIAS.
Brereton, Bonnie Pacala. 1995. *Thai Tellings of Phra Malai: Texts and Rituals concerning a Popular Buddhist Saint.* Tempe: Program for Southeast Asian Studies, Arizona State University.
Brown, Robert L. 2014. "Dvāravatī Sculpture." In *Lost Kingdoms: Hindu-Buddhist Sculpture of Early Southeast Asia*, edited by John Guy, 189–91. New York: Metropolitan Museum of Art.
Buckley, Brendan M., Roland Fletcher, Shi-Yu Simon Wang, Brian Zottoli, and Christophe Pottier. 2014. "Monsoon Extremes and Society over the Past Millennium on Mainland Southeast Asia." *Quaternary Science Reviews* 95:1–19.
"Burmese Invasion of Siam: Translated from the Hmanna Yazawin Dawgyi." 1959. In *Selected Articles from the Siam Society Journal*, vol. 5, *Relationship with Burma*, part 1, 3–84. Bangkok: Siam Society.
Busarin Lertchavalitsakul. 2017. "Living with Four Polities: States and Cross-border Flows in the Myanmar-Thailand Borderland." PhD diss., Universiteit van Amsterdam.
Casas, Roger. 2023. "Death of the Last King: Contemporary Ethnic Identity and Belonging among the Tai Lü of Sipsong Panna." In *Regional Identities in Southeast Asia: Contemporary Challenges, Historical Fractures*, edited by Jayeel Cornelio and Volker Grabowsky, 271–89. Chiang Mai: Silkworm Books.
Chandler, David, and Ian Mabbett. 2011. Introduction to *India Seen from the East: Indian and Indigenous Cults in Campa*, by Paul Mus, 1–14. Caulfield, Australia: Monash University Press.
Charan Chakandang. 1987. "Siam's Loss of Trans-Salween Territory to Great Britain in 1892." PhD diss., Pennsylvania State University.
Cheong, Conan. 2016. "The Art of the Shan State." In *Cities and Kings: Ancient Treasures from Myanmar*, edited by Stephen A. Murphy, 74–86. Singapore: Asian Civilizations Museum.
Chiu, Angela S. 2015. "Drawn to an 'Extremely Loathsome' Place: The Buddha and the Power of the Northern Thai Landscape." In *From Mulberry Leaves to Silk Scrolls: New Approaches to the Study of Asian Manuscript Traditions*, edited by Justin Thomas McDaniel and Lynn Ransom, 107–30. Philadelphia: University of Pennsylvania Press.
Chiu, Angela S. 2017. *The Buddha in Lanna: Art, Lineage, Power, and Place in Northern Thailand.* Honolulu: University of Hawai'i Press.
Cholthira Satyawadhna, 1991. "The Dispossessed: An Anthropological Reconstruction of Lawa Ethnohistory in the Light of Their Relationship with the Tai." PhD diss., Australian National University.

Churchman, Catherine. 2015. "Where to Draw the Line? The Chinese Southern Frontier in the Fifth and Sixth Centuries." In *China's Encounters on the South and Southwest: Reforging the Fiery Frontier over Two Millennia*, edited by James A. Anderson and John K. Whitmore, 59–77. Leiden: Brill.

Churchman, Catherine. 2016. *The People between the Rivers: The Rise and Fall of the Bronze Drum Culture, 200–750 CE*. Lanham, MD: Rowman & Littlefield.

Cohen, Paul T. 1998. "Lue Ethnicity in National Context: A Comparative Study of Tai Lue Communities in Thailand and Laos." *Journal of the Siam Society* 86:49–61.

Cohen, Paul T. 2001. "Buddhism Unshackled: The Yuan Holy Man Tradition and the Nation-State in the Tai World." *Journal of Southeast Asian Studies* 32 (2): 227–47.

Cohen, Paul T., ed. 2017. *Charismatic Monks of Lanna Buddhism*. Copenhagen: NIAS.

Collins, Steven. 1998. *Nirvana and Other Buddhist Felicities: Utopias of the Pali Imaginaire*. Cambridge: Cambridge University Press.

Collis, Maurice. 1938. *Lords of the Sunset*. London: Faber and Faber.

Condominas, Georges. (1974) 1990. "Notes on the Lawa History concerning a Place named Lua (Lawa) in Karen Country (Amphur Chom Thong, Changwat Chiangmai)." In *From Lawa to Mon, from Saa' to Thai: Historical and Anthropological Aspects of Southeast Asian Social Spaces*, edited by Gehan Wijeyewardene, 5–27. Canberra: Department of Anthropology, Research School of Pacific Studies, Australian National University.

Convery, Ian, Gerard Corsane, and Peter Davis, eds. 2012. *Making Sense of Place: Multidisciplinary Perspectives*. Woodbridge, UK: Boydell.

Conway, Susan. 2002a. *Silken Threads Lacquer Thrones: Lan Na Court Textiles*. Bangkok: River Books.

Conway, Susan. 2002b. "Court Dress, Politics and Ethnicity in the Shan States." In *Burma: Art and Archaeology*, edited by Alexandra Green and T. Richard Blurton, 133–42. London: British Museum.

Conway, Susan. 2003. *Power Dressing: Lanna Shan Siam 19th Century Court Dress*. Bangkok: James H. W. Thompson Foundation.

Conway, Susan. 2006. *The Shan: Culture, Art and Crafts*. Bangkok: River Books.

Conway, Susan. 2008. "Tai and Wa Textiles." In *Eclectic Collecting: Art from Burma in the Denison Museum*, edited by Alexandra Green, 123–44. Singapore: NUS Press.

Conway, Susan. 2014. *Tai Magic: Arts of the Supernatural in the Shan States and Lan Na*. Bangkok: River Books.

Cooler, Richard M. 1995. *The Karen Bronze Drums of Burma: Types, Iconography, Manufacture, and Use*. Leiden: Brill.

Crosby, Kate. 2014. *Theravada Buddhism: Continuity, Diversity, and Identity*. Chichester, UK: Wiley Blackwell.

Crosthwaite, Charles. 1912. *The Pacification of Burma*. London: Edward Arnold.

Davis, Richard B. 1984. *Mueang Metaphysics: A Study of Northern Thai Myth and Ritual*. Bangkok: Pandora.

Davis, Sara L. M. 2005. *Songs and Silence: Ethnic Revival on China's Southwest Borders*. New York: Columbia University Press.

de Maaker, Erik, and Monica Janowski. 2020. "Borderland Narratives." *Southeast Asian Studies* 9 (2): 151–60.

Dodd, William Clifton. (1923) 1996. *The Tai Race: Elder Brother of the Chinese: Results of Experiences, Exploration and Research*. Bangkok: White Lotus.

Doré, Mani-Samouth. 2008. "The Great-Drum among Northern Tai Buddhist Cultures: A Showcase of a Living Tradition." Paper presented at the 10th International Conference on Thai Studies, Thammasad University, Bangkok, January 9–11, 2008.

Durkheim, Émile. (1912) 2001. *The Elementary Forms of Religious Life*. Oxford: Oxford University Press.
Easum, Taylor. 2012. "Urban Transformation in the Colonial Margins: Chiang Mai from Lanna to Siam." PhD diss., University of Wisconsin–Madison.
Easum, Taylor. 2023. *Chiang Mai between Empire and Modern Thailand: A City in the Colonial Margins*. Amsterdam: Amsterdam University Press.
Egerod, Søren. 1959. "Essentials of Khün Phonology and Script." *Acta Orientalia* 24:123–46.
Enriquez, C. M. 1918. *A Burmese Loneliness*. Calcutta: Thacker, Spink.
Évrard, Oliver, and Chanthaphilith Chiemsisouraj. 2013. "The Ruins, the 'Savages' and the Princess: Myths, Migrations and Belonging in Viang Phu Kha, Laos." In *Mobility and Heritage in Northern Thailand and Laos: Past and Present*, edited by Oliver Évrard, Dominique Guillaud, and Chayan Vaddhanaphuti, 55–73. (Proceedings of the Chiang Mai Conference, December 1–2, 2011). Chiang Mai: Center for Ethnic Studies and Development, Chiang Mai University.
Ferguson, Jane. 2008a. "Rocking in Shanland: Histories and Popular Culture Jams at the Thai-Burma Border." PhD diss., Cornell University, Ithaca, NY.
Ferguson, Jane. 2008b. "Revolutionary Scripts: Shan Insurgent Media Practice at the Thai-Burma Border." In *Political Regimes and the Media in Asia*, edited by Krishna Sen and Terence Lee, 106–21. London: Routledge.
Ferguson, Jane. 2016. "Ethno-nationalism and Participation in Myanmar: Views from Shan State and Beyond." In *Metamorphosis: Studies in Social and Political Change in Myanmar*, edited by Renaud Egreteau and François Robinne, 127–50. Singapore: NUS Press.
Ferguson, Jane. 2021. *Repossessing Shanland: Myanmar, Thailand, and a Nation-State Deferred*. Madison: University of Wisconsin Press.
Fiskesjö, Magnus. 2021. *Stories from an Ancient Land: Perspectives on Wa History and Culture*. New York: Berghahn Books.
Forbes, Andrew. 2002. *A Forgotten Invasion: Thailand in Shan State, 1941–45*. Chiang Mai: CPA Media.
Forbes, Andrew, and David Henley. 2015. *Saharat Tai Doem: Thailand in Shan State, 1941–45*. Chiang Mai: CPA Media.
Formoso, Bernard. 2013. "To Be at One with Drums: Social Order and Headhunting among the Wa of China." *Journal of Burma Studies* 17 (1): 121–39.
Fraser-Lu, Sylvia. 1983. "Frog Drums and Their Importance in Karen Culture." *Arts of Asia*, September–October.
Fukuura, Kazuo. 2022. "From Ritual Traditions to Spirit Mediumship: The Evolution of Pillar Worship in Chiang Mai, Northern Thailand." In *Stone Masters: Power Encounters in Mainland Southeast Asia*, edited by Holly High, 216–41. Singapore: NUS Press.
Geertz, Clifford. 1973. *The Interpretation of Cultures: Selected Essays*. New York: Basic Books.
Geertz, Clifford. 1980. *Negara: The Theatre State in Nineteenth-Century Bali*. Princeton, NJ: Princeton University Press.
Ghose, Rajeshwari. 1998. "The Meeting of Minds: Buddhism as a Cross-Cultural Discourse." In *In the Footsteps of the Buddha: An Iconic Journey from India to China*, edited by Rajeshwari Ghose, 1–17. Hong Kong: University Museum and Art Gallery, University of Hong Kong.
Gibson, Richard M. 2011. *The Secret Army: Chiang Kai-shek and the Drug Warlords of the Golden Triangle*. Singapore: John Wiley & Sons.

Giersch, Charles Patterson. 2006. *Asian Borderlands: The Transformation of Qing China's Yunnan Frontier*. Cambridge, MA: Harvard University Press.
Gosling, Betty. 2004. *The Origins of Thai Art*. Bangkok: River Books.
Grabowsky, Volker. 1999. "Forced Resettlement Campaigns in Northern Thailand during the Early Bangkok Period." *Journal of the Siam Society* 87:45–86.
Grabowsky, Volker. 2003. "Cao Fa Dek Noi and the Founding Myth of Chiang Khaeng." In *Cultural Diversity and Conservation in the Making of Mainland Southeast Asia and Southwestern China: Regional Dynamics in the Past and Present; Collected Papers Originally Presented at Luang Prabang, Lao PRD 19–20 February 2002*, edited by Hayaskhi Yukio and Thongsa Sayavongkhamdy, 95–126. Kyoto: Center for Southeast Asian Studies.
Grabowsky, Volker. 2005. "Population and State in Lan Na Prior to the Mid-Sixteenth Century." *Journal of the Siam Society* 93:1–66.
Grabowsky, Volker. 2010. "The Northern Tai Policy of Lan Na (Ba-dai Da-dian) in the 14th and 15th Centuries: The Ming Factor." In *Southeast Asia in the Fifteenth Century: The China Factor*, edited by Geoff Wade and Sun Laichen, 197–245. Singapore: NUS Press.
Grabowsky, Volker. 2019. "Military Traditions and Society in Lan Na." In *Armies and Societies in Southeast Asia*, edited by Volker Grabowsky and Frederik Rettig, 29–59. Chiang Mai: Silkworm Books.
Grabowsky, Volker, and Renoo Wichasin. 2008. *Chronicles of Chiang Khaeng: A Tai Lü Principality of the Upper Mekong*. Honolulu: Center of Southeast Asian Studies, University of Hawai'i.
Grabowsky, Volker, and Andrew Turton. 2003. *The Gold and Silver Road of Trade and Friendship: The McLeod and Richardson Diplomatic Missions to Tai States in 1837*. Chiang Mai: Silkworm Books.
Griswold, A. B. 1975. "Wat Pra Yun Reconsidered." Monograph No 4. Bangkok: Siam Society.
Griswold, A. B., and Prasert Na Nagara. 1978. "Epigraphic and Historical Studies no 19: An Inscription from Keng Tung (1451 A.D.)." *Journal of the Siam Society* 66 (1): 66–88. Reprinted in *Epigraphic and Historical Studies*, 733–56. Bangkok: Historical Society, 1992.
Guy, John. 2014. *Lost Kingdoms: Hindu-Buddhist Sculpture of Early Southeast Asia*. New York: Metropolitan Museum of Art.
Hall, Rebecca S. 2008. "On Merit and Ancestors: Buddhist Banners of Northern Thailand and Laos." PhD diss., University of California.
Hall, Rebecca S. 2016. "Between the Living and the Dead: Three-Tail Funeral Banners of Northern Thailand." *Ars Orientalis* 46:40–60.
Higham, Charles. 2014. *Early Mainland Southeast Asia: From First Humans to Angkor*. Bangkok: River Books.
Higham, Charles, and Rachanie Thosarat. 2012. *Early Thailand: From Prehistory to Sukhothai*. Bangkok: River Books.
Holt, John Clifford. 2009. *Spirits of the Place: Buddhism and Lao Religious Culture*. Honolulu: University of Hawai'i Press.
Holt, John Clifford. 2017. *Theravada Traditions: Buddhist Ritual Cultures in Contemporary Southeast Asia and Sri Lanka*. Honolulu: University of Hawai'i Press.
Iijima, Akiko. 2009. "Preliminary Notes on the Cultural Region of *Tham* Script Manuscripts." *Senri Ethnological Studies* 74:15–32.
Iwamoto Yoshiteru, 2007. "Yamada Nagamasa and His Relationship with Japan." *Journal of the Siam Society* 95:73–84.

Johnson, Andrew Alan. 2014. *Ghosts of the New City: Spirits, Urbanity, and the Ruins of Progress in Chiang Mai*. Honolulu: University of Hawai'i Press.
Karlsson, Klemens. 1999. *Face to Face with the Absent Buddha: The Formation of Buddhist Aniconic Art*. Acta Univeritatis Upsaliensis, Historia Religionum, 15. Uppsala: Uppsala Universitet.
Karlsson, Klemens. 2006. "The Formation of Early Buddhist Visual Culture." *Material Religion* 2 (1): 68–95.
Karlsson, Klemens. 2009. "Tai Khun Buddhism and Ethnic-Religious Identity." *Contemporary Buddhism* 10 (1): 75–83.
Karlsson, Klemens. 2022. "Territory Cults and Power in the Eastern Shan State of Myanmar." In *Stone Masters: Power Encounters in Mainland Southeast Asia*, edited by Holly High, 242–67. Singapore: NUS Press.
Kerlogue, Fiona. 2004. *Arts of Southeast Asia*. London: Thames & Hudson.
Keyes, Charles. 1971. "Buddhism and National Integration in Thailand." *Journal of Asian Studies* 30 (3): 551–67.
Keyes, Charles. 1992. "Who Are the Lue? Revisited: Ethnic Identity within the Nations of Laos, Thailand, and China." Cambridge, MA: Massachusetts Institute of Technology, Center for International Studies. Working Paper.
Khammai Dhammasami. 2018. *Buddhism, Education and Politics in Burma and Thailand: From the Seventeenth Century to the Present*. London: Bloomsbury.
Khur Yearn and Loi Pang Lai. 2006. "History of Shan New Year and Its Celebrations." *SCA UK (Shan Cultural Association UK) Newsletter* 3:2–7.
Kinnvall, Catarina. 2004. "Globalization and Religious Nationalism: Self, Identity, and the Search for Ontological Security." *Political Psychology* 25 (5): 741–67.
Kirigaya, Ken. 2014. "Some Annotations to the Chiang Mai Chronicle: The Era of Burmese Rule in Lan Na." *Journal of the Siam Society* 102:257–85.
Kirigaya, Ken. 2015. "Lan Na under Burma: A 'Dark Age' in Northern Thailand?" *Journal of the Siam Society* 103:270–94.
Kreangkrai Kirdsiri. 2007. "Wat Lae Chumchon Baan Saen" (in Thai) [The Monastery and Community of Baan Saen]. *Muang Boran Journal* 33 (2): 80–93.
Kreangkrai Kirdsiri. 2008. *Cultural Landscape and Vernacular Architecture in Historic Town of Keng Tung, Shan State, Myanmar*. Bangkok: Silpakorn University.
Lagirarde, François. 2012. "Narratives as Ritual Histories: The Case of the Northern-Thai Buddhist Chronicles." In *Buddhist Narrative in Asia and Beyond*, vol. 1, edited by Peter Skilling and Justin McDaniel, 83–94. Bangkok: Institute of Thai Studies, Chulalongkorn University.
Leach, Edmund R. 1954. *Political Systems of Highland Burma: A Study of Kachin Social Structure*. London: Athlone.
Lehman, F. K. 2003. "The Relevance of the Founders' Cult for Understanding the Political Systems of the Peoples of Northern Southeast Asia and Its Chinese Borderlands." In *Founders' Cults in Southeast Asia: Ancestors, Polity, and Identity*, edited by Nicola Tannenbaum and Cornelia Ann Kammerer, 15–39. New Haven, CT: Yale University Southeast Asia Studies.
Leidy, Denise Patry. 2004. "Maṇḍala." In *Encyclopedia of Buddhism*, edited by Robert E. Buswell Jr., 508–12. New York: Macmillan Reference.
Li Song. 2015. *The Maguai Festival of the Zhuang People*. Reading, UK: Paths International; Anhui People's Publishing House.
Liangwen Zhu. 1992. *The Dai, or the Tai and Their Architecture and Customs in South China*. Bangkok: DD Books.
Lieberman, Victor. 1978. "Ethnic Politics in Eighteenth-Century Burma." *Modern Asian Studies* 12 (3): 455–82.

Lieberman, Victor. 2003. *Strange Parallels: Southeast Asia in Global Context, c. 800–1830.* Vol. 1, *Integration on the Mainland.* Cambridge: Cambridge University Press.
Lieberman, Victor, and Brendan Buckley. 2012. "The Impact of Climate on Southeast Asia, circa 950–1820: New Findings." *Modern Asian Studies* 46 (5): 1049–96.
Liew-Herres, Foon Ming, and Volker Grabowsky (in collaboration with Aroonrut Wichienkeeo). 2008. *Lan Na in Chinese Historiography: Sino-Tai Relations as Reflected in the Yuan and Ming Sources (13th to 17th Centuries).* Bangkok: Institute of Asian Studies, Chulalongkorn University.
Liew-Herres, Foon Ming, Volker Grabowsky, and Renoo Wichasin. 2012. *Chronicle of Sipsong Panna: History and Society of a Tai Lu Kingdom, Twelfth to Twentieth Century.* Chiang Mai: Mekong.
Lintner, Bertil. 2000. *The Golden Triangle Opium Trade: An Overview.* Asia Pacific Media Services. http://www.asiapacificms.com/papers/pdf/gt_opium_trade.pdf.
Lintner, Bertil. 2021. *The Wa of Myanmar and China's Quest for Global Dominance.* Copenhagen: NIAS.
Lintner, Bertil. 2023. *Burma's Path to Peace: Lessons from the Past and Paths Forward.* Loikaw, Myanmar: Researchers' Republic. https://researchersrepublic.org/publications/.
Lukas, H. 2012. "Ritual as a Means of Social Reproduction? Comparisons in Continental South-East Asia: The Lao-Kmhmu Relationship." In *Ritual, Conflict and Consensus: Case Studies from Asia and Europe,* edited by Gabriella Kilianova, Christian Jahoda, and Michaela Ferenfova, 103–17. Vienna: Austrian Academy of Sciences Press.
Malalasekera, G. P. 1974. *Dictionary of Pāli Proper Names,* vol. 2. London: Pali Text Society.
Mangrai, Sao Saimong. 1965. *The Shan State and the British Annexation.* Ithaca, NY: Cornell University Press.
Mangrai, Sao Saimong. 1981. *The Padaeng Chronicle and the Jengtung State Chronicle Translated.* Ann Arbor: University of Michigan, Center for South and Southeast Asian Studies.
Marshall, John, and Alfred Foucher. (1940) 1982. *The Monuments of Sāñchī.* 3 vols. Delhi: Swati.
Massieu, Isabelle. (1901) 2013. *Around Southeast Asia in 1897. A Frenchwoman's Observations in Vietnam, Cambodia, Thailand, Burma, and Laos.* Bangkok: White Lotus.
Maule, Robert Brice. 1993. "British Policy and Administration in the Federated Shan States, 1922–1942." PhD. diss., University of Toronto.
McDaniel, Justin. 2002. "Transformative History: Nihon Ryōiki and Jinakālamālīpakaraṇam." *Journal of the International Association of Buddhist Studies* 25 (1–2): 151–207.
McDaniel, Justin. 2007. "Two Bullets in a Balustrade: How the Burmese Have Been Removed from Northern Thai Buddhist History." *Journal of Burma Studies* 11:85–126.
McDaniel, Justin. 2008. *Gathering Leaves and Lifting Words: Histories of Buddhist Monastic Education in Laos and Thailand.* Seattle: University of Washington Press.
McDaniel, Justin. 2021. "Creative Engagement: The Sujavaṇṇa Wua Luang and Its Contribution to Buddhist Literature." In *Wayward Distractions: Ornament, Emotion, Zombies and the Study of Buddhism in Thailand,* 25–53. Singapore: NUS Press. Originally published in *Journal of the Siam Society* 88 (2000): 156–77.
Michaud, Jean. 2000. *Turbulent Times and Enduring Peoples: The Mountain Minorities of the South-East Asian Massif.* London: Curzon.

Milne, Leslie. (1910) 2001. *Shans at Home: Burma's Shan States in the Early 1900s*. Bangkok: White Lotus.
Mitton, G. E. [Lady Scott]. 1936. *Scott of the Shan Hills: Orders and Impressions*. London: John Murray.
Moerman, Michael. 1965. "Ethnic Identification in a Complex Civilization: Who Are the Lue?" *American Anthropologist* 67:1215–30.
Morgan, David. 2005. *The Sacred Gaze: Religious Visual Culture in Theory and Practice*. Berkeley: University of California Press.
Murakami, Tadayoshi. 2012. "Buddhism on the Border: Shan Buddhism and Transborder Migration in Northern Thailand." *Southeast Asian Studies* 1 (3): 365–93.
Mus, Paul. (1933) 2011. *India Seen from the East: Indian and Indigenous Cults in Campa*. Translated by Ian Mabbett. Caulfield, Australia: Monash University Press.
Narujohn Iddhichiracharas. 1980. "The Northern Thai Peasant Supernaturalism." In *Buddhism in Northern Thailand: The 13th Conference of the World Fellowship of Buddhists, 24–29 November 1980 at Chiang Mai*, edited by Saeng Chandrangaam and Narujohn Iddhichiracharas, 100–109. Chiang Mai: World Fellowship of Buddhists.
Nithi Sthapitanonda, 2016. *Architecture of Lanna: To Commemorate the 720th Anniversary of Chiang Mai City*. Bangkok: Li-Zenn.
Nora, Pierre. 1989. "Between Memory and History: Les Lieux de Mémoire." *Representations* 26:7–24.
Notton, M. Camille. 1926. *Annales du Siam: Première Partie*. Paris: Imprimeries Chales-Lavauzelle.
O'Connor, Richard A. 1995. "Agricultural Change and Ethnic Succession in Southeast Asian States: A Case for Regional Anthropology." *Journal of Asian Studies* 54 (4): 968–96.
O'Connor, Richard A. 2000. "A Regional Explanation of the Tai Müang as a City-State." In *A Comparative Study of Thirty City States*, edited by M. H. Hansen, 431–43. Copenhagen: Royal Danish Academy of Sciences and Letters.
O'Connor, Richard. 2003. "Founders' Cults in Regional and Historical Perspective." In *Founders' Cults in Southeast Asia: Ancestors, Polity, and Identity*, edited by Nicola Tannenbaum and Cornelia Ann Kammerer, 269–311. New Haven, CT: Yale University Southeast Asia Studies.
Panpen Kruathai and Silao Ketphrom. 2013. *Inscription of the Chiang Tung, Part 1*. Corpus of Lan Na Inscriptions, vol. 15. Chiang Mai: Archive of Lan Na Inscriptions, Social Research Institution, Chiang Mai University.
Peltier, Anatole-Roger. 1987. *La littérature Tai Khoeun: Tai Khoeun Literature*. Chiang Mai: École française d'Extrême-Orient and Social Research Institute, Chiang Mai University.
Peltier, Anatole-Roger. 1993. *Sujavaṇṇa*. Chiang Mai: Wat Tha Kradas.
Peltier, Anatole-Roger. 1999. *Kalae Ok Hno*. Bangkok: Princess Maha Chakri Sirindhorn Anthropology Centre (SAC).
Peltier, Anatole-Roger. 2006a. *Maghavā*. Phitsanulok: Naresuan University.
Peltier, Anatole-Roger. 2006b. *Chao Bun Hlong*. Chiang Mai: Wat Tha Kradas.
Peltier, Anatole-Roger. 2011. *Candasobhā: Les douze orphelines: The Twelve Orphan Girls*. Chiang Mai: Office of Arts and Culture, Chiang Mai Rajabhat University.
Peltier, Anatole-Roger. 2012. *Pèlerinage à Lanka: Pilgrimage to Lanka*. Chiang Mai: Rajabhat University.
Petit, Pierre. 2020. *History, Memory, and Territorial Cults in the Highlands of Laos: The Past inside the Present*. London: Routledge.
Plate, S. Brent. 2014. *A History of Religion in 5½ Objects: Bringing the Spiritual to Its Senses*. Boston: Beacon.

Prakong Nimmanahaeminda, 2012. "Tamnan Phra Chao Liap Loke (The Legend of the Buddha's Travels around the World): Lan Na Monastic Wisdom." In *Buddhist Narrative in Asia and Beyond*, vol. 2, edited by Peter Skilling and Justin McDaniel, 109–19. Bangkok: Institute of Thai Studies, Chulalongkorn University.
Ratanaporn Sethakul. 1988. "Political Relations between Chiang Mai and Kengtung in the Nineteenth Century." In *Changes in Northern Thailand and the Shan States, 1886–1940*, edited by Prakai Nontawasee, 296–327. Singapore: Institute of Southeast Asian Studies.
Ratanaporn Sethakul. 2018. "Lanna Buddhism and Bangkok Centralization in Late Nineteenth to Early Twentieth Century." In *Theravada Buddhism in Colonial Contexts*, edited by Thomas Borchert, 81–100. London: Routledge.
Reid, Anthony. 1988. *Southeast Asia in the Age of Commerce 1450–1680*. Vol. 1, *The Lands below the Winds*. New Haven, CT: Yale University Press.
Relph, Edward. 2008. "A Pragmatic Sense of Place." In *Making Sense of Place*, edited by Frank Vanclay et al., 311–23. Canberra: Australian National Museum.
Renard, Ronald D. 1988. "Social Change in the Shan States under the British." In *Changes in Northern Thailand and the Shan States 1886–1940*, edited by Prakai Nontawasee, 109–47. Singapore: Institute of Southeast Asian Studies.
Renard, Ronald D. 2000. "The Differential Integration of Hill People into the Thai State." In *Civility and Savagery: Social Identity in Tai States*, edited by Andrew Turton, 63–83. Richmond, UK: Curzon.
Renard, Ronald D. 2015. "Mon-Khmer Peoples and Thai Culture." In *Mon-Khmer: Peoples of the Mekong Region*, edited by Ronald D. Renard and Anchalee Singhanetra-Renard, 1–48. Chiang Mai: Chiang Mai University Press.
Rhum, Michael R. 1994. *The Ancestral Lords: Gender, Descent, and Spirits in a Northern Thai Village*. DeKalb: Northern Illinois University, Center for Southeast Asian Studies.
Robinne, François. 2003. "The Monastic Unity: A Contemporary Burmese Artefact?" In *The Buddhist Monastery: A Cross-Cultural Survey*, edited by Pierre Pichard and François Lagirarde, 75–92. Paris: École française d'Extrême-Orient.
Robinne, François, and Mandy Sadan. 2007. "Postscript: Reconsidering the Dynamics of Ethnicity through Foucault's Concept of 'Spaces of Dispersion.'" In *Social Dynamics in the Highlands of Southeast Asia: Reconsidering Political Systems of Highland Burma by E. R. Leach*, edited by François Robinne and Mandy Sadan, 299–308. Leiden: Brill.
Sai Kam Mong. 2004. *The History and Development of the Shan Scripts*. Chiang Mai: Silkworm Books.
Sarassawadee Ongsakul. 2005. *History of Lan Na*. Chiang Mai: Silkworm Books.
Schliesinger, Joachim. 2000. *Tai Groups of Thailand*. Vol. 2. Bangkok: White Lotus.
Schober, Juliane. 1997. "In the Presence of the Buddha: Ritual Veneration of the Burmese Mahāmuni Image." In *Sacred Biography in the Buddhist Traditions of South and Southeast Asia*, edited by Juliane Schober, 259–88. Honolulu: University of Hawai'i Press.
Schopen, Gregory. 1997. *Bones, Stones, and Buddhist Monks: Collected Papers on the Archaeology, Epigraphy, and Texts of Monastic Buddhism in India*. Honolulu: University of Hawai'i Press.
Schwartz, Barry. 2016. "Rethinking the Concept of Collective Memory." In *Routledge International Handbook of Memory Studies*, edited by Anna Lisa Tota and Trever Hagen, 9–21. Abingdon, UK: Routledge.
Scott, James C. 2009. *The Art of Not Being Governed*. New Haven, CT: Yale University Press.

Scott, J. George. 1932. *Burma and Beyond*. London: Grayson & Grayson.
Scott, J. George [Shway Yoe]. (1910) 1989. *The Burman: His Life and Notions*. Arran, UK: Kiscadale.
Scott, J. George, and J. P. Hardiman. 1900–1901. *Gazetteer of Upper Burma and the Shan States*. 5 vols. Rangoon: Superintendent, Government Printing, Burma.
Sen, Tansen. 2015. "The Spread of Buddhism." In *The Cambridge World History*. Vol. 5, *Expanding Webs of Exchange and Conflict, 500CE–1500CE*, edited by Benjamin Z. Kedar and Merry Wiesner-Hanks. Cambridge: Cambridge University Press.
Sengpan Pannyawamsa. 2009. "Recital of the *Tham Vessantara-Jataka*: A Social-Cultural Phenomenon in Kengtung, Eastern Shan State, Myanmar." *Contemporary Buddhism* 10 (1): 125–39.
Sengpan Pannyawamsa. 2016. *Dham Vessantara-Jataka and Its Recital in Kengtung*. Taunggyi, Myanmar: Centre for Tai Studies.
Shneiderman, Sara. 2015. *Rituals of Ethnicity: Thangmi Identities between Nepal and India*. Philadelphia: University of Pennsylvania Press.
Shorto, H. L. 1963. "The 32 Myos in the Medieval Mon Kingdom." *Bulletin of School of Oriental and African Studies* 26:572–91.
Simms, Sao Sandra. 2017. "Great Lords of the Sky: Burma's Shan Aristocracy." *Asian Highlands Perspectives* 48.
Singer, Milton. 1972. *When a Great Tradition Modernizes: An Anthropological Approach to Indian Civilization*. Chicago: University of Chicago Press.
Skilling, Peter. 2017. "Romance and Riddle: Buddhist Narratives of Siam." In *Imagination and Narrative: Lexical and Cultural Translation in Buddhist Asia*, edited by Peter Skilling and Justin Thomas McDaniel, 161–86. Chiang Mai: Silkworm Books.
Smith, John Sterling Forssen. 2013. *The Chiang Tung Wars: War and Politics in mid-19th Century Siam and Burma*. Bangkok: Institute of Asian Studies, Chulalongkorn University.
Smith, Jonathan Z. 1987. *To Take Place: Toward Theory in Ritual*. Chicago: University of Chicago Press.
Soangsak Prangwatanakun. 2008. *Cultural Heritage of Tai Lue Textile*. Chiang Mai: Thai Department, Faculty of Humanities, Chiang Mai University.
Sommai Premchit and Amphay Doré. 1992. *The Lan Na Twelve-Month Traditions*. Faculty of Social Sciences, Chiang Mai University.
Sommai Premchit and Donald K. Swearer. 1977. "A Translation of Tamnan Mulasasana Wat Pa Daeng: The Chronicle of the Founding of Buddhism of the Wat Pa Daeng Tradition." *Journal of the Siam Society* 65 (2): 73–110.
South, Ashley. 2008. *Ethnic Politics in Burma: States of Conflict*. New York: Routledge.
Spiro, Melford E. 1978. *Burmese Supernaturalism*. Expanded ed. Philadelphia: Institute for the Study of Human Issues.
Spiro, Melford E. 1982. *Buddhism and Society: A Great Tradition and Its Burmese Vicissitudes*. 2nd expanded ed. Berkeley: University of California Press.
Stadtner, Donald M. 2011. *Sacred Sites of Burma: Myth and Folklore in an Evolving Spiritual Realm*. Bangkok: River Books.
Stratton, Carol. 2004. *Buddhist Sculpture of Northern Thailand*. Chiang Mai: Silkworm Books.
Strong, John S. 2004. *Relics of the Buddha*. Princeton, NJ: Princeton University Press.
Stuart-Fox, Martin. 1998. *The Lao Kingdom of Lan-Xang: Rise and Decline*. Banglamung, Thailand: White Lotus.
Sunait Chutintaranond. 2002. "Leaning Port Cities in the Eastern Martaban Bay in the Context of Autonomous History." In *Recalling Local Pasts: Autonomous History in*

Southeast Asia, edited by Sunait Chutintaranond and Chris Baker, 9–24. Chiang Mai: Silkworm Books.
Swanson, Herbert R. 1982. "The Kengtung Question: Presbyterian Mission and Comity in Eastern Burma, 1896–1913." *Journal of Presbyterian History* 60 (1): 59–79.
Swearer, Donald K. 1976. *Wat Haripunjaya: A Study of the Royal Temple of the Buddha's Relic, Lamphun, Thailand*. Missoula: University of Montana, Scholars Press.
Swearer, Donald K. 1987. "The Northern Thai City as a Sacred Center." In *The City as a Sacred Center: Essays on Six Asian Contexts*, edited by Bardwell Smith and Holly Baker Reynolds, 103–13. Leiden: Brill.
Swearer, Donald K. 1995. "Hypostasizing the Buddha: Buddha Image Consecration in Northern Thailand." *History of Religions* 34 (3): 263–80.
Swearer, Donald K. 1999. "Centre and Periphery: Buddhism and Politics in Modern Thailand." In *Buddhism and Politics in Twentieth-Century Asia*, edited by Ian Harris, 194–228. London: Pinter.
Swearer, Donald K. 2004a. "Signs of the Buddha in Northern Thai Chronicles." In *Embodying the Dharma: Buddhist Relic Veneration in Asia*, edited by David Germano and Kevin Trainor, 145–62. Albany: State University of New York Press.
Swearer, Donald K. 2004b. *Becoming the Buddha: The Ritual of Image Consecration in Thailand*. Princeton, NJ: Princeton University Press.
Swearer, Donald K., and Sommai Premchit. 1978. "The Relation between the Religious and Political Orders in Northern Thailand." In *Religion and Legitimation of Power in Thailand, Laos, and Burma*, edited by Bardwell L. Smith, 20–33. Chambersburg, PA: Anima Books.
Swearer, Donald K., and Sommai Premchit. 1998. *The Legend of Queen Cāma: Bodhiraṃsi's Cāmadevīvaṃsa, a Translation and Commentary*. Albany: State University of New York Press.
Swearer, Donald K., Sommai Premchit, and Phaithoon Dokbuakaew. 2004. *Sacred Mountains of Northern Thailand and Their Legends*. Chiang Mai: Silkworm Books.
Tambiah, Stanley J. 1970. *Buddhism and the Spirit Cults in North-East Thailand*. Cambridge: Cambridge University Press.
Tambiah, Stanley J. 1976. *World Conqueror and World Renouncer: A Study of Buddhism and Polity in Thailand against a Historical Background*. Cambridge: Cambridge University Press.
Tambiah, Stanley J. 1982. "Famous Buddha Images and the Legitimation of Kings: The Case of the Sinhala Buddha (Phra Sihing) in Thailand." *Res: Anthropology and Aesthetics* 4 (September): 5–19.
Tanabe, Shigeharu. 1984. "Ideological Practice in Peasant Rebellions: Siam at the Turn of the Twentieth Century." *Seri Ethnological Studies* 13:75–110.
Tanabe, Shigeharu. 1988. "Spirits and Ideological Discourse: The Tai Lü Guardian Cults in Yunnan." *Sojourn* 13 (1): 1–25.
Tanabe, Shigeharu. 2000. "Autochthony and the Inthakhin Cult of Chiang Mai." In *Civility and Savagery: Social Identity in Tai States*, edited by Andrew Turton, 294–318. London: Routledge.
Taylor, Robert H. 1988. "British Policy and the Shan States, 1886–1942." In *Changes in Northern Thailand and the Shan States 1886–1940*, edited by Prakai Nontawasee, 13–62. Singapore: Institute of Southeast Asian Studies.
Taylor, Robert H. 2007. "British Policy towards Myanmar and the Creation of the 'Burma Problem.'" In *Myanmar: State, Society and Ethnicity*, edited by N. Ganesan and Kyaw Yin Hlaing, 70–95. Singapore: ISEAS.
Telford, J. H. 1937. *Animism in Kengtung State*. Rangoon: Zabu Meitswe Pitaka. Reprinted from *Journal of the Burma Research Society* 27 (2), 1937.

Terwiel, Barend Jan. 2012. *Monks and Magic: Revisiting a Classic Study of Religious Ceremonies in Thailand*. 4th ed. Copenhagen: NIAS.
Thant Myint-U. 2001. *The Making of Modern Burma*. Cambridge: Cambridge University Press.
Thant Myint-U. 2020. *The Hidden History of Burma: Race, Capitalism, and the Crisis of Democracy in the 21st Century*. London: Atlantic Books.
Thongchai Winichakul. 1994. *Siam Mapped: A History of the Geo-body of a Nation*. Honolulu: University of Hawai'i Press.
Thongchai Winichakul. 2005. "Trying to Locate Southeast Asia from Its Navel: Where Is Southeast Asian Studies in Thailand?" In *Locating Southeast Asia: Geographies of Knowledge and Politics of Space*, edited by P. H. Kratoska, R. Raben, and N. S. Nordholt, 113–32. Singapore: Singapore University Press.
T'ien Ju-K'ang. 1986. *Religious Cults of the Pai-I along the Burma-Yunnan Border*. Ithaca, NY: Cornell University Press.
Trankell, Ing-Britt. 1995. *Cooking, Care, and Domestication: A Culinary Ethnography of the Tai Yong, Northern Thailand*. Acta Universitatis Upsaliensis, Uppsala Studies in Cultural Anthropology, 21. Uppsala: Uppsala Universitet.
Trankell, Ing-Britt. 1999. "Royal Relics: Ritual and Social Memory in Louang Prabang." In *Laos: Culture and Society*, edited by Grant Evans, 191–213. Chiang Mai: Silkworm Books.
Turner, Victor. 1974. *Dramas, Fields, and Metaphors: Symbolic Action in Human Society*. Ithaca, NY: Cornell University Press.
Turner, Victor. 1987. *The Anthropology of Performance*. New York: PAJ.
Veidlinger, Daniel M. 2006. *Spreading the Dhamma: Writing, Orality, and Textual Transmission in Buddhist Northern Thailand*. Honolulu: University of Hawai'i Press.
Walker, Andrew. 2014. "Seditious State-Making in the Mekong Borderlands: The Shan Rebellion of 1902–1904." *Sojourn* 29 (3): 554–90.
Walton, Matthew J. 2008. "Ethnicity, Conflict, and History in Burma: The Myths of Panglong." *Asian Survey* 48 (6): 889–910.
Wimmer, Andreas, and Nina Glick Schiller. 2002. "Methodological Nationalism and Beyond: Nation-State Building, Migration and the Social Change." *Global Networks* 2 (4): 301–34.
Wolters, O. W. 1982. *History, Culture, and Religion in Southeast Asian Perspectives*. Singapore: Institute of Southeast Asian Studies.
Woodward, Hiram. 2005. *The Art and Architecture of Thailand: From Prehistoric Times through the Thirteenth Century*. Leiden: Brill.
Wyatt, David K. 2003. *Thailand: A Short History*. 2nd ed. Chiang Mai: Silkworm Books.
Wyatt, David K., and Aroonrut Wichienkeeo. 1998. *The Chiang Mai Chronicle*. 2nd ed. Translated by David K. Wyatt and Aroonrut Wichienkeeo. Chiang Mai: Silkworm Books.
Yos Santasombat. 2001. *Lak Chang: A Reconstruction of Tai Identity in Daikong*. Canberra: Pandanus Books.
Younghusband, G. J. (1888) 2005. *The Trans-Salween Shan State of Kiang Tung*. Edited by David K. Wyatt. Chiang Mai: Silkworm Books.
Yu Shi-jie. 2001. "Zhuang Frog-Worship." In *The Tai World: A Digest of Articles from the Thai-Yunnan Project Newsletter*, edited by Nicholas Tapp and Andrew Walker, 42–46. Canberra: Australian National University.

Index

Introductory Note
References such as "178–79" indicate (not necessarily continuous) discussion of a topic across a range of pages. Wherever possible in the case of topics with many references, these have either been divided into sub-topics or only the most significant discussions of the topic are listed. Because the entire work is about Chiang Tung, the use of this term (and certain others which occur constantly throughout the book) as an entry point has been restricted. Information will be found under the corresponding detailed topics. Cross-references in a form such as "monasteries. *See also individual monasteries*" direct the reader to headings in a particular class (e.g. in this case "Wat Baan Saen") rather than a specific "*individual monasteries*" entry.

abbots, 27, 121, 153, 166, 200
AFPFL (Anti-Fascist People's Freedom League), 82
agriculture, 44, 124–28, 156, 162, 192
  slash-and-burn, 36
  wet rice, 25, 126–28, 156, 162, 186, 189, 192
Alaunghpaya, king, 54
alliances, 40, 47–49, 53, 55, 57, 68, 80, 86
Amarapura, 60, 62, 67, 146, 159
Amporn Jirattikorn, 88–89, 153
Anaukhpetlun, king, 53
Anawrata, king, 93
ancestor cults, 130–31
ancestors, 14, 97, 123, 129, 133, 157, 161, 192
ancestry, common, 22, 59, 65, 105, 123, 191
Anderson, Benedict, 20, 31
Angkor, 44, 48, 127, 202
Anglo-Burmese Wars, 61–62, 67
animals, 107, 110–11, 113, 170–71, 177
annual ceremonies, 119, 133, 135
anti-British nationalism, 76
Anti-Fascist People's Freedom League (AFPFL), 82
Anuman Rajadhorn, Phya, 166
Arakan, 61, 94–95, 146, 159
architecture, 25, 48, 98, 100, 102, 139
area studies, 22–24
armed groups, ethnic, 14, 87–88
armies, 9, 18, 34–35, 40, 53–54, 60–61, 72, 87
artistic expressions of Buddhism, 25, 136, 194
assassinations, 70, 79, 147
assembly halls (*vihan*), 6, 26, 98–100, 102–6, 108–12, 114–16, 118–19, 122
atyatham, 151–52, 159, 163, 194
Aung San, 80, 82

Aung Tun, 67, 75–76, 79, 81–82, 86
autochthonous people. *See* indigenous people
autonomy, 23, 53, 78, 82, 85–86, 96, 203
Ava, 47, 52, 54, 57
Aysaengto, 40
Ayutthaya, 10, 29, 41, 50–55, 140, 143, 201

baan. See villages
Baan Yipun, 41–42
Bagan, 6, 44, 48, 92–94, 127, 195, 203
Bagyidaw, king, 67
Bangkok, 4, 9–10, 57, 59, 61–62, 73, 79–81, 149–52
banishing, symbolic, 37–38, 43, 188
banners, 105–8, 110, 166, 202
Baptists, 78, 201
baskets, 44, 178, 200
bathing, ritual, 165–66
Bayinnaung, king, 50–53, 64, 91, 97
beliefs, 94, 100, 131, 133, 135, 157, 166, 192
belonging
  local, 6, 16–30
  rythm of, 178–82
  sense of, 190–97
Blackburn, Anne M., 138, 145
Bodawpaya, king, 66, 94–95, 146, 159
Bodh Gayā, 137, 145
bodhi trees, 99, 140, 142, 166
bodyguards, 63, 71–72
Boon Tip, Sao, 39, 153–54
Border Area Development Program, 90
borderland, 1–2, 7, 9, 22–23, 53, 65–66, 118, 153, 163
Buddhism, 24–25

217

borders, 13–15, 22–23, 66–67, 85–88, 90–91, 96, 148–49, 153
  regional, 22
British, 5–6, 29, 61–64, 74–84, 96, 150–51, 162, 194
  annexation of Chiang Tung, 66–73
British Burma, 9, 29, 69, 71, 77
British Ceylon, 79, 96, 147
British India, 67, 74, 77, 89, 147
bronze drums, 111, 113, 169–74, 176, 178
Buddha, 31–33, 100, 103–4, 106–8, 117–18, 144–46, 155–56, 158–63
  images, 103–4, 136–37, 142, 144, 155, 158–61, 165–67, 193 (see also individual images)
  statues, 91–93, 200, 204
Buddhavaṃsa sutta, 173, 182
Buddhism, 3, 24–25, 28, 37, 46, 50, 57, 78–79
  adoption, 14, 44, 48, 136, 143–44, 156, 193
  artistic expressions, 25, 136, 194
  between borders, 148–55
  in Chiang Tung, 4, 78, 95–96, 115, 147, 149, 151, 194
  in Lan Na, 136–47
  protectors, 57, 78, 96, 146–47, 191
  royal protection, 79, 139, 147
  Sinhalese, 148, 163
  and spirit cults, 155–63
  Theravāda, 93, 138, 160–61
  Yuan, 148, 203
Buddhist architecture, 108
Buddhist buildings, 99–100, 139, 159
Buddhist culture, 4, 6, 99, 138–39, 144, 148–49, 163, 194
Buddhist monasteries. See monasteries
Buddhist monks. See monks
Buddhist rituals, 114, 120, 149, 155, 163, 190, 194
Buddhist texts, 108, 115, 138, 140, 142, 194
Buddhist traditions, 4, 25, 46–49, 136–37, 139–41, 148, 151, 193
Buddhist worldview, 27, 143, 156–57, 162, 193
buffaloes, 34, 107, 174
buildings, 21, 39, 47, 91, 100, 102, 121, 153–55
  Buddhist, 99–100, 139, 159
bulls, 108, 110–11, 113, 174
Bunchum, Khruba, 92–93, 153
Burma, 29–30, 59–64, 69–70, 75–76, 78–84, 86–90, 96, 201–2 (see also Myanmar)
  British, 9, 29, 69, 71, 77
  court, 62, 72, 75, 201
  kings, 60, 68, 74, 78 (see also individual names)
  Lower, 51, 63, 70, 139, 199
  Southern, 54, 61–62, 67, 69
Burmanization, 90–97
Burmese, 10–12, 51–52, 54–57, 60–63, 66–67, 94–95, 151–52, 190–92
Burmese army. See Burmese military
Burmese dynasties, 51, 53–54, 90–91, 95, 97, 99, 162, 190
Burmese military (Tatmadaw), 54, 85–86, 90–92, 95, 97, 178–79, 188, 194–96

cakkavattin, 46, 143, 162, 203
calendars, 113, 120, 133–35, 152
Cāmadevī, queen, 14, 203
Cāmadevīvaṃsa, 14
Cambodia, 8, 42, 48
Cao No Kham, 60–61
castings, 79, 96, 144, 146, 162, 170
celebrations, 89, 110, 131, 133–34, 146, 159, 166, 168, 176, 179, 181, 187–88, 195–96, 203
Central Thais, 80, 150
ceremonies, 103, 109–10, 115, 118–19, 131, 135, 164–65, 202–3
  annual, 119, 133, 135
  consecration, 91, 160
  drumming, 38, 179, 188
  religious, 99, 115, 123, 147, 164
ceremony masters, 182–83
Cham, 48, 127
Chanthaphilith Chiemisouraj, 35, 200
Chao Sua Khan Fa, 11
charismatic monks, 5, 149–50, 152–55, 163, 194
charismatic personality, 143, 162
chedis, 3, 33, 39, 52, 57, 79, 99–100, 111, 136–37, 141–42, 144–45, 154, 158, 166, 187
  See also stupas
Chiang Kai-shek, 81, 85
Chiang Khaeng, 28, 57, 201
Chiang Mai, 7–10, 49–51, 53–59, 61–63, 73, 136–43, 192–94, 199–204
  ancestors, 133, 204
  Treaty, 149–50
  See also individual rulers
Chiang Mai Chronicle, 40, 49, 56, 58, 109, 127, 200
Chiang Man, 200
Chiang Rai, 7–9, 34–36, 43, 54, 56, 69, 137, 191
Chiang Rung, 7, 40, 52–53, 59–61, 63, 148, 150, 158
Chiang Saen, 7–9, 48–49, 53–56, 61, 69, 73, 140, 153

Chiang Tung
 attacks on, 50, 61
 British annexation, 66–73
 culture, 99, 105–6, 163, 195, 197
 exposed location, 82–84
 mythical origin, 32–36
 palace, 37–38, 43, 195
 repopulation, 5, 8, 63, 82, 144, 162, 194
 rulers (*saopha*), 7, 38, 63, 74, 76–77, 79, 83, 90, 130, 143, 151, 181 (*see also individual rulers*)
 as Saharat Thai Doem, 6
 spirit of, 7, 123, 129–34, 157–60, 162, 182–83, 193, 196
 Wars, 59, 61, 63, 144, 162, 194
 See also introductory note to this index
Chiang Tung Chronicle (CTC), 13, 19, 22, 27–28, 32–37, 39–41, 50, 53–57, 64, 127, 137, 145, 157, 172–73, 199–200
China, 4–5, 7–9, 12, 34–35, 59–61, 70, 85–87, 97
 South, 3, 25, 47, 125, 127, 169–70, 192, 204
 southern, 24, 70, 87, 114, 125–28, 172
Chinese, 10–12, 33–34, 39–41, 51, 60, 80–81, 97, 200
Chinese emperors, 32–33, 39–40, 59
Chinese invasions, 50, 200
Cholthira Satyawadhna, 37
chosen glories, 21, 44, 48
chosen history, 18, 21, 42, 190, 192
chosen trauma, 21, 52
Christian missionaries, 78, 184
chronicles, 11, 13, 26–28, 33–36, 53–54, 137–39, 141–42, 182
Churchman, Catherine, 125, 169, 171
city walls, 8, 57, 69
city-states, 4, 7, 13, 19, 27, 40, 46–47, 52, 57, 59, 96, 124, 126, 129–30, 133, 139, 144–45
 important, 7, 50, 64, 156, 193
 independent, 56, 73
 in Lan Na, 26, 46, 73, 144
 political geography of, 47, 156
 small, 7, 56, 68, 136, 143, 156, 162, 193
 See also *mueang*
climate, 81, 126–27, 165, 202
clothes, 135, 154–55, 203
Cohen, Paul T., 19, 36, 59, 148, 153
collective memory, 21, 42
colonial period, 23, 66, 74–79, 94, 96, 146, 151, 191
colonial policy, 73, 149
colonial powers, 23, 66, 73, 78, 80, 83, 149
colonial rule, 74–78, 85, 99, 149, 191, 202

common ancestry, 22, 59, 65, 105, 123, 191
common identity, 17, 21–22, 31, 95, 99, 103, 122
Communist Party of Burma (CPB), 85–88, 96–97
conflicts, 54, 57, 59–60, 67, 85–86, 95, 99, 192
conquest, 35, 49, 53, 57, 69, 191
consecration, 112–13, 173–74
consecration rituals, 155, 161
control, 14–15, 51, 55, 75, 95–96, 149–50, 160, 195–96
 of human power, 17, 191
Conway, Susan, 12, 18, 154, 201, 203
cooperation, 74–75, 81, 128
coronation ceremony/ritual, 37–38, 43, 143, 175, 179, 188, 195
countryside, 8, 16, 102, 120, 129, 156, 162–63, 193
coups, military, 24, 79, 86, 89, 95, 151, 160, 188
courts, 5, 12–13, 38–39, 60–62, 74–75, 143, 180–81, 194–96
CPB. *See* Communist Party of Burma
craft workers, 45, 57–58, 108, 159, 171
Crosthwaite, Charles, 70, 78
CTC. See *Chiang Tung Chronicle*
cults, 45, 100, 130–31, 155–56, 158, 192–93, 196, 203
 ancestor, 130–31
 of frogs, 172, 174
 phallic, 42, 168, 176, 184
 spirit, 44–45, 124, 129, 134, 136, 155–64, 193
 of territory spirits, 25, 45–46, 123, 125, 127–30, 156, 192–93, 203
cultural exchange, 118, 151, 201
cultural identity, 99, 118
cultural performances, 1, 3, 164–65, 175
culture, 10–11, 14–15, 64–66, 118, 125–26, 163–64, 191, 196–97
 Buddhist, 4, 6, 99, 138–39, 144, 148–49, 163, 194
 Indic Hindu-Buddhist, 44, 48, 136, 162, 175, 177, 193, 195–96
 indigenous monsoon, 177, 184, 188, 190, 195
 Khuen, 26, 37, 111, 161, 192
 material, 6, 25, 98–99, 122, 149, 190, 194
 monsoon, 3, 111, 126, 148, 164, 171, 195, 197
 religious, 6, 24–25, 123–63, 191
 visual, 5, 95, 98–99, 156, 162–63, 193

Dammilap, 13, 32
Davis, Sara, 20, 93, 109, 130, 165, 203
defensive wall, 39, 57, 59, 63, 144, 192, 200
Dehong Dai. *See* Tai Neua

Delhi Durbar, 77
dependence, mutual, 3, 13, 36–39, 43, 188, 195
Dham Vessantara Jātaka, 109–10, 115, 118–19, 202
Dīgha Nikāya, 203
Dodd, William Clifton, 9, 29, 38, 76, 167–68, 179
Doi Suthep, 14, 49, 203
donations, 140–42, 153–54, 178, 202
Dong Son drums. *See* bronze drums
Dong World, 125
Doré, Amphay, 114, 119–21, 133, 165–66, 203–4
drinking, 135, 166, 175–76
droughts, 127, 172–73, 203
drug trade, 1, 85–87, 97
drumming, 3, 131, 175, 178–80, 182, 184, 188, 195–96
  ceremonies, 38, 179, 188
  rhythmic, 182–83, 185, 188–89
drums, 111–15, 176, 180–82, 184–86, 188, 195–96
  bronze, 111, 113, 169–74, 176, 178
  frog, 169–70
  in monsoon culture, 169–75
  rain, 169, 176
  ritual, 111, 113, 173–74
  Songkran, 173, 175–76, 178
  temple, 111–15, 122, 173–75, 182
  wooden, 173–74
Dvāravatī, 48–49, 136

earth gods, local, 45–46
earthborn Lua, 43, 134, 187
Easum, Taylor, 8, 202
education, 41, 62, 75–76, 154
elders, 39, 89, 150, 166
elephants, 9, 34, 39, 56, 58, 75–76, 107–10, 172
  royal, 76
  white, 53, 109, 118
Emerald Buddha, 80, 161
emperors, 33, 40, 77
  Chinese, 32–33, 39–40, 59
Eng, 14, 113, 173–74
Enriquez, C. M., 38, 76–77, 168, 179, 184
ethnic groups, 9–14, 17–19, 22–23, 26–27, 35–37, 57–59, 82–83, 191–92
ethnic identity, 14, 16–19, 36–37, 43, 59, 167
  localized, 19, 36, 55, 59, 65, 190–91
ethnic markers, 36, 43
ethnic minorities, 74, 82, 86, 109, 153, 167
Évrard, Olivier, 35, 200
exposed location of Chiang Tung, 82–84

FACE. *See* Frontier Areas Committee of Enquiry
Faihin, Khruba, 150
families, 56–57, 62, 116, 119, 122–23, 134–35, 147, 182
Feast of Lights, 120
federal Shan State, 75
female spirits, 33, 35, 182, 184
Ferguson, Jane, 85, 87–88
fertility, 3, 89, 167, 169, 171–72, 175–76, 179, 187–89
festival sites, 175–76, 182–83
festivals, 1, 3–4, 16, 25, 99, 131, 157, 164–65, 175–76, 178–79, 182, 187, 196
First Anglo-Burmese War. *See* Anglo-Burmese Wars
Flower Garden order. *See* Suan Dok (Puppharam)
folder books, 11, 98, 116, 122
food, 32, 81, 99–100, 123, 131–32, 135, 176, 183
forced resettlements/relocations, 17–18, 22, 56, 58, 65, 148, 191
foreign rulers, 66–97, 201
foreign visitors, 28–30
forests, 13, 58, 81, 109, 125, 127, 130, 192
French Indo-China, 70
French Mekong Exploration Commission, 29, 68
frog drums, 169–70
frogs, 164, 176, 182–84, 186, 188, 195
  cult of, 172, 174
  in monsoon culture, 169–75
  worship, 171–72, 174
Frontier Areas, 78, 82–83, 96, 151, 191
Frontier Areas Committee of Enquiry, 83
frontier states, 7, 34–35, 37, 191
funeral monuments, 175

gates, 8, 57, 171, 183
Geertz, Clifford, 164–65, 175
generosity, 108–9, 118–19, 122
geopolitics, 71, 125–26, 157
gifts, 49, 110, 120, 202
gold leaf, 112
gold painting, 108
gold stenciling, 111, 122
Golden Age, 42, 50, 138
golden stag, 34, 200
Grabowsky, Volker, 7, 11, 13, 40–41, 55–56, 58, 60, 126, 200–202
group identity, 16–17, 19, 98, 194
Guangdong, 169, 204
Guangxi, 126, 169, 172, 204

INDEX 221

Guangzhou Ji, 170
guardian spirits, 32–33, 119, 128, 130, 133, 166, 203–4

Hall, Rebecca, 106
Haripuñjaya, 7, 13–14, 48–49, 55–56, 61, 136–37, 139–40, 201
  Mon tradition of, 136–37
headmen. *See* village headmen
hermits, 14, 32–33
hierarchy, 4, 134, 149, 154, 163, 193–94
highland people, 13, 23, 25, 37, 43, 188, 195
highland river valleys, 47, 125, 156
Hindu-Buddhist worldview, 45–46, 129
Hkun Kyi, Sao, 64
Holt, John Clifford, 129, 134, 156, 158–59, 161, 167
horses, 9, 56, 107–10, 118, 172, 177, 185
  statues, 110
houses, 20, 96, 123, 146, 161, 166, 173, 184
Hsinbyushin (Mangra), king, 54–55
Hsipaw, 51, 67, 84

identity, 6–7, 16–17, 19–22, 58–59, 65, 83, 99–100, 161
  collective, 59, 65
  common, 17, 21–22, 31, 95, 99, 103, 122
  cultural, 99, 118
  ethnic, 14, 16–19, 36–37, 43, 59, 167
  group, 16–17, 19, 98, 194
  religious, 17, 148
images, 20–21, 91, 93–99, 103–4, 144–46, 159–61, 163, 182
  Buddha, 52, 103–4, 109, 136–37, 140, 142, 144, 155, 158–61, 165–67, 193
  Mahāmuni, 94–95, 133, 144, 146, 159–60, 162–63
  See also individual images
imagined community, 89
independence, 7, 68, 80, 85, 87–89, 96, 151, 190–91
India
  British, 67, 74, 77, 89, 147
  South, 13, 136
Indianization of Southeast Asia, 44–48
Indic Hindu-Buddhist culture, 44, 48, 136, 162, 175, 177, 193, 195–96
indigenous monsoon cultures, 177, 184, 188, 190, 195
indigenous people, 13, 43, 127, 200, 204
Indra, 159, 164, 166, 176–77, 179, 185–86, 188, 195
  statue, 171, 176, 180–81, 184–86, 188

informal political contract, 37–38, 43, 175, 180, 188, 195
inscriptions, 11, 26–28, 49, 92, 117, 136–37, 140–42, 145–46
Intaleng, Sao, 38, 71, 76–79, 81, 94, 96, 108, 144, 146–47, 162–63, 167–68, 179, 184–85
integration, 18, 36, 41, 43, 48, 191
intermarriage, 12, 18, 60, 84, 192
interviews, 26, 112, 156, 200
Inthakhin, 203–4
  city pillar, 133
irrigation, 127–28, 162, 169, 192
  See also wet rice cultivation

Japan, 29, 41, 79–80
Japanese, 5, 29, 41–42, 80–81
Japanese origin, 42, 184
Jātakas, 109–11, 115, 117–19, 122, 194, 202
Jinakālamālī, 27, 40, 141

Kachin, 12, 59, 80, 82
Kaeo, Phaya, 50–51, 140, 142
Karen, 58, 77, 80, 82, 85, 171, 201
Kawila, 1, 6, 44, 55–59, 62, 151, 200
Kawn Kiao Intaleng, Sao. *See* Intaleng, Sao
Kawng Kham Hpoo, Sao, 72
Kawng Tai, Sao, 30, 47, 63–65, 68–69, 71–72, 79, 84, 147, 201
Keng Tung, 1, 6
Keyes, Charles, 19, 36, 59, 148–49
Kha, 13, 199–200
khruba, 93, 152–54
  See also individual names
Khuen, 10–12, 19, 21–22, 24–27, 33–35, 37–38, 41–43, 178–80, 187–91
  dependence and loyalty between Khuen and Lua, 36–39
  language, 27, 117, 122, 149, 163, 180, 188, 194, 199
  literature, 25, 116–18, 122, 197, 202
  monasteries, 99–105, 109, 111, 122–23
  origin, 35–36
  temple drums, 111–15, 122, 173–75, 182
kingship symbolism, 108–11
KMT. *See* Kuomintang
KNU (Karen National Union), 85
Konbaung dynasty, 51, 54–55, 59, 61, 64, 66–67, 94, 190
Kreangkrai Kirdsiri, 8, 102, 104, 200
Ku Kut, 136–37
Kuena (Ku Na), Phaya, 49–50, 139, 143
Kuomintang (KMT), 81, 85–86, 96
kuti, 99

Lagrée, Ernest de, 29, 68
Lak Thai, 9
Lampang, 7, 54–56, 61, 73, 131, 153, 199, 201
Lamphun. See Haripuñjaya
Lan Na, 4, 6–7, 48–56, 59–62, 106–8, 117–20, 147–53
  Buddhism, 136–47
  golden age, 42, 44, 48–51, 64, 138, 143, 191
Lan Xang, 158, 167
land ownership, 3, 37–38, 143, 175, 179–80, 188, 190, 195–96
landscape
  political, 48, 127
  sacred, 32–33, 46, 118, 143–45, 148–49, 156, 162–63, 193
Lanka, island of, 6, 28, 46, 118, 136, 138–42, 144–45, 147–48
Laos, 8–9, 12, 19, 114–15, 118–19, 158, 160–61, 165–67
  northern, 4, 114, 200
  northwestern, 7, 106
Lawa. See Lua
laypeople, 102, 110, 113, 156–57, 160, 187
leadership, 7, 34, 66, 136, 140
legends, 11, 13–14, 21–22, 27, 33–35, 100, 136–37, 143–44
legitimation, 44, 48, 79, 136, 143–44, 156, 158, 193
  symbolic, 187–88
libraries, 28, 99, 116, 142
Lieberman, Victor, 17–18, 51, 127, 202
lightning, 40, 92, 172, 176
Limbin, prince, 64
Limbin Confederacy, 63–64
liquor, 131–32, 135
living traditions, 6, 41, 138, 157–58
local belonging, 6, 16–30, 33, 36, 42, 55–59, 123–24
local history, 21–24, 148–49, 163
local lords, 74, 106
local places, 19, 65, 145, 148, 156, 162, 193
local spirits, 45–46, 156, 162, 193, 203
local traditions, 24–25, 29, 46, 148, 151, 193–94
localized ethnic identity, 19, 36, 55, 59, 65, 190–92
  See also local belonging
Loi-mila, 200
Lower Burma, 51, 63, 70, 139, 199
lowlands, 13, 23, 37, 125, 127
loyalty, 3, 36, 49, 76, 80
Lua (Lawa), 12–14, 34–39, 43, 48–49, 173–76, 178–80, 184–89, 195–97
  dependence and loyalty between Khuen and Lua, 36–39
  earthborn, 43, 134, 187
  See also Tai Loi

Luang Prabang, 9, 59, 61, 114, 158–59, 167, 196, 200
Lue, 11, 19, 58–59, 199, 202
Lvas, 34, 36–38, 199

McDaniel, Justin, 52, 98, 115–17, 145
McLeod, William C., 13, 29, 56–57, 60, 62, 68, 200–201
Mae Sai, 1, 51, 56, 85
magical powers, 67, 139, 142
Maguai festival, 172
Mahā Dhammikarājā, 53, 144
Maha Hpom, Sao, 68
Mahābodhi monasteries, 137, 142
Mahachat (Vessantara) ceremony, 118, 120
Mahakhanan, Sao, 5, 56–57, 60, 62–63, 151, 162, 192, 200–201
Mahāmuni Buddha, 66–67, 79, 94–97, 144, 146–47, 159–60, 162–63, 202
Mahaphom, Sao, 60, 62
Mahāvihara, 138–39, 142
  See also Udumbaragiri
Mahawang, 60
Malai, Phra, 119
mandala, 7, 46–47
Mandalay, 8–9, 47, 63–64, 67, 96, 146, 151, 159
Mangra. See Hsinbyushin, king
Mangrai, 33–35, 43–44, 48–49, 78, 136–37, 143–44, 156, 193
  dynasty, 38, 50, 143, 196
Mangyoy, 34–35, 37
manuscripts, 27–28, 93, 202
  palm-leaf, 11, 98, 116, 122, 142, 144, 150
map, religious, 45, 156, 162, 193
markets, 30, 81, 108, 176, 179
Martaban, 139, 147
māt poem, 116–17, 131–32, 135, 147, 176, 183, 185, 188–89
material culture, 6, 25, 98–115, 122, 149, 190, 194
meditation, 33, 121, 152–53
Mekong, 5, 8–9, 29, 58, 68–69, 73, 96, 126
memories, 5–6, 16, 21–22, 31–44, 98–99, 105, 123
  collective, 21, 42
  shared, 16, 20–21, 42, 123
merit, 95, 114, 116, 119–20, 122, 147, 165–66, 187
  donations, 140–41, 153–54
  sharing, 93, 153
Milakkha. See Lua
military commanders, 95, 97, 160, 188
military coups, 24, 79, 86, 89, 95, 151, 160, 188

military custodians, 24, 79, 86, 89, 95, 151, 160, 188
Mindon, king, 62–64, 67, 72
Ministry for the Progress of Border Areas and National Races, 90
minorities, ethnic, 74, 82, 86, 109, 153, 167
minority regions, 6, 90–91, 93, 97, 194
Miss Lao New Year, 159, 167, 196
missionaries, Christian, 78, 184
Mitton, Geraldine, 67, 71–72
Mon tradition of Haripuñjaya, 136–37
monasteries, 98–102, 112–16, 119–23, 146, 149–52, 158–63, 193–94, 202
See also individual monasteries
in Chiang Tung, 26, 102–4, 108, 115, 122, 151, 160, 194
Khuen, 99, 109, 111, 122–23
Mahābodhi, 137, 142
village, 100, 120, 159, 161, 163, 166, 187, 193
monastic rules, 140, 142
money, 119, 135, 140–41, 176
Mong La, 87, 91, 104
Mong Mao (Mueang Mao), 11
Mong Nai, 64, 77
Mong Pan, 81, 91
Mong Yang, 56, 82, 85
Mong Yong, 19, 56, 58, 65
Mongkut. *See* Rama IV
Mongols, 7, 34–35, 37, 39–41, 48, 127, 191
Mon-Khmer. *See* Palaungic Mon-Khmer
monks, 4–5, 102–3, 113, 119–21, 137–42, 144–48, 152–57, 160–63
Buddhist, 45, 139, 144, 157
charismatic holy, 5, 149–50, 152, 154, 163, 194
Sinhalese, 139, 142
See also individual names
Monsoon Asia, 24–25, 125–26, 128–29, 156, 161, 169, 171, 195
monsoon climate, 44, 124, 126–27, 156, 169, 192
monsoon culture, 3, 111, 126, 148, 164, 171, 195, 197
drums and frogs, 169–75
indigenous, 177, 184, 188, 190, 195–97
Moulmein, 9, 69–70, 201
mountains, 7–9, 35–37, 39, 43, 80–81, 125–27, 153–54, 179
Muang Sam, Sao, 55
mueang, 4, 7–8, 35, 43, 47, 56, 65, 83, 124, 129, 131, 134, 144, 156–60, 163, 193, 203
See also city-states
Mueang Mao. *See* Mong Mao
Mus, Paul, 24, 45–46, 125, 128–29, 135, 158
mutual dependence, 3, 13, 36–39, 43, 188, 195

Myanmar, 4–8, 10–12, 89–91, 94–95, 148–49, 152, 176–78, 196–97
See also Burma
Myanmar Population and Housing Census, 10
mythical origin of Chiang Tung, 32–36
myths, 21–22, 24–27, 31–43, 98, 128, 172, 177, 200–203

Nagamasa, Yamada, 29, 41–42
Namthum, 39–40, 137
Nan, 7, 28, 54, 61, 73, 199, 201, 203
Nāṇagambhīra, 140–41
Nangklao. *See* Rama III
Naresuan, king, 53
nat, 130, 166
See also spirits
nation states, 10, 66, 96, 115, 148–50, 167
Nationalists, 76, 85–87
nationhood, 88–89
nation-state-centric studies. *See* area studies
Ne Win, 86, 97
negotiations, 15, 39, 64, 67, 71–72, 83
New Year, 88–89, 120, 152, 165–67, 176, 180, 186, 195
See also Shan New Year; Songkran
Nora, Pierre, 21, 98
North Vietnam, 125, 169–70
northern Laos, 4, 114, 200
Northern Thailand, 11, 58–59, 101–2, 106–7, 114–15, 118–20, 148–49, 152–53
novice ordination, 119–20
novices, 26, 39, 99, 146, 153–54, 202

objects
phallic, 42, 176, 184
sacred, 98–99, 112, 122, 174, 194
O'Connor, R. A., 7, 127–28, 130, 192, 202
offerings, 36, 52, 119, 131–32, 135, 158, 172, 182–85
Old Royal Market Day, 120, 131, 134, 158
opium, 13, 85, 87
ordination, 138, 140–42, 151–52
halls, 99, 146
novice, 119–20
ownership, of land. *See* land ownership

Pa Daeng monastery/order, 12, 27–28, 50, 100, 119–21, 123, 138–43, 145–46
pagodas. *See chedis*
palaces, 35–38, 40, 76–77, 90, 114–15, 137, 168, 200–201
royal, 58, 78, 90, 97, 133, 160
Palaungic Mon-Khmer, 3, 7, 12–14, 25, 48, 126–27, 167, 173

INDEX

Pāli, 4, 13, 27, 117–18, 141, 150, 166, 177
 canon, 115, 118
palladia, 158–60, 163, 167, 193, 196, 203–4
palm-leaf manuscripts, 11, 98, 116, 122, 142, 144, 150
Panglong Agreement, 82
Panglong Conferences, 5, 82–83, 86, 96
Paññāsa Jātaka, 117
pan-Thai nationalism, 5
Parivaskam, 120–21
participant observations, 26
paui sang long (novice ordination), 119–20
peacocks, 107–9
Pearl Harbor, 80–81
Pearl River, 125, 169
Pegu, 47, 52–54, 58, 137
Peltier, Anatole-Roger, 111, 115, 117, 147, 197, 202
phallic cults, 42, 168, 176, 184
Phayao, 7, 49, 54, 199–200
phi, 130, 203
 See also spirits
Phibun, 6, 80–81
Phra Bang Buddha, 158–60, 167, 196
Phra Sihing Buddha, 167, 196
Phrae, 7, 54, 61, 73, 199, 201
Phrom Lue, Sao, 79
pilgrimages, 79, 96, 147, 153
poems, 116, 131, 147
political agenda, 88–89
political contract, informal, 37–38, 43, 175, 180, 188, 195
political decisions, 5, 35–36, 43, 82–83, 191
political landscape, 48, 127
political power, 95, 97, 109, 144, 156, 193
political-economic system, 14, 36
power, 62–65, 78–79, 88–90, 95–97, 108–9, 156, 187–89, 195–96
 magical, 67, 139, 142
 political, 95, 97, 109, 144, 156, 193
 state, 17, 55, 65, 192
 symbolic, 74, 95, 160, 191
 universal, 44, 48, 136, 143–44, 156, 193
precolonial period, 17–18, 28, 44–65, 192
processions, 3, 76, 164, 168, 176, 179, 182
 Songkran, 184–89
pronunciation, 28, 115–16, 141, 150
prosperity, 38, 49, 67, 175–76, 178, 180, 188, 195–96
protective power, 135, 154–55
protectors of Buddhism, 57, 78, 96, 146–47, 191
provinces, 6–7, 52, 66, 69–70, 149
Pu Sae Ya Sae, 133, 203–4
Puppharām. *See* Suan Dok

Qing dynasty, 55, 59, 61, 66

rain ceremonies, 176
rain drums, 169, 176
Rama I, king, 59
Rama III (Nangklao), king, 61
Rama IV (Mongkut), king, 61, 63
Rangoon. *See* Yangon
Rattanakosin dynasty, 59, 66
rebellions, 54, 64, 72–73
recitations, 110, 115, 117–19, 131–32, 135, 139, 141, 165, 176, 183, 185, 188–89, 202
Red Forest order. *See* Pa Daeng, order
refugees, 42, 81, 87, 201
relics, 57, 100, 102, 138–39, 142, 144–45, 160, 203–4
religion, 25–26, 46, 90, 98–99, 118, 148, 163, 194–97
religious buildings, 90, 99, 107, 144, 154
religious ceremonies, 99, 115, 123, 147, 164
religious culture, 6, 24–25, 123–63, 191
religious environment, 103, 122
religious map, 45, 156, 162, 193
religious traditions, 108, 148, 152, 161, 169
Relph, Edward, 16, 20
repopulation of Chiang Tung, 5, 8, 63, 82, 144, 162, 194
resettlements, forced, 17–18, 22, 56, 58, 65, 148, 191
resistance, 46, 60, 70, 88, 163
 movement, 80, 88
rhythmic drumming, 182–83, 185, 188–89
rice, 7–8, 39, 53, 126–27, 169, 200
 See also wet rice cultivation
righteous rulers, 143, 156, 162, 193
rites, 130–31, 152, 165, 168
ritual bathing, 165–66
ritual drums, 111, 113, 173–74
 wooden, 173–74
rituals, 25, 38, 112–22, 154–55, 160–61, 164–67, 183–84
 Buddhist, 114, 120, 149, 155, 163, 190, 194
 consecration, 155, 161
 coronation, 143, 179, 195
river valleys, fertile, 125–26, 192
rivers, 3, 5, 8, 40, 70, 126, 130, 158, 164, 168, 171–72, 176, 178–79, 182–88, 199
 See also individual rivers
roads, 9, 70, 75, 85
royal elephants, 76
royal palaces, 58, 78, 90, 97, 133, 160
royal protection of Buddhism, 79, 139, 147
rulers, 39–40, 47–51, 60–64, 67–79, 129–30, 134, 139–47, 192–96

of Chiang Tung, 39, 49, 60–61, 64, 69, 72, 77, 90, 100, 114, 146–47, 167, 175, 181, 191, 201
local, 52–53, 73, 78–79, 96, 130, 145–46, 151, 196
new, 38, 60, 63, 78, 83, 143, 179, 195–96
righteous, 143, 156, 162, 193
See also individual names

sacred landscape, 32–33, 46, 118, 143–45, 148–49, 156, 162–63, 193
sacred objects, 98–99, 112, 122, 174, 194
sacred places, 99, 122, 145, 202
sacred space, 6, 21, 98–122, 161, 202
sacred water, 135, 152
Saddhamma Rāja Cuḷāmaṇi, 145
Saharat Thai Doem, 6
Sai Ling Tip, 83–84
Sai Long, Sao, 79, 83, 133, 144, 188
Saimong Mangrai, Sai, 27, 33, 38, 139, 199
Salween, 7–9, 11–12, 67–71, 81, 96–97, 147, 151, 162
Sam Fang Kaen, 50, 140
samurai, 41–43
sanads, 72, 74, 76, 78, 147
Sāñcī, 45, 118
sand *chedi*. See *chedis*
saṅgha, 4, 38, 139–40, 148–50, 154, 163, 194, 196
organization, 151–52
and state, 143–47
Sangha Administration Act, 4, 149–50
Sangha Council, 151–52, 163, 194
sao baan, 8, 120, 123–24, 130, 134, 157, 202
sao mueang. See spirit of Chiang Tung
saopha (rulers), 38, 74, 76–77, 79, 83, 90, 130, 143
See also individual names
Sarassawadee Ongsakul, 13, 48–53, 55, 143, 200
Scott, J. George, 12, 14, 38, 40–41, 71–72, 166–68, 173–74, 184
scripts, 5, 11, 37, 115–17, 122, 131, 142, 149–50, 162–63, 183, 190, 194, 202–3
Second Anglo-Burmese War. *See* Anglo-Burmese Wars
Second World War, 26, 30, 76, 79–82, 84–85, 87, 89, 96
secrets, 3–4, 31, 164, 188, 196
self-identification, 18, 21, 24, 31
seniority, 4, 149, 151–52, 163, 194
sense of place, 16, 20–22, 31, 36, 42–43, 145, 180, 188–91, 196
See also local belonging
Shan Chinese. *See* Tai Neua
Shan New Year, 88–90

Shan Rebellion 1902–1904, 73
Shan State Army (SSA), 86, 96
Shan State Progress Party, 86–87
Shan states, 29–30, 63–64, 67–70, 73–75, 81, 83, 96, 201
armed conflicts, 84–88
Shan States Federation, 5, 83–84, 96
Shanland, 88–90
Shans (Tai Yai), 9, 11–13, 102, 149, 154, 163, 192, 202
shared ancestry, 31, 42
shared memories, 16, 20–21, 42, 123
Shneiderman, Sara, 18
Shrin Araham, 93
shrines, 123–24, 131, 133–35, 152, 175, 183, 202
spirit, 7–8, 123–25, 133–34, 156, 162, 183, 193, 202
Shwedagon Pagoda, 79, 91, 94, 147, 201
Shwegiyn Nikāya, 4, 148
Siam/Siamese, 4–6, 51–52, 55, 57–63, 66–70, 72–73, 83–84, 148–51
See also Thailand
Sihing Buddha, 161
silver, 39, 41, 110, 113, 152, 171
Sing Zai, Sao, 83–84
Singer, Milton, 3, 164–65
Sinhalese, 140–41
Sinhalese Buddhism, 137–39, 142, 148, 163
Sinhalese orders, 137–39, 141–42, 151
Sipsong Panna, 4, 7, 10–12, 19, 55–56, 58–60, 106–9, 150
See also Chiang Rung
Siridīghā, queen, 146
sites of memory, 21
See also collective memory
Siwichai, Khruba, 150, 152–53
skin color, 74
SLORC (State Law and Order Restoration Council), 88, 90, 97
Smith, John Sterling Forssen, 60–63
Smith, Jonathan Z., 161
Soangsak Prangwatanakun, 106–7
soil, 32–34, 127–29, 157–58
soldiers, 35–36, 43, 52–54, 57, 59–63, 80–81, 85, 97
Sommai Premchit, 14, 28, 137, 139–40, 165, 200
Songkran, 3–4, 38, 41–43, 157–58, 164–90, 195–97
beating the rythm of belonging, 178–82
cultural performance, 175–89
drums, 173, 175–76, 178
procession, 184–89
second day, 171–72, 177, 182–84
in Southeast Asia, 165–68

sons, 32–34, 40, 50, 60, 69, 75–76, 145, 201
South China, 3, 25, 47, 125, 127, 169–70, 192, 204
South India, 13, 136
Southeast Asian Massif, 125
Southern Burma, 54, 61–62, 67, 69
southern China, 24, 70, 87, 114, 125–28, 172
space, sacred, 6, 21, 98–122, 161, 202
spirit cults, 44–45, 124, 129, 134, 136, 155–64, 193
spirit houses, 114, 134, 174
    See also spirit shrines
spirit of Chiang Tung, 7, 123, 129–34, 157–60, 162, 182–83, 193, 196
spirit of place, 20, 192–93
spirit shrines, 7–8, 123–25, 133–34, 156, 162, 183, 193, 202
spirit world, 124, 129–30, 193
spirits, 32–34, 123–25, 127–35, 155–59, 182–85, 187–90, 193, 202–4
    female, 33, 35, 182, 184
    guardian, 32–33, 119, 128, 130, 133, 166, 203–4
    local, 45–46, 156, 162, 193, 203
    territory, 25, 44–46, 123, 125, 127–35, 143–44, 156–57, 192–93
    village, 123–24, 129, 131–35, 155, 157–58, 162, 192–93
Sri Lanka, 6, 13, 133, 136, 138
    See also Lanka, island of
SSA (Shan State Army), 86, 96
SSA-North (SSA-N), 87
SSA-South (SSA-S), 87
SSA/SSPP, 86–87
standing Buddha, 6, 93–94, 136, 163
State Law and Order Restoration Council. See SLORC
state power, 17, 55, 65, 192
statues, 91–95, 110, 146, 176–78, 182, 184–86, 195–96, 204
    Indra, 171, 176, 180–81, 184–86, 188
sticks, walking, 32–33
stupas, 91, 99–100, 102, 147, 160, 172. See also chedis
Suan Dok (Puppharam), monastery/order, 28, 50, 137–41
subordination, 37, 43, 79, 188, 195
Suchawan, 60–61
Sudhamma (Thudhamma) Nikāya, 4, 148
Sujavaṇṇa Wua Luang, 110–11, 117–18, 120
Sukhothai, 7–8, 10, 44, 49, 139–40, 147
Sumana, 137, 139
Sunait Chutintaranond, 23, 52

Suvaṇṇabhūmi, 137
Swearer, Donald K., 14, 22, 28, 137, 139–40, 144–45, 149–50, 155
symbolic agreement, 35, 37, 175, 180, 195
symbolic banishing, 37–38, 43, 188
symbolic imagination, 184, 188
symbolic language, 95, 99
symbolic legitimation, 187–88
symbolic meanings, 90, 99–100, 106, 179, 189
symbolic ownership of land. See land ownership
symbolic power, 74, 95, 160, 191
symbolism, 92, 131, 172, 176, 183
    kingship, 108–11
symbols, 90–91, 96, 108, 142, 165, 167, 170, 195

Tachileik, 51, 85, 91
Tagata Shrine, 42, 184
Tai, 9, 12–13, 32–35, 48–49, 58–59, 125–27, 179–80, 202–4
    conquerors, 13–14, 153, 180, 196
    groups, 11–12, 35–36, 126, 192
    language, 115, 150
Tai Dam, 10, 22
Tai Khuen. See Khuen
Tai Loi, 3–4, 14, 35–39, 43, 153–54, 178–80, 184–89, 195–97
    earthborn, 37, 167
    indigenous, 43, 164, 175, 179
    young, 39, 179, 187
    See also Lua
Tai Lue, 10, 12, 19, 49, 102, 107–8, 149, 163
Tai Neua, 12, 149, 163, 192
Tai New Year. See Shan New Year
Tai Yai. See Shans
Tai Yuan-Khuen-Lue culture, 10–12, 22, 25–27, 101–2, 106, 116–17, 148, 190–95
Taksin, king, 54–55
Tambiah, Stanley J., 47, 155, 203–4
Tamnan Mūlasāsanā Wat Pa Daeng (TMWPD), 27–28, 139–41
Tanabe, Shigeharu, 13, 73, 133, 153, 158, 180
Tatmadaw. See Burmese military
Taunggyi, 9, 75, 84, 147, 151, 201
tea cultivation, 14
teachers, 71, 141, 147, 151
temple banners, 105–8
temple drums, 111–15, 122, 173–75, 182
temples, 26, 39, 96, 112–13, 146, 153–54, 159–60, 196
    See also individual temple names
territory spirits, 25, 44–46, 123, 125, 127–35, 143–44, 156–57, 192–93
    See also spirit cults

textiles, 18, 107–8, 203
Thailand, 4–5, 7–9, 80–81, 84–87, 96–97, 115, 118–19, 165–66
  Central, 136, 155
  See also Siam
tham script, 5, 11, 37, 115–17, 122, 131, 149–50, 162–63, 183, 190, 194, 202–3
Thao Chiang Khong, 50–51
"theatre state," 175
Thein Sein, 91, 160
Theravāda Buddhism, 93, 138, 160–61
Thibaw, king, 47, 63–65, 68, 70–72
Thongchai Winichakul, 7, 23, 66, 145
thrones, 37, 60–64, 67, 71, 79, 114, 195, 201
Thudhamma. See Sudhamma Nikāya
Tiloka, king, 140–42, 145, 201
TMWPD. See *Tamnan Mūlasāsanā Wat Pa Daeng*
ton bun, 93, 152–54
ton bun khruba, 153–54
Tooth Relic, 96, 144, 147
Toungoo, 51–54, 190
tourists, 91, 106–8
trade, 9, 45, 73, 75, 87, 151, 162, 194
  drug, 1, 85–87, 97
  routes, 1, 8, 70, 73
traditions
  Buddhist, 4, 25, 46–49, 136–37, 139–41, 148, 151, 193
  living, 6, 41, 138, 157–58
  local, 24–25, 29, 46, 148, 151, 193–94
  religious, 108, 148, 152, 161, 169
Trans-Salween Territory, 67
trees, 27, 45, 110, 113–14, 123–24, 130, 133, 175
Triangle Region Command, 91, 160, 181, 196
tribute, 7, 54–55, 57, 59–60, 68, 71–72, 78, 191
Tripitaka, 115
Tuṅga Rasī, 32, 35
Turner, Victor, 3, 185

U Nu, 86
ubosot, 99
Udumbaragiri, 139
  See also Mahāvihara
United Wa State Army. See UWSA
universal power, 44, 48, 136, 143–44, 156, 193
Upper Burma, 29–30, 67, 70, 167, 201
UWSA (United Wa State Army), 14–15, 87, 97

Veidlinger, Daniel M., 49–50, 138, 142
veneration, 92, 95, 131, 159, 167, 196, 202
  communal, 187–88
Vessantara ceremony. See Mahachat ceremony

Vessantara compilation, 107, 109–11, 115, 118–19, 122, 194
Vessantara Jātaka, 109–10, 115, 118–19, 202
Vietnam, 8–9, 29, 48, 125, 169–70, 203
vihan. See assembly halls
Vilanga, king, 14
village communities, 127, 156, 192
village headmen, 129–30, 134–35, 156–57, 162, 192–93
village monasteries, 100, 120, 159, 161, 163, 166, 187, 193
  See also individual monasteries
village spirits, 123–24, 129, 131–35, 155, 157–58, 162, 192–93
villagers, 100, 120, 123–24, 128–30, 134–35, 159, 161, 192
villages (*baan*), 8, 12, 14, 20, 34–36, 38, 58–59, 85, 87, 99, 102, 104–5, 116, 119, 121, 123–25, 128–31, 133–35, 150, 156–57, 159, 161–62, 166, 174, 179, 186–87, 192–93, 200, 202–4
visual culture, 5, 95, 98–115, 156, 162–63, 193

Wa, 14–15, 35, 82, 87, 97, 113–14, 173–74, 204
  territory, 14, 35, 87
walking sticks, 32–33
walls
  city, 8, 57, 69
  defensive, 39, 57, 59, 63, 144, 192, 200
Wan Zai, 39
war, 21–22, 50–51, 53, 55–56, 62, 80–82, 94, 148
  captives, 55–58, 201
Wat Baan Saen, 105, 116, 200
Wat Chet Yot, 142
Wat Chiang Jan, 103
Wat Chom Kham, 33, 79, 100–101, 144–45
Wat Ho Khong, 101, 115
Wat In, 104
Wat Nong Kham, 120
Wat Pa Daeng, monastery/order, 12, 27–28, 50, 100, 119–21, 123, 138–43, 145–46
Wat Pa Daeng Chronicle (WPDC), 27–28, 32, 37, 119, 140–41, 146, 172–73
Wat Phra Kaeo, 80
Wat Phra Sao Luang, 96, 115, 133, 146, 159, 176, 202
Wat Phra Singh, 154, 196
Wat Phra Yun (Haripuñjaya), 137, 139
Wat Suan Dok (Puppharam), monastery/order, 28, 50, 137–41
Wat Yang Kuang, 139
Wat Zom Loi, 38–39, 57, 120, 153, 202

water, 32–33, 40–41, 165–66, 168, 176–77, 181–82, 188–89, 195
  sacred, 135, 152
  splashing, 165–66, 168, 178, 182, 185–86, 188
wealth, 175, 178, 180, 186, 188–90, 195–96
welfare, 130, 159, 167–68, 177, 184
Western Shans. *See* Shans
wet rice cultivation, 25, 126–28, 156, 162, 186, 189, 192
white elephants, 53, 109, 118
Wiang Kum Kam, 49, 137
Wichitmatra (Wichit), 6, 10
wives, 29, 33, 71–72, 76, 91, 95, 97, 108, 118, 160, 168, 201
Wolters, O. W., 46–47
women, 26, 76, 85, 106, 155, 176

wooden ritual drums, 173–74
World War II. *See* Second World War
worldview, Buddhist, 27, 143, 156–57, 162, 193
WPDC. See *Wat Pa Daeng Chronicle*

Yangon, 9, 71, 79, 91, 147
Yawnghwe, 67, 77
Yong, 19, 56, 58–59
Younghusband, G. J., 9, 29, 66, 69–70
Yuan Buddhism, 148, 203
Yuan dynasty, 7, 34
Yuan-Khuen-Lue culture. *See* Tai Yuan Khuen-Lue culture
Yunnan, 7–8, 10, 12, 40, 56, 70, 106, 203–4

Zhuang, 172, 204
Zomia, 125

www.ingramcontent.com/pod-product-compliance
Lightning Source LLC
Chambersburg PA
CBHW030824230426
43667CB00008B/1372